If It Fitz

The Best of Jim Fitzgerald

Jim Fitzgerald
and granddaughter Emily

Published by the Detroit Free Press
321 W. Lafayette Blvd.
Detroit, Michigan 48231

If It Fitz
The Best of Jim Fitzgerald

Design: Dick Mayer
Illustrations: Roy Beaver
Photography: John Collier
Copy editing: Emily Everett
Editor: Bill Diem
Co-ordinator: Michele Kapecky

Manufactured in the United States of America

ISBN 0-9605692-8-6

Introduction

The thing that amazes me about Jim Fitzgerald's columns is they can veer off in unexpected directions, appear to be topic-hopping, observe llamas and Lee Iacocca in the same piece, but always manage to get back in time to arrive at a perfectly logical conclusion.

Within this sometimes astonishing structure is an essay composed of clear, expository sentences. There's never a hint of affectation or strain; the words seem to fall effortlessly into place. You hear Jim's voice and get the feeling he would break his own fingers before ever attempting to show off with cute-clever words or images. What he is is an awfully good writer.

I've been reading and admiring Jim's work ever since he came to the Free Press from The Lapeer County Press, nine years ago. By now Jim has written close to 2,000 columns for us (he's also syndicated in more than 50 other newspapers), has taken clean, deft swipes at some of our dearest customs, and has come to know personally every cocktail piano player in the city.

Jim loves music. He laughs easily and isn't afraid to reveal himself or show affection. Just don't tell him when to celebrate St. Patrick's Day or a national holiday; Jim is moved spontaneously, not by strict observance.

Best of all he approaches his work with an eye, awareness. He spots the incongruous, the absurd, the pretentious, then treats them with a wry form of logic, straight-faced, that would bring cheers from Mark Twain and Will Rogers. They'd welcome Jim in a minute into their exclusive club ... but wait. There'd better not be any cars double-parked in front. If you can't double up in front of the Anchor Bar, Jim would ask somewhat innocently, why is it permitted in front of private clubs? Logic: Jim Fitzgerald's long, strong suit. Turn the page and see what I mean.

— *Elmore Leonard*

Dedicated to
Michele, Melissa and John,
Who came before Emily

If It Fitz

Just for laughs

My St. Patrick's Day
tie wears better in June

April 10, 1976

These words are being typed not long after St. Patrick's Day, in the fourth month of this glorious year of the bicentennial. Which seems an appropriate time to confess to my two most grievous sins, currently:

1. Although my lineage is 100 percent Irish all the way back to the Olde Sod, I do nothing whatsoever to celebrate St. Pat's Day.

2. Although I think this is a fine nation and I wouldn't live anywhere else, I don't give a hoot about its 200th birthday.

Some might say this makes me a traitor twice, to my ethnic group and to my nation. I plead not guilty. I might plead guilty to being an eccentric, even a curmudgeon. But sentence me to 30 days for a misdemeanor, please. Don't hang me without a hearing.

When the mood is right, my eyes mist at the singing of the "The Star-Spangled Banner." I bawled outright when Jose Feliciano sang it with a rock beat in Tiger Stadium in 1968, the glorious year our guys won the World Series. Which is a tip-off to my hang-up.

Most people were outraged at the sacrilege. But I gushed at the kick of living in a nation where a blind Puerto Rican was able to do his thing in center field, with no shots fired from right or left.

Likewise, there is nothing I enjoy more than drinking too much and singing "McNamara's Band" too loud. But another tip-off is I'd rather do it because the company is right, my sister Terrible Jean is leading the chorus with great swoops of her lengthy arms, and some Jewish fellow is picking up the tab. Not because it's March 17.

It is true it is a fine thing to be Irish, and a grand thing to be a U.S. citizen. But it is also true an excess of nationalism often leads to barroom brawls — or wars. I like my pride lit from a spontaneous spark. I love a parade that starts because the music sets feet to marching, not because the calendar says today is the day to put the flag out.

Today's mail brought me a 400-page book titled "Comprehensive Calendar of Bicentennial Events — East of the Mississippi." It is the third such book I've received from the American Revolution Bicentennial Administration in Washington. It tells me such marvel-

3

ous things as the dates of the Norris Dogwood Trail Festival in Norris, Tenn.

Such books are being delivered to most newspaper offices in the United States. As an ex-printer, I know the publishing costs must run into the millions. As an ex-mailman, I know the delivery costs are enough to hire sufficient postal employes to deliver a 13-cent letter from New York to California in one day. They could line up and hand it across the nation.

And as an ex-editor, I know those books will never be read by anyone. They are as visually appealing as a book of zip codes. They are a total waste of money.

I would like to celebrate the bicentennial by spending that money to feed hungry kids, or fill chuckholes, or buy one-way tickets to the moon for the numskulls in Washington responsible for such foolishness.

If the numskulls ever should escape back to Washington, they should be drowned the next March 17th in all the lousy green beer that wasn't consumed because St. Patrick's Day was cancelled. The Irish should skip the saloons and simply go to church, or kneel at home, and pray for an unorganized life.

There are benefits for renegades who don't check if 30 days has September before they get emotional over five-day deodorant pads. Any slob can give his wife a toaster on Dec. 25. But give her a negligee because it's Tuesday and you might hope Wednesday never comes.

In my friskier days, I owned a green tie with white shamrocks on it. I wore it once a year, usually in June to a Greek restaurant. When someone asked why, I told them it was National Trifoliate Plant Week. This is a good way to meet new people, especially the kind who collect nuts. The out-of-season tie never gained me a dance with Zorba, but it broke a lot more ice in June than it would have on March 17.

This nation will go wild next July 4, selling red, white and blue hot dogs on Benjamin Franklin plates, $15.50, with 13-star shaped onion rings. I will celebrate my independence by smuggling an amnesty birthday cake into Canada. More crumbs for the unpardoned patriots who refused to dump tea in Vietnam harbors.

I'll be the last to wish the United States a happy birthday next New Year's Eve, while everyone else is sloshing up statistics for the Auto Club.

The moral is clear: Birthdays and holidays should not be observed in close-order drill. Everyone fall out; smoke 'em if you got 'em. ■

Pigeons do justice
to a reporter's court story

April 13, 1976

There were no bees buzzing and no pigeons depositing in Judge James Churchill's Detroit courtroom last week. But there was the sharp smell of heroin, thousands of dollars' worth.

Jim Churchill has come a long way.

When I met him he was circuit judge in Lapeer which, says a plaque in the front yard, boasts Michigan's oldest courthouse. The plaque isn't necessary. A quick glance tells the most uninterested passerby that Christopher Columbus paid a parking ticket here. If the passerby is blind, he still can learn that the courthouse is early medieval by listening to the yelps of anguish coming from the judges inside. They don't like dispensing justice within sight of torture racks. Besides, there's no air conditioning.

Or the yelps might come from the jurors who must cross the street to go to the john. It's not only the walk. Some of the jurors resent being accompanied by a deputy whose assignment is to make sure they don't discuss the case with the gas station attendant.

Once I wrote a news story about a trial held in the third-floor courtroom, which is reached by a circular stairway modeled after a cliff. There's no elevator. Actually, the easiest way to reach the courtroom is to be born there.

Anyway, the first paragraph of the story may be the nearest I'll come to a classic. It said: "No dove of peace was cooing as opposing attorneys battled in Michigan's oldest courtroom Monday. But there was a pigeon, defecating."

Honest. The bird came through a hole in the roof and swooped overhead throughout the day, dropping remembrances to all below. I was afraid to look up, and afraid not to.

(An award-winning journalism student at Wayne State University asked me how to write such brilliant leads. "The first thing you must learn," I answered, "is to always carry a pigeon with you.")

On another memorable day, a case had to be recessed because the courtroom was invaded by a swarm of bees.

I was remembering the bees and the pigeons as I headed for the Federal Building to visit Judge Churchill, who escaped the oldest

5

courthouse via appointment. President Ford named him one of Detroit's 12 federal judges about 15 months ago. The move was similar to being traded from the Tigers to the Red Sox and marrying Ethel Kennedy: The federal appointment is for life. As a circuit judge in the pigeon loft, Churchill faced re-election regularly.

But let's get back to how Judge Churchill is surviving in the big city. Before I could board an elevator to his federal courtroom, I had to pass between two electric eyes to prove I wasn't carrying an anti-judicial missile. The policeman in charge gave me a quick OK. He also gave me a funny look when I asked him if he'd had any trouble with out-of-town pigeons trying to gain entrance unstooled.

After passing inspection I discovered Judge Churchill hearing the trial of some guys accused of possessing heroin. A succession of narcs were testifying and I didn't understand a word they said. The trial has been going on for seven weeks and it was the same as arriving at the theater after the popcorn machine has been turned off.

Later, at lunch, Judge Churchill refused to talk about that case, or any of the cases he's heard since shifting to a roofed courtroom. Judges must be careful what they say to newsmen for fear we'll publish something for the 155th appeal. But he did reveal that the pile of evil-smelling stuff in front of his bench was 12 pounds of heroin. I thought it was pigeon remembrances.

Before saying "goodby" (I could quote that), the judge showed me around his suite of offices. In Lapeer his administrative facilities consisted of two memo pads in his pocket and one secretary who also worked for the county clerk and waited tables on weekends. In Detroit he has a secretary, two law clerks and a court recorder scattered throughout five handsomely furnished rooms.

That's not counting the huge courtroom where, in his judicial wisdom, the judge has hung a photo of Michigan's oldest courthouse. Whenever the smell of heroin gets too strong, he looks at the picture, thinks pigeon, and remembers how much he likes his new job.

I asked him who takes his jurors across the street to the john.■

Those football announcers
are just too, too sweet

May 29, 1976

The voice on the phone asked me to please hold the line for J.P. McCarthy.

J.P. McCarthy? Detroit's most famous disc jockey on WJR, the world's greatest radio station? The sometimes TV substitute for the immortal Bill Kennedy? J.P. wanted to talk to me, on the air? Wow. This is big-time stuff, I thought. He usually phones Sonny Grandelius.

McCarthy was calling to welcome me to town, while his millions of listeners wondered why he didn't play some good music instead. The call came almost two months ago and I wanted to write about it sooner, but J.P. has been sick. I didn't want to say anything to make him feel worse.

Not that I don't agree he is a great disc jockey and raconteur. I am temporarily a commuter, on the freeway an hour every morning, and J.P. makes the driving fun.

When he was ill and off the air for several weeks, much of Michigan ached and mourned. Every Big Name except the Pope substituted for him and came up short. Not even Shirley Eder could stop McCarthy's listeners from yearning for his return. Me, too.

But now that he's back to work, maybe I can explain something about that phone call without getting punched by his fans.

When McCarthy got me on the air, he asked: "Didn't you once write something about me being too sweet?" I had to admit it, although I'd been hoping he wouldn't remember.

It happened several years ago when J.P. first began doing the color commentary for Detroit Lions football games. This means he was one of Bill Ford's hired cheerleaders. I wrote something about him cheering too, too sweetly. And he answered with a note saying one "too" would have been sufficient.

McCarthy was simply the latest victim of my long-standing gripe against sports announcers who phony it up to help the club owners sell tickets, rather than tell the truth so listeners will know enough to stay home.

When I say long-standing, I mean I go all the way back to Harry

7

Wismer. He started on the road to wealth by broadcasting Lions games back in the 1930s. He never told the truth until 1966 when he wrote a book called "The Public Calls It Sport." That's when he admitted his job had been to make the Lions sound great to the radio audience, even when they stunk out the joint. The Lions then were owned by George Richards. Wismer wrote: "I could hardly have been an objective reporter. My first responsibility was to Richards, not the fans of Detroit."

Nothing much has changed since then. Club owners still have control over who is hired to broadcast their games. Some of them do their best to be objective but they remain suspect, always short of 100 percent credibility.

Would you trust this newspaper's labor writer if he couldn't have been hired without General Motors' approval?

In the case of the Lions, such suspect reporting today could be tougher on Joe Slob than in Wismer's day. Michigan taxpayers, without their consent, are paying $800,000 a year to finance the Lions' domed stadium in Pontiac.

It's one of the most outrageous rip-offs. Bill Ford should buy his own toys.

But you don't hear many taxpayers gripe about it. They know the Lions are worth every cent because their broadcasters tell them so.

All of which is pretty heavy stuff for a column about J.P. McCarthy, who always sounds light enough to talk on cotton batting. So here's a more frivolous reason for disc jockeys leaving sports to un-biased experts like me . . .

One of McCarthy's on-the-air phone callers last Monday was a woman who wanted to know what years the modern Tigers had won pennants. He told her 1934, 1935, 1945 and 1968.
Bobo Newsom would never forgive J.P. Bobo pitched the Tigers to a pennant in 1940. They lost the World Series to Cincinnati.

That woman was making a Tiger hat to enter in a Downtown Detroit Days contest. She wrote the pennant-winning years all over the hat. But, because she received bum information, there was no 1940. And she didn't win the contest. I know, because I was one of the judges.

I asked if the loss made her angry at McCarthy. "I could never get mad at him," she said. "He is too sweet."

"But not too, too," I said. ■

Friends of the deceased
will meet on the 18th green

June 24, 1976

Last week, on a short Southern vacation, I foolishly resumed my annual participation in that stupid game called golf. While hacking through the underbrush, I thought about the Massachusetts man who was buried beneath the 18th green at his favorite golf course. I guess he was dead.

If I am ever buried on a golf course it will be because I committed suicide there and my partner refused to drag my body away. He probably stomped on my face before going on to the next hole.

Golf is a foolish way to waste time. Hit a ball and then look for it and then hit it again. I don't know why I play. Tennis is really my game but I can never get a court. It has been 32 years since I played tennis, which will give you an idea how crowded the courts are.

On TV, the golfers never talk to each other. They show a little respect. I should play on TV. Instead, I play with a bunch of hustling wise guys who keep mouthing insincere cliches that upset my game and my stomach.

For instance, I slam my usual limp drive smack down the center of the fairway, at least 30 feet. "That won't hurt you," says Harvey Hustler.

What he really means is that lousy drive won't kill me, it will just leave me maimed and limping. It is the lousiest shot he ever saw and 15 more just like it might get me on the green, which is that pretty patch of grass with the hole in it, in case I've never been there before.

Another smart thing Harvey often says is: "You had the distance."

This means I walloped the ball 250 yards. The trouble is I hit it north and the green is south.

The reverse of this inanity comes when Harvey says: "You hit it right on line."

This means I pounded the ball straight at the hole which is 350 yards away. But the ball fell 340 yards short.

And after we walk 10 yards to my ball Harvey looks at it admiringly and says: "You sure know how to stay out of trouble."

If we were playing baseball, he would praise me for knowing how

9

to keep the ball in the park. Instead of hitting home runs, I strike out.

And at the end of the game, as he takes my money, Harvey always explains that I got a lot of tough breaks out there today, while he was lucky, and if a couple of putts had dropped for me it would have been a different story, fella, and I'm sure to get my money back next week.

Harvey knows it wouldn't help my game if I were Arnold Palmer's little brother. He knows if a long putt had dropped for me I would have got seven on the hole, instead of eight. He knows I have been playing the stupid game for 25 years and I still address the ball as if I'm afraid it will attack my right foot.

He knows all these things, but he still spouts the baloney for fear I might quit playing him and he'd have to get his booze money by some more honorable means — such as pawning his mother's wheelchair.

The only time Harvey's language gets precise is when he asks for my score on a hole.

"Let's see," I say, and then I get a faraway look in my eyes and move my lips slowly as my mind backtracks through two traps, the right rough, the woods on the left, a rock pile, the freeway, and that lake where two fishermen threatened to sue. "I think I got a five."

"You got an 11," Harvey says, and produces two witnesses to back him up, one a priest and the other a CPA.

Owners of the club were so enthusiastic about the idea that they erected a plaque to mark the grave. The possibilities do appear promising. Why not a grave or two at every green, and perhaps some by the traps and rough?

A guy wouldn't mind attending a funeral if he could chip up onto the burying surface. Of course, the undertaker would have to add a few services — such as caddies for pallbearers — but I'm sure all such problems could be solved with a minimum of keening.

Just so long as slow funerals allow faster funerals to play through.   ■

A pocket full of spirits,
a bra stuffed with popcorn

July 1, 1976

The pure clarinet of Benny Goodman brought back bittersweet memories to thousands of aging swingers at the Meadow Brook Music Festival Friday night.

I was reminded of Depression days when Mother lined my pockets with oilcloth so it would be easier for me to steal soup.

Amazingly, Goodman sounds as fine in 1976 as in 1936. His "Sing, Sing, Sing" and "Lady Be Good" almost made me weep for the sheer joy of the music and the nostalgia. But I would have been happier if I'd had oilcloth pockets. My wife forbids me to tell you why. But this is not yet a matriarchal society. I am going to tell you why, from the beginning . . .

As you know, if you have any culture at all, the Meadow Brook Music Festival is held outdoors every summer at Oakland University in Rochester. Most of the listeners pay $3 to sit on a grassy hillside. The swells pay $6 to sit in the pavilion with the orchestra.

For either price, the acoustics are great. But sometimes the weather isn't. The grass sitters must gamble, especially when they buy tickets ahead of time.

For instance, the night before Goodman performed, some grass sitters took shelter from wind and rain in pup tents to hear the Detroit Symphony Orchestra, led by Aldo Ceccato, who was safe in the pavilion. It was as though the Italians had won World War II.

The hillside is marvelous for top-flight hedonists. There's lots of room to spread a satin blanket under the chateaubriand and champagne. It is not unusual to see the picnickers sipping from crystal and pondering which fork is obligatory during an obbligato.

There are also the grassers with six-packs and old Army blankets, which is more my speed. But either way, slob or couth, that's the way to attend a concert. If the music is lousy, you still can save the evening with a good wallow in the potato salad.

I've enjoyed Meadow Brook's hillside many times. But there were also those occasions when I froze, or floated down the hill. So this year I bought pavilion tickets to the Friday jazz series. It cost around

11

$80 but what is money when Oscar Peterson and the Preservation Hall Jazz Band are coming to town.

Besides, you don't have to spread a blanket to enjoy popcorn and lemonade with jazz. I figured there was no good reason why pavilion sitters couldn't have circumspect picnics in their laps. We'd have to leave the six-foot pepper mill home, and there could be no more tap dancing on our knees. But there would be no need for dehydration.

So, in preparation for opening night with Benny Goodman, I circumspectly mixed the juice of lemons and grains into a circumspect red gallon thermos. Inside the Meadow Brook gate, I bought a circumspect washtub full of popcorn. The music was beginning as we arrived at the pavilion.

"No refreshments are allowed in the pavilion," the usherette said.

In my most circumspect tone, I pointed out that the surrounding hills were alive with the sound of people chomping and gulping. They had paid $3 per ticket less than I did to get inside. What kind of reverse discrimination was this?

She merely pointed to a sign that said "No Refreshments Allowed in Pavilion."

"They don't have that sign on your popcorn stand," I snarled circumspectly.

The usherette explained it was too hard to clean up the mess left behind by pavilion diners. It is simple to rake and vacuum the hillside, but the cleaning equipment won't fit between the rows of seats.

I wasn't impressed. It would be easy to hire Oakland students to do a little stoop labor. But I was challenged. I couldn't abandon that booze and popcorn.

I located some friends on the grass, just a few feet behind our seats. They agreed to guard our treasure, from which I made frequent withdrawals. The juice went into a plastic cup and the popcorn went into napkins.

Fortunately, the usherette gave me a good-sized program from behind which I drained the cup. This covert operation made my wife so nervous she threatened to relieve the tension by turning me in to Donald O'Dowd, Oakland president. But she didn't because she knew I'd squeal about the popcorn stuffed inside her blouse.

We have five more jazz concerts to go in the antiseptic pavilion. Oilcloth linings are now being fashioned by my favorite seamstress.

See you at Meadow Brook. Just watch for a man who sloshes when he walks. He'll be escorting a woman with a size 50 bust.

Criminals are made, not born. ◼

Please do sit on the grass;
it keeps you down-to-earth

August 3, 1976

"Friday, in our never-ending quest for culture, we will sit on the hill," I told my wife. "But on Sunday we will eschew the grass and dine in the palace with the president."

"I don't think you chew grass; I think you smoke it," she said.

"This will be another fine opportunity for me to test the White Star Phenomenon," I said, ignoring her poor pun. She needs culture more than I do.

Anyway, we did it.

On one night we sprawled on the grass at the Meadow Brook Music Festival and listened to Maynard Ferguson defy death by hernia, wailing his trumpet to the shrillest notes this side of a dog whistle. We wore tennis shoes, ate cold chicken from a box, and avoided windburn by crawling into a Thermos bottle.

Two nights later we ate a three-fork dinner at the Sunset Terrace, the splendid home of Donald O'Dowd, president of Oakland University. The Terrace overlooks the Meadow Brook ampitheater, so it was possible to look down on the peasants as we ate kabobs and brown tomatoes. At show time, we descended to stage front, snug in the pavilion, to enjoy a scholarly program presented by the New England Conservatory Ragtime Ensemble.

The contrast between the two evenings at Meadow Brook was extreme — which is what I was seeking. I wanted to find out if, when it comes to culture, I still take after my father. This brings us to what I always have called the White Star Phenomenon.

The White Star stands no more. Long ago it fell to urban renewal, that gigantic bruiser of childhood memories. The White Star once was the sleaziest saloon in my hometown, Port Huron. It occupied a scruffy corner near the St. Clair River, in the red light district, where decent people never went.

I first went inside the White Star when I was 18. I was one of several brave soldiers home on furlough during World War II, and we had spent the night celebrating in the ribald manner befitting young men who knew this might be their last hurrah — death could be waiting in the next foxhole. (I was a clerk-typist assigned to the chaplain's office).

Somehow it was decided that we should climax the evening by invading forbidden territory — the White Star. All our lives our parents had instructed us to beware of that bar. We had been warned against everything from opium addiction (from drinking from unsterilized glasses) to being shanghaied by Great Lakes sailors and forced to spend the rest of our years on Lake Erie, off Cleveland.

But this was war. Into the White Star we went.

It appeared as bad as advertised. The floor was dirt, most of the customers carried their heads between their feet, and the bartender's face looked like two blocks of broken sidewalk.

In those days you had to be 21 to drink. The bartender asked me for proof and I showed him a photostat of my birth certificate. The birth date had been suitably altered but the rest of the information was legitimate.

"Hey," said the bartender, "you must be Eddie Fitzgerald's son."

I was. And my companions fell on the floor laughing, splendor in the dirt.

It turned out my father was an old and favored customer. I soon became the same thing. And when my mother found out, she explained the phenomenon succinctly: "You're just like your father. You'd rather hang around with bums than bank presidents."

This is pretty much the truth, but I've always fought it.

That's why the Meadow Brook experiment was so appealing. If I liked Sunday's plush better than Friday's slush, I could pronounce myself cured. I could phone Mother and tell her it was finally OK to eschew my old cuspidor.

But it didn't happen that way.

Sunset Terrace is a lovely place. The free parking and preferred sitting made me feel important. And President O'Dowd is an unusually gracious host, forever youthful. He could be Gov. Milliken's younger brother, another cousin of Dorian Gray. It was a charming time.

But when Maynard Ferguson blew "I Can't Get Started With You," I was flat on my back, searching the sky for yesterdays, and my favorite girl tickled my shin with her big toe. It could never have happened in row HH, seats 32 and 34. It was a moment made for sighing.

"We should never eschew the grass," I sighed, in cultured tones.■

Let's see what skip ropes
do for an old goat's sex life

August 17, 1976

Psychologist Dr. Joyce Brothers has written a book called "Better Than Ever," about middle age.

As she approached age 50, Dr. Brothers started skipping rope regularly. As a result, she said, her husband turned into a madly exciting lover.

Today, Dr. Brothers is well-known as the newspaper columnist with a paralyzed upper lip whose knees are riveted together for all appearances on TV talk shows.

But I can remember long ago when Dr. Brothers first gained fame. It was in the 1950s, on a TV quiz show. She answered questions about prizefighting and won enough money to go to psychology school and buy a skip rope.

Dr. Brothers drew a lot of attention because no one could understand how a dainty little blond lady could know so much about the rugged sport of boxing. Later it was revealed the quiz show was rigged and many of the contestants had been reading their answers off the quiz master's forehead.

There was an immediate suspicion that perhaps Dr. Brothers had not gotten her numb lip in the fight ring. But the investigators never laid a glove on her and to this day her reputation remains as pure as her posture.

Which is why I don't hesitate to accept her advice. Everyone knows prizefighters train by skipping rope. Now Dr. Brothers has revealed it is good training for more than boxing.

Last week I mourned my 50th birthday. I wasn't going to say a word about it, partly to make a liar out of a fellow columnist who recently became 40. He said columnists love to reach such milestones so they can write the ultimate truths about cold peas and hot flashes.

This is not necessarily so. When I reached 40, I didn't write a word about it for fear the news might reflect badly on my column photo which then featured a crew haircut received at Ft. Knox in 1944.

For a better reason, I also was determined to remain non-public about attaining Number 50. When I was born, my mother was 26

15

years older than I was. Today the gap has narrowed to about 10 and it is getting embarrassing for both of us.

But then I arrived home from work on my birthday to discover silence was futile. My oldest daughter had painted me a birthday card on a bed sheet and hung it from our carport. The "50" could be read from the next county. The photographer from the local weekly was taking a picture of the giant card, to publish opposite the obituary page.

Later there was a party at the home of Terrible Jean, my sister who is older than our mother. The birthday decorations featured Terrible Jean's drawing of a huge goat chewing on newsprint. The face on the goat was mine. The message, in block letters, was "Happy 50th, You Old Goat."

So it's no use, Mother. Your son is 50 and the whole world knows you honeymooned in kindergarten. And I might as well deal publicly with the terrible trauma of becoming half a century old.

I know it's a terrible trauma because I read Dr. Brothers and the other menopause experts who continually are quoted in the newspapers, usually on the same page as Ann Landers.

They say a man my age has reached a crisis. I should look back at what I have accomplished in 50 years, and own up realistically to the fact that I'll probably never play second base for the Tigers.

Also, I must decide what I am going to do with my remaining years. As a headline on the Women's Page said last week: "Middle Age: Change or Die . . . Grow or Stagnate."

Younger men are eager to take my place and I must learn to adjust gracefully to the inevitable truth that someday someone else will change the ribbon on this typewriter.

To help him accept middle age, a man needs the help of an understanding woman. Possibly his wife. In their book, "Making It from 40 to 50" (Random House, $8.95), experts Joel and Lois Davitz say the husband needs "her reassurance, her flattery, her total acceptance and encouragement." She must treat him as a "strong, sensitive and powerful man."

Yeah.

I was going to buy the Davitz book for my wife, but then I read a succinct review of Dr. Brothers' "Better Than Ever" (Simon and Schuster, $7.95).

And instead I bought his-and-her skip ropes (K mart, $2.02).■

Restaurants just aren't fit
for shy, single diners

November 19, 1976

It is a fine idea to reserve sections of restaurants for people who do not smoke. Another good idea would be to designate special areas for people who do not want to eat in the dark.

During my first week as a downtown Detroit resident, my wife left me. It was not another urban problem. She had to go sit up with a sick grandson. My wife can hear her grandchildren sneeze 300 miles away, and she resents anyone who beats her to the scene with a Kleenex.

Anyway, I can prepare my own meals, as long as I want to eat peanut butter sandwiches. After a couple of days, the entire apartment was sticking to the roof of my mouth. So I forced myself to eat in some restaurants.

It's not that I don't like to eat out. I love it. But not when I'm alone. I want someone at the table with me. Preferably my wife, but almost any warm body will do in an emergency.

Good conversation makes a good dinner better, I suppose. But I will not try to kid you. Conversation isn't what I want mostly from a dinner companion. My insecurity goes deeper than that.

What I want most is simply someone to share my table, so the rest of the people in the restaurant won't feel sorry for me.

I can't stand the pity of chewing strangers. Why is that, doctor?

When I am dining alone in a crowded restaurant, the first thing I notice is that I am the only lone diner. Every other table contains couples, or quadruples, or Rotary clubs. All of these people are having a grand time, laughing and talking loudly.

Except every once in a while, singularly or in unison, these tables full of people grow quiet. This is when they are looking at me, and wondering why I don't have any friends.

I can always imagine what they are thinking. They are thinking my wife threw me out of the house, but I still must make the mortgage payments, and the YMCA caught me cooking in my room.

Or they are thinking I am a traveling salesman, written by Arthur Miller, who no longer knows the territory and who has become crazed from sitting on curbs because motels don't have lobbies.

Whatever they are thinking, it isn't true and it isn't fair. In the

17

worst way, I want them to know I am eating alone because all my friends were killed in an international cataclysm, or simply because I like to eat alone and, despite invitations from Joe Namath and Truman Capote, I have to be me.

But I am too shy to talk to strangers. So I simply sit there and bear their stares and whispers. And the paramount question becomes, where do I look? Especially, where do I look until the waiter brings some food to study?

A lonely diner can spend only so much time investigating ice cubes and expressing sincere concern for the silverware. There comes a time when my gaze must wander around the crowded room.

And I always lock eyes with a retired policeman who knows I am eating alone because I molest children. Naturally, I forgot to take off my raincoat.

There is only one way I can feel halfway comfortable while eating alone in a restaurant. I must read a newspaper or a book. The printed page furnishes acceptable refuge from the glances of a prying, pitying world.

Which brings us back to the opening paragraph wherein I suggested restaurants should have special sections for diners who do not want to eat in the shadow of a smile.

Not everyone goes into a restaurant to play kneezies, or to lurk. There should be well-illuminated areas for lonely, guilt-ridden men who like to eat behind sports pages. Just like breakfast at home.

A newspaper even can come in handy when you can't read it. In one murky restaurant, I faked it. I couldn't see the paper but I kept looking at it anyway, so I wouldn't have to look at the people.

But then I noticed silences falling upon the crowded tables around me. And I knew they were thinking I was a phony, pretending to read, when in reality I was simply afraid to unduck my head and face the public scrutiny which might uncover the evil secrets in my mind, or in my room at the YMCA.

So I improved my disguise. I moved my lips.

Onward and Upward.

Who needs a coat rack
when you're this virile?

In a recent newspaper interview, News Director Phil Nye of Detroit TV Channel 7 took a swipe at his competition.

"Channel 2 has gone down the tubes because they do shtik over there, they don't do news," Nye said. "They're a disgrace to the industry."

My wife reads all that kind of good stuff. "What is shtik?" she asked me.

"You asked at exactly the right time," I answered, pointing at the TV set. "That is shtik."

Coincidentally our TV was tuned to Channel 7. The station was kissing itself, showing one of its own commercials. It stars Jim Osborn, Channel 7's general manager, who was filmed in an "office situation."

This means Osborn doesn't simply look into the camera and give his spiel. He comes out from behind his desk and walks around his office while he thoughtfully explains why Channel 7's news programs are the hardest-hitting in town.

This was the second time I had seen the Osborn commercial that evening, and probably the 30th time since Christmas. TV stations always do a lot of self-advertising after Christmas because they can't sell the commercial spots to regular advertisers who exhausted their advertising budgets heralding the birth of Jesus Christ, all major credit cards accepted.

The TV stations can do two things to fill this unsold time, which otherwise would hum blankly between scheduled programs, much like Ozzie Nelson reruns.

The stations can air public-service announcements, urging everyone to join the Marines or get checked for venereal disease. There is no money in this for the TV stations, but they make points with the Federal Communications Commission, which is favorably impressed by stations that demonstrate an ungreedy concern for the security and health of the nation, if only at 2:30 a.m. on the first Tuesday between Christmas and the January white sales.

The other alternative to pausing for silent, unillustrated messages

19

is for the TV channels to fill the cracks with unpaid advertising for their own programs. Effective self-advertising can boost future audiences, thus enabling the TV stations to raise the rates for paid advertising.

Obviously, the TV stations have more to gain from self-advertising than from public service announcements. Which explains why Jim Osborn has been walking around on my TV screen so much lately, and why there is so much venereal disease in this nation.

But back to shtik. Osborn is in his shirt-sleeves as he strides purposefully around his office, but he is carrying his suit coat slung over his right shoulder.

"Most business executives don't carry their coats around their offices. They either hang them up or put them on," I explained to my wife. "But Osborn wants viewers to see that he and his news crew are a gutsy bunch who will report the news no matter how many fat toes they must step on. So he is carrying his coat over his shoulder to prove his virility. That is shtik."

My limited research indicates that Frank Sinatra started the whole thing. He has always projected an I-don't-give-a-damn attitude, tough and sexy. He often performs with his coat draped carelessly over one shoulder, leaving his arms unencumbered, ever-ready for love or war, with no danger of losing the mood while searching for a coat rack.

The image caught on. Men with coats slung over one shoulder appear in all sorts of advertising. Camel cigarets used the slung look to illustrate that brave men aren't afraid to risk cancer for pleasure. High school seniors pose for graduation pictures with their best coat hung on their shoulders. It's manly.

That's where Channel 7's general manager is coming from. Osborn wants viewers to realize his news crew is a shirt-sleeve bunch that will roll them up to get a tough story, but still has sense enough to keep a coat handy in case someone turns off the heat.

Before anyone at Channel 7 news criticizes a competitor for using shtik, they should first tell their boss to put his coat on, or hang it up. ∎

There's a whole lot to love in a Henry Ford mansion

February 20, 1978

Movie critics generally agree that "The Betsy" is a glossy piece of trash. It is ironical that Cristina Ford is the person who may have inadvertently put her finger on just exactly where the movie went wrong.

The purpose of "The Betsy" is to titillate the peasants with graphic portrayals of how very wealthy people get their jollies. Most of the stars and featured players have sex with each other, regardless of family relationships or gender. Sir Laurence Olivier, for instance, makes it with his daughter-in-law while her son watches and while her husband is making it with his top aide who is a him.

But no one in the movie becomes emotionally involved with a kitchen table.

In court testimony the other day, Cristina Ford said it is possible for a person to be emotionally attracted to an inanimate object. She said she feels an emotional attachment to every piece of property owned by her estranged husband, Henry Ford II. It must be assumed that this includes his kitchen furniture.

If you care at all, you understand the irony of Cristina Ford revealing, however unintentionally, what important phase of the ultra-rich life was omitted from "The Betsy." The movie was made from Harold Robbins' book, which many people think is a roman a clef aimed at the Ford family.

As explained here several months ago, I once explained, a roman a clef is not an Italian with a speech impediment. It is a French phrase used to describe a novel which disguises fact as fiction. The names are changed to protect the writer from being sued.

"The Betsy" revolves around an auto company which is run by the same family for three generations. There's the strong-willed grandfather who started the business, the comparatively weak son who never can really take his father's place, and the hard-nosed grandson who wants to make a buck almost as much as he wants to divorce his first wife so he can marry a beautiful foreigner.

This plot doesn't remind many people of the Herman Jeep family. But author Robbins denies he was thinking strictly of the Fords. He mentions the Dodges and the Chryslers and says there's lots of juicy sin to be squeezed from the history of automobile families.

That's probably true. The rumble seat may have been invented by a little-known auto magnate with a giraffe fetish. Robbins' research might have uncovered more dirt than even he could shovel into a roman a clef. But I'll still bet he wishes he hadn't finished "The Betsy" before Henry Ford II tried to sell his snuff boxes.

When Henry decided to auction about $2 million worth of his antique snuff boxes and other expensive items collected through the years, Cristina protested. She took him to court in an attempt to block the sale, and some of her testimony has been the stuff from which romantic novels are written.

Cristina told the judge she burst into tears when she learned Henry had taken the furnishings from the drawing room of their 76-room mansion in Grosse Pointe Farms and planned to sell them.

"It was the only room I loved . . . I mean I love beautiful things," she testified.

Henry's lawyer asked Cristina if she feels the same emotional attachment for "every piece of property this man owns." She said yes, she did.

Not even Henry Ford knows exactly how much he is worth, but he estimates around $70 million. When you realize how big a pile of possessions equals $70 million, you realize that Cristina has got a lot of unrequited lovin' to do.

By her own admission, that woman is emotionally attracted to a virtually unlimited number of unemotional things. Such a one-sided romance must be somewhat similar to going steady with a string of hardware stores.

I don't pretend to know the true significance of such a phenomenon. But if Harold Robbins had been able to investigate it in "The Betsy," the book and subsequent movie might have earned a more respectful reception from the critics.

Surely "The Betsy" would have done a more complete job of telling what it's like to be ultra-wealthy if it had included a scene showing Laurence Olivier climbing into bed with a tudor sedan. Just in case, there could have been a jumper cable on the nightstand.

Onward and Upward. ■

Dumb drivers abound, but Nerd tops them all

March 15, 1978

There were charges of nepotism when , a year ago, I awarded my son first place in my Dumb Driver contest. To refute the critics, I'm here today to submit further proof of Nerd's right to the championship, regardless of who his father is.

Nerd is a good kid and he worked hard for the honor. It wouldn't be fair to deny him his due simply because my blood squirts from his veins when I hit him on the face.

It must be admitted that, being 19 years old, Nerd has a built-in advantage in a Dumb Driver contest. It has been my experience that persons in their upper teens automatically are several lengths ahead of everyone else when it comes to doing dumb things with cars. For instance, if it weren't for upper teenagers, the world wouldn't know that tires can be screeched while the car is still parked.

But it would be as unfair to deny Nerd his prize because of his age as it would be to deny him because of his father. After all, it's not his fault he was born 19 years ago; it's his parents' fault. My wife has forgiven me, and perhaps someday, when Nerd is 32 and working steady, I will forgive her.

It's not surprising that my Dumb Driver contest resulted, many years later, from something I did when I was a teenager. What I did was pick up my father's 1940 Plymouth at the bump shop after he'd spent $80 to have wrinkles removed from its fenders. I smashed that refurbished Plymouth into two parked cars before I got out of the bump shop parking lot. The damage was $150.

That evening my father said I had set a world's record for dumb driving. He said never before in history had any driver wrecked a newly bumped-out car while still in the bump shop.

That record stood until 1976 when Nerd wrecked two cars at once and neither car had its engine running. Both cars belonged to me.

He was backing my Pacer out of the driveway. It's downhill, so he coasted. He opened the door so he could look back to see where he was going. The Pacer door hooked the fender of my Oldsmobile parked innocently beside the driveway. The Pacer door came off and the Olds fender dimpled deeply. Marvelous. Blood will tell.

23

When I crowned the new champion in print, the Dumb Driver contest began. Several readers questioned Nerd's claim to the throne. They described dumb things they or their children had done with cars. They suggested I'd been hasty in declaring Nerd the dumbest driver in the land.

I'll admit some of the entries were good. I was most impressed by the driver who, Nerd-wise, also opened his door while backing up. The door was unhinged by a tree. A friend in the passenger's seat heard the noise and opened his door to see what it was. That door was unhinged by a bush.

To continue driving, that dumb driver had to tie the two doors to each other. This was in 1948 and the clothesline holding the doors shut was the auto industry's first seat belt.

Not bad. But I still awarded first place to Nerd, mainly because he'd accomplished his double crash with no engines running. There are always some sore losers, and I was accused of nepotism. This hurt. My choice was based purely on merit, and I resented any implication that I'd been influenced by natural desire to keep the championship in the family.

That's why I was happy to hear of Nerd's latest achievement. While not as dramatic as the dumbness which originally won him the championship, this most recent gem of stupidity is still unique and certainly supports his claim to the top spot.

The other night he locked himself out of the Pacer. Anyone can do that, you say? Sure. But Nerd takes no chances. He had both Pacer keys with him, and he locked both keys inside the car.

Naturally, you're impressed, and you wonder how he did it. I'm not telling. My family may some day lose the Dumb Driver championship, but it won't be because we were dumb enough to leak the secrets of our success to the competition. You'll just have to take my word for it. Nerd did it, and I'm proud of him.

How did he get back inside the car? Easy. He knew that a semi-dumb driver would use a wire coat hanger if one key were locked inside. So Nerd walked to the nearest home and asked to borrow two hangers. ■

You can't have your
lunch and be skinny, too

June 9, 1978

Because I don't run around the block 10 times every morning, a reader has bet that "Fitzgerald looks like a 200-pound turnip." This is nonsense, of course.

Sometimes I think you people aren't paying close enough attention to my wisdom. Only a few weeks ago I have pointed out that people don't get fat from not running. They get fat from eating too much.

Running to lose weight makes as much sense as eating spaghetti to win a foot race. Think about it.

Don't start reading this paragraph yet. Think some more about what I just told you.

OK. Now we can get on with today's wisdom. It concerns the wise way to shed fat and keep it shed. No weird diets are required. You don't have to eat boiled dandelions while sitting on your feet in downtown Bombay. And you don't have to jog.

All you have to do is quit eating lunch.

Nutritionally, lunches are overrated. People eat them out of habit, not hunger. Lunches have become rituals which must be performed before two people can talk business, or make love, or plan dinner.

A boss will take an employe to lunch to promote him or fire him. World War III will be declared over lunch. Years later, the survivors will delay signing the peace treaty until the luncheon dishes have been cleared.

A person invited to lunch may weigh 400 pounds. He doesn't need lunch, he needs therapy. But he goes to lunch because to refuse would be rude, or poor business, or fatal to a romantic liaison he's been enjoying with a 250-pound beach ball.

Lunch is traditional, something like Bob Hope. It doesn't have to be good, it has to be consumed. Just as it is unpatriotic to admit Hope hasn't been funny in 20 years, it is uncivilized to skip lunch.

Working people who can't get out to a restaurant still don't flout the tradition. They brown bag it and drip mustard all over that day's

25

gross national product. Automobiles that went through the assembly line during lunch often are recalled because of bread crumbs.

When I tell fat people they should skip lunch, they get angry. They deny that they eat lunch for social or economic reasons, or simply out of habit. They say they eat lunch for their health.

One fatty said he gets a dull ache in his stomach when he misses lunch. He said he can't stand the pain. So to lose weight, he runs every night until his legs throb and his lungs burn and he throws up.

Another fatty said her head aches if she doesn't eat at noon. Medical men say her headache it caused by worry, not hunger. She worries that, if she doesn't eat lunch with her friends, they will be free to gossip about how fat she is getting.

In 1973, I did look like a 200-pound turnip. That's when I quit eating lunch. It took me four months to lose 25 pounds. Every time the scale said I'd shed five pounds, I invited friends and strangers to a candlelight ceremony in which I punched another hole in my belt. This is the secret to keeping the fat shed.

Brag about your new slimness and the steel willpower which made it possible. Demonstrate by putting your skinny body and a living room couch into your old pants. Be an obnoxious bore. Tell the world lunch isn't necessary, just as I've told you. Everyone will hate you, but that's good.

No one will ask you to lunch.

Now you know the wise way to lose fat. Running doesn't do it. Running is for catching buses. Not eating lunch is for getting slim. Think about that.

Never mind what's in this paragraph. You should be thinking. ■

Weird birds of a feather
flock to the big city

October 9, 1978

On a recent afternoon, the sound of chirping birds came through my office window. This seemed unusual in downtown Detroit. I looked out and saw a middle-aged man standing on the sidewalk below. He was looking up at the sky and the bird chirps were coming out of his mouth.

This man did not appear to be the sort of nut who would come downtown on a busy afternoon and stand around imitating birds. He was well-dressed in a business suit, white shirt and conservative tie. He carried a Bible in one hand and an expensive-looking briefcase in the other.

He stood there making bird sounds for a full hour. Occasionally he would put the Bible and the briefcase on the sidewalk so he could raise both arms toward the sky. Dozens of people walked by the chirper, hardly giving him a glance. No one stopped to ask him what the hell he was doing.

I called a co-worker, a hardened newspaper reporter, to come look at the chirping man. All big-city newspaper reporters are hardened because they have seen all of life's tragedies and quirks, and nothing surprises them. And if life's experiences don't make them hard enough to control their emotions while reporting bloodbaths or looking at their paychecks, they sleep in chest freezers and eat plaster of Paris.

"Oh, that's just the birdman. He is one of life's quirks. He performs downtown quite often," my hardened co-worker explained.

"He's pretty good at birdcalls," I said.

"He's probably a phony," my hardened co-worker said. "He probably has a bird in his briefcase and the bird is a ventriloquist."

Still seeking to amaze, I left my cynical co-worker and went home to tell my wife about the chirping man. When a hick doesn't want to stand in awe alone, all he has to do is find another hick to stand with him. My wife often comes in handy this way.

As I expected, Pat she gave me the reaction I thought the birdman deserved. "That's really weird," she said.

Until moving into the city a couple of years ago, Pat my wife and I

27

always lived in small towns. I was a softened reporter on a weekly newspaper. Well-dressed, middle-aged men never stood outside my window and chirped like birds. A bruised knee was a bloodbath. Every payday, I cried.

"You mean that man stood there making bird noises for an hour in the middle of downtown and the people walking by didn't even look at him? Big-city people are crazy," my wife said.

At this point in the conversation, our youngest child toddled through the room on his way out the front door. He is 20 and he never before lived in a city with more than 6,000 population.

He was wearing dirty tennis shorts, a large hiking boot on his right foot, and a tennis shoe on his left foot. His mother didn't blink.

"Did he hurt his foot or something?" I asked.

"No, but he's going to drive the car," Pat she explained. "Whenever he drives, he wears the heavy boot on his right foot because he says it helps him keep his foot down on the accelerator."

"Oh," I said. "Where is he going?"

"He is going to play tennis and then he's going to a concert."

"Is he going to wear those dirty tennis shorts to the concert?"

"No, he always keeps a change of clothes in the car."

"Does he change in the car or at a gas station?" I asked.

"He says he always likes to change in the bathroom at the Grosse Pointe library," she said.

"It's certainly comforting to know that all weird people come from big cities," I said. "If he ever meets the birdman, our son will know how to react. He will throw him bread crumbs." ■

I'll not be caught providing fodder for your juicy gossip

February 14, 1979

Lee Marvin is the subject of gossip because of whom he lived with. She wasn't his wife. Nelson Rockefeller is the subject of gossip because of whom he died with. She wasn't his wife.

Maybe that says it all. If you're living or dead, the gossips will get you if you don't watch out.

Everybody loves to gossip. Why? What is it about gossip that makes it so popular?

Lee Marvin once won an Academy Award which officially made him the best movie actor of a particular year. He didn't get as much publicity for that achievement as he has for refusing to pay a woman what she wants for living with him in unwedded bliss for six years.

Nelson Rockefeller was once the vice-president of the United States, the traditional breath away from the biggest job in the world. Nothing he did as vice-president has put Nelson Rockefeller's name into as many cocktail party conversations as what he did when he was a breath away from no more breathing. He apparently died in the company of a young woman, not his wife, to whom he had lent $45,000, which, according to his will, she doesn't have to pay back.

Don't you just adore it, darlings? But why?

Why are we all more interested in the private lives of celebrities than we are in the public lives which made them celebrities?

I'm certainly glad I asked.

The answer is that Joe and Jane Average can identify with the domestic problems of the king and queen of England, even if Joe and Jane can't imagine how it feels to go to bed wearing diamond crowns.

Life is pretty much the same for all of us between the sheets, or across the breakfast table, except for a few exotic brands of oatmeal not cooked in the average kitchen.

For Joe and Jane, it's an impossible dream to be movie stars, or millionaire vice-presidents. But it's not impossible that Joe could cheat on his wife, and get sick in his girlfriend's apartment. Or that Jane could wash a guy's dirty socks for six years, and then the bum could take a walk, leaving her with soapy hands and no water to rinse them.

29

Take me, for example. The other night, I fell out of bed and cracked a rib. You probably thought only little kids fall out of bed. What do you know? Actually, I didn't really fall, I dived, head first, smack onto the hard floor.

It was a nightmare. That evening I'd seen "The Deer Hunter," a powerful, frightening war movie. In one sequence, prisoners of war were locked in a cage and submerged in a river. In my nightmare, there were dogs in the cage and I was determined to dive deep enough to rescue them.

So I dived on the floor, wham, and there I sat, nude, holding my sore rib, when the woman on the other side of the bed asked what the hell was going on. I'd taken all the blankets with me, to wrap the dogs in.

A cracked rib was bad enough, but I easily could have cracked my skull, requiring immediate medical attention. What if the woman trying hard not to laugh at my embarrassment hadn't been my wife?

For one thing, if she owed me $45,000, she'd be sorry she laughed. For another thing, there would have been no spokesman to explain to my wife that the young woman who called the ambulance was someone I'd hired to help me write a book on how to give mouth-to-mouth resuscitation to wire-haired terriers.

Of course, it was my wife who pulled me back into bed by the blankets. I'm no Lee Marvin. If a woman isn't my wife, I don't want to live with her one night, let alone six years. There's something to be said for old-fashioned oatmeal, and I just said it.

But I understand how another guy might get in trouble reaching for forbidden breakfast. And when the other guy is a movie star, or a big-shot politician, I understand why Joe and Jane enjoy the gossip. They are delighted to know that fame and wealth are no guarantee against a person getting caught diving after drowning dogs from the wrong bed.

Gossip is not the most admirable human trait, but it's human, and being human is what we're all stuck with. Psst . . . ∎

Not all conceptions are pregnant — get the idea?

July 30, 1979

In a radio interview, Richard Nixon said if he had it to do all over again, he'd be a sportswriter.

"I can conceptualize that," my friend Ralph said.

Ralph had just read the report card that Hamilton Jordan, the White House chief of staff, asked department heads to use in rating the job performance of their subordinates. Among many other skills, employes are graded on their "conceptualizing" ability.

Several department heads refused to report on conceptualizing, saying it is none of the government's business how good its employes are at having babies.

This was a misunderstanding. There is more than the pregnant type of conception. Ideas, as well as children, can be conceived. Ideas also can be aborted. It's easy to get federal money to finance the abortion of an idea. In fact, it's generally believed that more ideas are aborted in federal offices than anywhere else in the world.

No one ever complains that an aborted idea, if it had been allowed to live, would have saved the world, or even an empty lot. The evidence of bureaucratic history suggests too strongly that the most likely result of a non-aborted idea is a much slower death caused by incessant coffee breaks.

Bureaucrats are forever grateful there is no widespread objection to the abortion of ideas in the sterile environment of government offices. Otherwise, it would be necessary to have ideas aborted in back alleys, which often are filthy because the idea of having municipal employes collect garbage on time was aborted.

Anyway, my friend Ralph simply was showing off his vocabulary when he said he could conceptualize Richard Nixon as a sportswriter. Ralph wanted me to know he is at least as smart as Hamilton Jordan.

"If Nixon covered baseball, he wouldn't report stolen bases. He'd cover them up," Ralph said. "He would do the same thing with intercepted footballs and stolen basketballs.

"If his editor asked him if there wasn't a base stolen in last night's game, Nixon would perspire on his upper lip. He would insist he wasn't in on the planning of the theft and didn't know a thing about it

31

until the next morning when he woke up in bed with second base."

It seemed like a good time to change the subject, before Ralph conceptualized that Nixon would prove he was an honorable sportswriter by marrying second base, even though he'd never gotten to first base. So I asked Ralph what he thought of the recent shuffle in Jimmy Carter's cabinet.

"The best replacement was Charles Duncan in for James Schlesinger as energy secretary," Ralph said. "I can conceptualize Duncan doing great things to keep this nation rolling on the freeways."

This surprised me. All I knew about Duncan was that he is from Georgia. Most of the political pundits insist the biggest trouble in Washington is too much Georgia. So what's so promising about Duncan?

"He used to be president of Coca-Cola," Ralph explained. "All my life I've heard about the amazing things Coca-Cola can do besides relieve thirst. I know people who say they use Coke to scrub rust off bumpers and glass rings off coffee tables. I met a lady who grew huge tomatoes in her basement. She said she watered them with Coca-Cola.

"I fully expect Charles Duncan to announce soon that American-made automobiles will run on Coke, at about 280 miles per six pack. This immediately will erase the fuel shortage. Coca-Cola is available everywhere at all times of the day or night. The people who dug up King Tutankhamen's tomb in the 14th Century had to shove aside a Coke machine to get in," Ralph said.

I have to admit that Duncan may have a marvelous conception. I only hope it isn't aborted before it is thoroughly tested. If the idea of Coke for gas must die, it should be from coffee breaks. ∎

I'm all for blue jeans that
will get women off the floor

November 9, 1979

It's not easy to be a woman. This fact often has been brought to the husband's attention, but never more vividly than when he read what some women must do to put on long pants.

During an interview with a fashion writer, Gloria Vanderbilt was praising the fit of the blue jeans she has designed. She said: "The jean that has been available till now that a lot of women wore had to be put on by lying down on the floor to zip up."

The husband couldn't help wondering: If all the women zipping up their jeans were lying end to end, would they stretch all the way around the world, only halfway, or just far enough to make it impossible to close the door of a public rest room?

The husband never has claimed to be a stylish dresser. The evidence to the contrary always has been too convincing. For example, he recently had the slob label pinned on his feet by no less a sartorial expert than Alex Karras, eminent actor and a former football lineman. Karras was discussing his former boss, Russ Thomas, general manager of the Detroit Lions, a former football team.

"I'll just never forget the time Russ called me into his office to talk about my image," Karras said. "He told me he didn't like the fact I never wore a tie. I looked at him and said, 'Russ, you're wearing Hush Puppies! Hush Puppies! You're telling me I don't wear a tie and you're wearing $12 shoes.' "

The husband has been wearing the same pair of Hush Puppies shoes for 25 years. They cost $9 new, including the cleats on the bottoms. He wears them for golfing and for making acoustical tile floors. Just last summer, on the golf course, he accidentally ran into Ray, the shoe salesman who sold him the Hush Puppies back when both of them were boys.

Ray couldn't help sobbing at the sight of his old friend in the old Hush Puppies. "You can't possibly be still wearing those shoes," Ray said. "How can you expect shoe salesmen to make a living if you spend your entire life in one unfashionable pair of shoes?"

33

"It isn't my fault that these shoes refuse to wear out," the husband explained. "Let us all pay homage to the electric golf cart."

The husband always has believed clothing shouldn't be replaced until it's worn out. In view of this unstylish attitude, it isn't surprising he was confused when he read that Gloria Vanderbilt is keeping women off their backs in bathrooms by selling them "callipygian pants." He thought these pants might be designed to be worn while dancing to calliope music in Egypt.

The dictionary straightened him out. "Callipygian" is an adjective meaning "having well-shaped buttocks." Gloria's jeans help women to have attractive rear ends.

The husband quickly decided to support callipygian pants for women. He has long been crestfallen by the fight of large-reared women in tight jeans, although until now he has hesitated to voice his dismay out loud in the supermarket. He realizes that fat men also look silly in tight pants and that all consenting adults should be allowed to wear whatever they choose just so long as no innocent cities are shattered by bursting hip pockets. He didn't want to get into trouble with liberal dresses of either sex.

But the advent of callipygian pants has encouraged the husband to speak out. Until reading Gloria Vanderbilt's advertising, he hadn't realized that some women wearing non-callipygian pants had to lie down to zip up. These women could be putting themselves into a dangerous position, not to mention embarrassing.

The husband has seen many women who, if they were to lie down with their toes up in a supermarket rest room, might not be able to get back up again without assistance. They might have to yell for the aid of a check-out boy. Or they might get stepped upon by some unfashionable acoustician wearing Hush Puppies. Either way, it's too high a price to pay for the gravity required to deflate a tummy.

Gloria Vanderbilt claims her jeans are designed to make life more comfortable for women with larger-than-average rumps. The husband thinks callipygian pants are a fine idea. He says life is tough enough for women, and they shouldn't have to zip it lying down before dancing to steam whistles along the Nile. ∎

34

Men in the Twilight Zone
don't need remote controls

April 9, 1980

Lately the husband has discovered he can adjust his TV set simply by leaning toward it. Like penicillin, it was an accidental discovery.

One night, in the middle of "M*A*S*H," the color suddenly left Hawkeye's face. The husband never has owned one of those remote control gadgets that allow a man to control a TV set several feet away without leaving his chair. He always has wanted one, but his wife has forbidden it for selfish reasons, worrying that if he weren't forced to stand up to switch channels, he might forget how to walk and she would have to carry him to bed every night.

So when Hawkeye paled, the husband struggled toward the TV. Before he got there, the color returned. He figured that was life.

"A watched pot never boils," he explained in memory of his grandmother.

"What does that mean?" asked the pampered wife for whom boiling pots have always whistled.

"It means if you watch a pot to make sure it doesn't boil over on the stove, it never will. But the minute you go into the pantry to churn butter, the pot begins boiling," he answered. "As long as I sit in my chair, there will be no color on that TV. But the minute I stand up, the color will return, before I touch the set. That is the perverse nature of life. If life weren't supposed to be that way, God would have commanded us to spread the churned butter on both sides of the bread."

Sure enough, when the husband sat back down, the TV turned black and white again. And when he stood up, the color returned before he got halfway to the set. After this procedure was repeated several times, and the husband was beginning to pound his head against his knees, he turned sly. He pretended to get out of his chair but actually only leaned forward. The TV set was fooled and the color came on. But when he leaned back, the color disappeared again.

This was when the husband knew he'd crossed over into the Twilight Zone. Simply by rocking back and forth in his chair, he could control the hues on his TV set across the room. "You are

35

married to a man with mysterious powers," he told his wife as he rocked and the TV chameleoned.

At first, the wife insisted the co-ordination was coincidence. She said the TV would lose color even if the husband didn't lean back, and vice versa. But it never happened that way. She finally was convinced when he orchestrated the changing shades of "M*A*S*H" merely by thrusting his arms toward the set while remaining seated, much like Leonard Bernstein conducting from his piano bench.

"I'll concede you are controlling the color, but you don't have any mysterious power. I could do the same thing if I were sitting in your chair," she said. "When you lean forward your body somehow interferes with the TV signal. Our antenna probably needs adjusting. There is a logical explanation for everything."

"No one else will ever sit in my chair. My power might be diluted by the presence of a foreign body," he proclaimed. "For my next demonstration I will float in the air and eat off our best dishes."

It has always disturbed the husband that the best-looking dinner plates in their home are hung on the wall, close to the ceiling. Even if someone could get high enough to eat off them, the food would slide off the plates. The husband often calls these plates to the attention of guests eating off chipped saucers from K mart. He tells the guests that after dinner they are welcome to take a walk on the handsome rug hanging on the wall in the family room. The wife thinks he is the funniest thing since butter churners.

"I would like to watch you float. In fact, I would be satisfied to just watch you get out of that chair and walk," she said. "It is always a rare pleasure to watch you do anything except sit."

"What you are forgetting," he said, "is that a watched pot never boils, especially in the Twilight Zone." ■

I don't like magazines that advertise my unimportance

April 19, 1980

Actor George Kennedy stars in a TV commercial for Tums. He drops a Tums into a glass jar, which, he says, contains stomach acid. Where did he get that stomach acid?

My wife asked me that question. I wish she hadn't. I usually try to ignore TV and radio advertising. Whenever I pay attention to those ads, they start me to thinking about things I don't want to think about.

For instance, U.S. News & World Report keeps saying on the radio: "We spare our advertisers unimportant readers." Think about that. The publisher of that magazine is claiming people who don't read it are unimportant. I don't read it.

It's not nice for a big magazine to tell me I'm not important. It's snobbish. Snobs make me angry, and I'd rather not think about them.

The only magazine I read regularly is Newsweek, and then I start at the back and never make it to the front. At the barbershop, I flip through Playboy or Penthouse, but I don't like the pictures — too clinical — and I can't read the words because I can't wear my glasses while getting my hair cut. Actually, I look at the magazine so I won't have to talk hockey with the barber. I'm afraid I might let it slip that I think hockey is a stupid game, which could cost me my ears.

I do read every page of at least two newspapers every day, and I read all sorts of paperback books. I don't like to read hardcover books because I feel guilty when I smear chocolate on them. This makes me a slob, but it doesn't make me unimportant.

I'm not saying U.S. News & World Report is a bad magazine, I'm saying I don't read it. There are thousands of magazines I don't read, but U.S. News & World Report is the only one that calls me unimportant. Not only that, it uses me in its advertising, without my permission.

The cost of magazine ads is based on demographics — not only how many people read the magazine, but also how rich they are, or how tweedy. When U.S. News & World Report brags that "we spare our advertisers unimportant readers," it is saying you can run an ad

37

in the magazine without worrying about me reading it. The idea is that if I did read your ad, I would be too dumb or too gabardine to buy what you're selling, so you shouldn't have to waste your money sending your message into my leisure suit.

There is nothing wrong with specialty magazines aimed at special audiences. It makes sense to advertise yachts in Yachting magazine, which is read by yachters, rather than in People magazine, which is read by people. People can't afford yachts, and yachters don't have time to read People because they're too busy spending two years before the mast, in tweed yardarms.

But Yachting magazine doesn't go on the radio and call me unimportant, and use my unimportance to lure advertisers. Neither does People magazine. (I read a People magazine once, and on Page 22 I asked my barber if we could go somewhere and play hockey.) I don't see why U.S. News & World Report has to denigrate me in its advertising, and I don't like to think about it.

I also don't like to think about where George Kennedy got the jar of stomach acid to drop Tums in. It seems to me that if stomach acid could be manufactured outside the stomach it wouldn't be stomach acid. Maybe it would be battery acid. What do I know?

There are laws against false advertising, so Kennedy wouldn't dare say that was stomach acid in the jar if it were really battery acid. And if stomach acid can come from nowhere except a stomach, where did Kennedy get it? How did he get it?

Before he became a Tums salesman, George Kennedy was seen most frequently in disaster movies, and he always survived while all those around him became corpses. I will leave you with that thought. You will think it the next time you see that Tums commercial, and you will realize how easy it was for me to become unimportant.

Onward and Upward. ∎

What if I should lose myself once I've finally found me?

May 24, 1980

A reader named Carol Murray figures writing a column takes only a few minutes a day, and she wonders what I do with the rest of my time. What I do is look behind bushes and under beds, searching for myself. Hoping to weather the male midlife crisis, I am trying to find my identity so I can have it altered.

Carol put her question this way:

"If your job is to help me start out my day on the right foot, then you are successful. But I imagine you typing some funny short story, which would take about an hour, and the rest of the day is spent sitting with your feet up on the desk and drinking coffee. Somehow your job seems too easy. There must be more to it than what I can think of. Please describe your job . . . "

Carol's description is accurate, except I don't drink coffee. In my younger years, I worked much harder. I was an assembly line worker for Chrysler, a mailman, an advertising salesman, a sports writer, an editor and several other things. I didn't have all these jobs at the same time, but sometimes it seemed that way. In those days, the only time I put my feet on a desk was to change a light bulb on the ceiling.

But about five years ago, I suddenly realized I was middle-aged and I still didn't know who I was, or where I was. I decided to cut my working hours so I'd have sufficient time to find myself. As a steady reader of interviews with psychologists and movie stars and other experts on functional living, I knew how important it is for a person to find himself or herself, whichever the case may be.

Once I read that Burt Reynolds didn't find himself until he was 40 years old. At the time, this made me feel smug. I had thought I found myself when I was only 30, while looking in a mirror. But, after serious reflection, I realized it was shallow of me to think I could polish my image simply by rubbing it with Windex. I kept looking.

My concern deepened when I read about Dom DeLuise, the chubby comedian, who said: " . . . It's so easy to lose who you are."

This raised the possibility of more than one search for the same me. Even if I did find myself, I could later lose myself. Repeated searches would leave me no time for work at all, not even as a one-hour-a-day columnist. I vowed that once I did find myself, I would never let myself out of my sight.

Then I read an interview with Michael E. McGill, a PhD from the University of South Carolina. He wrote a book called "The 40- to 60-Year-Old Male," in which he said every male has a midlife crisis. By age 50 I had experienced no hot flashes and no impulse to wear a pizza-sized medallion around my neck, so I naively hoped I had slept through my midlife crisis. Dr. McGill convinced me I was mistaken.

"The midlife crisis stops when the man alters his identity in such a way that he is no longer vulnerable to threats to that identity which brought about the crisis in the first place," Dr. McGill said. "If there is no fundamental alteration in his identity, the man will remain ever vulnerable to those same threats, ever vulnerable to crisis."

This means when I finally do discover my identity, my task won't be completed. I must also take it in for alterations. Naturally, there is no way I can know whether I should be shortened or lengthened until I find me. Maybe all I will need is a tuck under the chin.

Obviously, my time is running out. I don't want to be an old man before I know who I am. Certainly, I don't want my survivors to say I died of midlife crisis, at the age of 80, without ever knowing who I was.

So, in answer to Carol Murray's question, that's what I do when I'm not writing a column. I try to find myself.

And that's all for today. Not only is my hour up, but I just glanced out the window and I think I saw me walking down the street, toward a saloon. ■

The waiting game comes with a new set of dangers

January 17, 1981

Some people, mostly historians, insist there is nothing new in the world. They say all things are reruns and recycles. Don't believe it. In this world today, there is a new way of waiting.

I don't mean there is a new reason for waiting. Yesterday, today and tomorrow, people stand in line, or sit in waiting rooms, for only one reason — there are too many of them and not enough of what they are waiting for.

Usually, people wait for service. They wait for beyond their appointment times to see a doctor because they need the doctor more than the doctor needs them, and the doctor knows it. They wait for hours in checkout lines because there isn't another supermarket in their neighborhood, a fact which allows strategically located supermarkets to keep half their checkout counters closed at all times without fear of losing customers.

Of course, within this one, broad, supply-demand reason for waiting, there is room for interpolation, thus making it possible for secondary sources to increase the aggravation of the people waiting. That is, you can wait one hour because your greedy doctor overbooked his appointments, and you can wait an extra 15 minutes because the patient ahead of you can't find the Blue Cross card in her suitcase-size purse.

Likewise, when you have no appointment, as at the bank, it isn't always fair to blame management for all of your long wait. You can wait 90 minutes because six out of 10 teller windows are closed, and you can wait 30 extra minutes because two customers ahead of you didn't begin making out their deposit slips until they reached the teller.

Usually, an interpolator is more agonizing than the original source of a wait. This is because the interpolator, before she is unmasked, appears to be just the person ahead of you in line, a fellow victim of the waiting process, someone who should share your misery, not add to it. (I use the female pronoun because it has been my experience that most waiting interpolators are women. I don't know why this is, but I think it has something to do with purses.)

41

No matter what they're waiting for, interpolators fail to prepare for the time when they will reach the head of the line. Interpolators never have the correct change ready. I have waited at a bus stop with a woman for 20 minutes, then waited several more minutes inside the bus while she searched her purse for bus fare. She had 20 minutes to do that. Dear Lord, why didn't she?

Some Sundays, in church, I see a woman who begins writing a check for the collection plate when the usher is 10 pews away from her. She had all week plus the first 70 minutes of the church service to write that check, but the usher has to wait for it.

Obviously, there is room for waiting interpolators to be innovative. But, while their ingenuity may add immeasurably to the unhappiness of the people behind them, interpolators add nothing new to the manner in which this waiting is done. And that's what I started to tell you about — a new way of waiting, created by automation.

Traditionally, people standing in line have closed ranks tightly, shuffling ever forward, never leaving gaps to tempt interlopers. But now there is a new type of line in which the waiting people purposely leave large gaps between each other.

These gapped lines can be seen at those automated banking devices into which each customer must punch his or her secret number to withdraw money. Waiting customers don't stand close to each other for fear of being accused of trying to see another guy's person's secret number. In acceptably civilized fashion, no one expects to be trusted.

The hardest part about this new way of waiting is that each waiter in a gapped line must be ever alert that no interloper lopes into a gap. Special vigilance is required against interpolating interlopers, which are the worst kind. ■

Game shows easier to take
if your mind's on vacation

May 2, 1981

While we were sitting in a CBS-TV studio in Hollywood, waiting for the show to start, a young man leaned into my view, looked me over closely and said: "Tell me the truth. You've never seen 'Price Is Right' on television, have you?"

I confessed I not only had never seen the program, I'd never even heard of it before that very day, and, once more, the few TV game shows I had watched were so bad they made my socks unravel.

"I knew it. I can always tell," said the young man, who was a CBS employe. If he worked in a theater, he would be called an usher. But people who usher in TV studios are called pages. I don't know why this is. I wanted to ask the young man why he wasn't an usher, but before I could he turned and walked away.

"That's the other side of the page," I told my wife, pointing at his back.

The page's acute observation concerning my presence at a taping of "Price Is Right" raised two questions that certainly should be dealt with as part of my never-ending study of the human condition, particularly as it is reflected in the strange behavior of people who talk smarter than they act.

First, how could that page tell, just by looking at me, that I was not a "Price Is Right" habitue? Second, if I can't stomach game shows, why did I voluntarily, of my own free will, spend almost three hours surrounded by deranged people who kept screaming right prices at Bob Barker, the boyishly handsome host who obviously must be aging horribly on a kinescope of a 1950 episode of "Truth or Consequences" currently stored in the attic of a Screen Gems warehouse abandoned many years ago in rural Pasadena?

It was apparent that the answer to the first question would be found on my face. At first, I figured the page could tell from my pursed lips that the only reason I own a TV set is to watch National Geographic specials. But my wife pointed out that many other people in the audience also had pursed lips, and the page hadn't accused any of them of being infiltrators sent by public television.

43

We finally decided the page was tipped off to my unfamiliarity with "Price Is Right" by the extremely astounded look in my eyes.

I was astounded by the crowd's reaction to the warm-up entertainment provided by Johnny Olsen, the program's triple-tongued announcer. To get the studio audience in a happy mood before the taping began, he told several jokes concerning older people's alleged lack of sexual prowess, and the resulting laughter was uproarious. Olsen didn't say anything remotely funny, but everyone laughed as though Jack Benny had been reincarnated. Astounding. The only explanation is that the entire audience was in California on vacation. Because of the high cost of vacations, tourists are determined to have a good time no matter what. If they'd been born earlier, the tourists who laughed at Olsen might have chuckled while going down with the Titanic.

The program itself is a fascinating exhibition of orchestrated greed. Selected members of the audience are loudly instructed by Olsen to "C'mon Down," an order which causes them to leap screaming from their seats and trample everyone nearby while running to the stage where they trade spasms for prizes.

I am told that "Price Is Right" is aired for an hour ever weekday and millions of people watch it. Astounding. Which brings us to the second question prompted by the inquiring page. If I think TV game shows are so dumb, why did I watch one being taped?

My answer is borrowed from the intrepid people who climb mountains. I watched "Price Is Right" because it was there. And that same day, climbing the highest peak, I watched the taping of the last "Laverne and Shirley" show of the current season. It was bad enough to make even tourists frown.

Take it from me, it's not easy to be intrepid in TV land. How would you like to climb a mountain while your socks unravel? ■

Even this old father
can disspend face

May 18, 1981

"This is a good place to dissave," I told my wife. We were in Caesars gambling casino in Lake Tahoe, Nev., and had lost $20 to the slot machines in 15 minutes.

"Dissave" is my favorite new word. I learned it from Michael Evans, who is a Washington economist. He told Congress' Joint Economic Committee that "consumer surveys show that half the nation's households dissave on balance at a rate of about five percent."

A household that dissaves money spends more than it earns and goes into debt. This is the opposite of a household that earns more money than it spends, or disdebts.

You can probably remember when a household that spent more than it earned was described as losing ground. But "losing" is a negative word. It sounds much more positive to say the household is dissaving ground. And when dissaved ground is recovered, it is dislost. Tomorrow's children, picking coins off the street, will shout: "Finders keepers, disfinders dislaughers."

There is a mind exercise designed to help mentally sluggish people who have trouble understanding such words as dissave. These disforward people are advised to meditate while repeating a mantra concerning the true meaning of the word "dismantle." To dismantle is to take a center fielder apart. The mantra is "Mickey Dismantle."

Similarly, to discover is to pull back the blanket, to dissuade is to take off suede shoes, to dislodge is to exit from the Lodge freeway and to dispair is to split a pair of jacks.

End of English lesson. Return with me now to the land of chance, where it was decided that a good way to stop dissaving amid the slot machines would be to see a lounge act. Readers who don't frequent gambling casinos in Lake Tahoe and Las Vegas may be surprised to learn that lounges act. They don't do drama. Lounges act as a refuge for tourists who want to sit down but can't afford the main act.

Main acts are performed in huge room inside which hundreds of people who don't know each other share the same table and encroach upon each others' thighs while rising to give standing ovations in

45

recognition of the rare talent displayed by waitresses who get an order right. Lounge acts are performed in little saloons which usually are comfortable because whenever a lounge act attracts large crowds, it is promoted to a main act. Many of today's best-known main acts used to be lounge acts. When Errol Flynn was alive, Ronald Reagan was a lounge act.

The evening we were at Caesars, the main act was Chicago and the cover charge was $30 per person, a dissaving price I wouldn't pay to see all of Illinois. We sat in the lounge where, for the price of our drinks, the act was the Four Freshmen. My youngest daughter was present, and after she explained that Chicago is a musical group, I also explained something. I said I'd often seen the Four Freshmen perform in Detroit when I was a college freshman myself. "That explains why they look so old," my daughter said.

Phooey on her. I like the Four Freshmen because they sing songs that can be hummed, which is my only musical talent. Young people today don't hum as they leave rock concerts, they reverberate. By coincidence, I'd done much humming on our U-turn motor trip toward Lake Tahoe, which included stops at Amarillo, Tex.; Gallup, N.M.; Flagstaff and Kingman, Ariz., and San Bernardino, Calif. My companions reacted doubtfully — even derisively — when I said I was humming a song about all those towns. They said there was no such song.

That's where the marvelous coincidence came in. At Caesars lounge, the first song the Four Freshman sang was "Get Your Kicks on Route 66." Ah. It was immensely satisfying to watch my daughter as she heard our itinerary in rhythm and rhyme and was forced to admit her old Dad had been humming sense.

Life can be beautiful. I felt like a main act, or dislounged. ■

Of 18-hour bras and
five-day deodorant pads

June 24, 1981

Usually, I don't question TV commercials. I ignore them, or enjoy them, or curse at their stupidity, but I don't worry about what they mean. That's why I was surprised to hear myself ask my wife, "What is an 18-hour bra?"

Jane Russell was selling them on Channel 7 to women with mature figures. Maybe that's why I was unusually curious. I'm old enough to remember when Jane became famous for wearing a bra especially invented for her by Howard Hughes. At least, that's the legend.

I never have known exactly what a five-day deodorant pad is, and I have never cared that I didn't know. I've probably seen or heard more than a thousand advertisements for the five-day pad, but I've never read enough, or listened enough, to learn exactly how it works. I'm just not interested enough, probably because there is no legend attached to the five-day deodorant pad.

This isn't surprising. I'm not sure, but I imagine the deodorant pad is worn in armpits. It would be difficult to carry a legend around under each arm, no matter how firmly the legends were attached to the pads.

Of course, it also must be difficult to wear a bra to which a legend is attached. This probably explains why you seldom see Jane Russell without her teeth clenched. Whatever. My point is that I was content to live my entire life without ever knowing much about the five-day deodorant pad, but the minute I heard Jane Russell mention the 18-hour bra, I wanted to know precisely how it works.

I'm sure the difference in my reaction to these two timed products isn't because of the 102-hour gap, but rather because of the aura of mystery surrounding any bra worn by Jane Russell. This aura, provided by the mysterious Howard Hughes, undoubtedly supplies the buoyancy required to keep the attached legend from becoming too much of a drag on the bra.

Lately I've been intrigued by the advertising for Mitchum stick and spray deodorant. Mitchum claims to be so effective that "sometimes you can skip a day." I guess this means Mitchum applied on Monday will keep you smelling nice until Wednesday if the weather isn't too warm Tuesday. This makes me suspect that a five-day deodorant pad is worn continuously for five days, which seems like an awfully long time to keep your arms close to your sides. But I don't know if this is true and, as long as the five-day pad has no aura-wrapped legend attached to it, I don't care.

The only reason I mention the Mitchum advertising is to speculate on the fascinating possibilities it suggests. The deodorant industry is fiercely competitive, and when one deodorant claims to be effective "X" number of days, an escalation of claims is inevitable. The logical winner is a deodorant that has to be applied only "once in a lifetime." Or perhaps a deodorant that doesn't have to be applied at all, but merely lived in the same city with. Now that is a really great idea if I do say so myself. I think I smell a legend.

But back to the 18-hour bra. My wife said it is called that because it can be worn for 18 hours. Does that mean it is thrown away, like a disposable diaper, after being used less than a day? No, my wife said, it means the bra can be worn comfortably for 18 hours.

What happens if the bra isn't removed after 18 hours? Does the wearer begin to itch, or topple, or constrict? My wife said this isn't really important because almost no one stays awake for more than 18 hours a day and no woman wears a bra to bed. I don't know about that.

I knew an old-fashioned woman who couldn't sleep in her train berth because of the jiggling. So she put her corset on beneath her nightgown and slept soundly. That is a true story, reprinted by Readers Digest, many years before Charlie's Angels.

Another thing: How many hours' rest does an 18-hour bra require before it can be worn comfortably again? And if there is a legend attached to the bra, does it sleep with the legend above or below the covers? ∎

48

Chocolate sauce causes less talk than a trumpet in bed

October 18, 1982

The way I figure it, if a wealthy person can't go to bed with a trumpet without getting a mess of bad publicity, what's the good in having enough money to buy all the horns you want?

Recently a young woman and I got stuck to each other with Hershey's chocolate sauce. Now that's kinky. But no TV reports or headlines or lawsuits resulted from our unusual relationship. I'm convinced we were allowed to get sticky together in relative anonymity simply because we don't have much money.

Conversely, life is a much different bowl of fish for Peter and Roxanne Pulitzer of Palm Beach, Fla. In a deposition made before their divorce trial, according to the Associated Press, Peter Pulitzer testified that Roxanne used a trumpet during seances she regularly conducted in her bedroom with 10 or 15 friends.

"Roxanne would lie on the bed and, at the foot of the bed, would be a trumpet with a black cape," Peter testified.

Subsequently, these headlines appeared in the New York Post — "Pulitzer Sex Trial Shocker: 'I Slept with a Trumpet!'" and "Trumpet Was Her Bedmate." And now Roxanne is suing the Post for $10 million in damages, claiming the newspaper exposed her to ridicule.

I don't know why Roxanne Pulitzer crawled into bed with a trumpet on seance nights. She testified she'd been told it was symbolic of the trumpet that Archangel Michael used to summon other archangels. Maybe Roxanne used it to summon the spirits of all dead people who wanted to see a trumpet with its cape off.

It doesn't matter. I'm not concerned with the reason for Roxanne's relationship, whatever it is, with a trumpet. For me, as an avid anthropologist, it is more interesting to ponder the social customs that allow me and a partner to wallow anonymously in Hershey's chocolate sauce while someone like Roxanne Pulitizer becomes front page news for nothing more than allegedly sleeping with a trumpet instead of, say, a teddy bear.

The difference, of course, is money. Roxanne Pulitzer claims her husband is worth $25 million. Peter is the grandson of Joseph

49

Pulitzer, who launched a newspaper empire and founded the annual journalism prizes named for him. And now, simply because the media panders to a public fascinated by rich people, Peter Pulitzer can't get a divorce from a woman and her horn without suffering embarrassing publicity.

Every time Peter and Roxanne accuse each other of such insignificant aberrations as promiscuity, dope smuggling and incest, the media makes a big deal out of it. By the time the Pulitzers are divorced and the custody of their five-year-old twin sons is awarded, the couple will be the hoot of Palm Beach. And journalists who win Pulitzer prizes will hear more snickers than applause.

That's the price of great wealth, and it sometimes is paid by innocent people.

On the other hand, except for this personal confession, you wouldn't have heard the slightest whisper about the girl and me sticking together through thin (hot fudge is thick, but we didn't have any).

The girl was Emily, my youngest grandchild, who recently spent a few days visiting my home to celebrate her first birthday. Every night after dinner she sat on my lap and we shared a large bowl of ice cream awash in Hershey's chocolate sauce. I used one spoon and Emily used two hands. And when the bowl was emptied, and it came time for the two of us to separate, it hurt — something like removing an adhesive bandage.

It is a great joy to see what a lovely mess a one-year-old can make if given half the chance by a sappy grandfather. But I wouldn't want to read about it in the New York Post ("Old Man and Tot Get Sauced").

I would never be corny enough to tell Peter and Roxanne that the best things in life, such as five-year-old twins, are free. That would be dumb economics. But a can of Hershey's chocolate sauce costs only 75 cents, which is probably cheaper than buying a trumpet from an archangel. ∎

Steamed thorn birds not palatable to McDonald's

March 30, 1983

According to legend, a thorn bird lives long enough to sing only one song before being either fried or broiled to death in a fast-food restaurant.

Whether a broiled or fried thorn bird tastes better currently is the subject of an advertising war between Burger King and McDonald's. Ironically, some of that advertising is being televised during "The Thorn Birds," a four-part series which, according to my favorite TV critic, contains "one of television history's truly steamy love scenes."

McDonald's reportedly advised its franchise holders not to advertise during "The Thorn Birds" unless the ads aired before the steamy love scene. Some veteran observers of fast food believe McDonald's took that stand because steam fogs windows and encourages customer graffiti. No McDonald's franchise wants "Ronald McDonald Is No Celibate" lettered on its front window.

However, a McDonald's spokesman said the company had nothing against steam in itself, but only against the steam generated when a Catholic priest broke his vow of celibacy in "The Thorn Birds." Such steam is not suitable for family viewing, the spokesman said.

And he added that McDonald's prefers its cooking process to be called grilling, not frying. It is believed the only difference is that a grilled thorn bird is questioned about its chastity; if the answers aren't family-oriented, the bird isn't fried, it is shooed down the street to a Burger King.

According to my monitoring, my local ABC-TV station didn't air any McDonald's ads before the steamy love scene. Sponsors of "The Thorn Birds" on Detroit Channel 7 included Burger King, Denny's restaurants, Renault cars, Jeep Scramblers, Commodore computers, Gallo wine, E.F. Hutton, Oil of Olay, Blue Cross-Blue Shield, Maybelline lipstick, American Greeting Easter cards, Calvin Klein jeans, Prell shampoo, Scope mouthwash, Toyota, Lady's Choice deodorant, Jell-O, American Airlines, Tampax, Permalens contact lenses, Sunoco and Independent Insurance Agents.

That last sponsor doesn't surprise me. My friend Howard Bon

Vivant is an independent insurance agent and I always suspected he wasn't suitable for family viewing. But what about all those other advertisers? Is the public to believe Blue Cross-Blue Shield and E.F. Hutton approve of a Catholic priest and a married woman getting steamy during prime time?

What about American Greeting Easter cards? Along with McDonald's, the United States Catholic Conference and many members of the clergy publicly objected to "The Thorn Birds," especially to its timing — it began on Palm Sunday and runs deep into Holy Week. If McDonald's wouldn't use the adulterous conduct of a priest to sell fast food, how could American Greeting use it to sell cards celebrating the resurrection of Jesus Christ?

But that is an unimportant question. Probably those advertisers think it's silly to require celibacy of a priest, not to mention Ronald McDonald, so why worry about sponsoring a soap opera in which Richard Chamberlain acts more like Dr. Kildare than Pope Paul?

The important question concerns the comparative advertising used by Burger King during "The Thorn Birds." It claimed a recent taste test revealed that people prefer broiled burgers to fried burgers, not to mention thorn birds. When Burger King used similar advertising last year, McDonald's filed a lawsuit, which wasn't dropped until Burger King reportedly agreed to stop the ads. But now Burger King is back at it again, and God knows what will happen next.

How about a taste test to discover which is worse — people's taste in TV shows or their taste in fast food?

Also, McDonald's should admit the only reason it shoos an occasional bird down the street to a Burger King is that the lyrics to some thorn birds' love song are too kinky for family hearing: "Give yourself a beak today." ■

I'd have more hair appeal
if my wife weren't so thrifty

April 4, 1983

A few months ago, it was reported here that although I was then using Suave shampoo, people never called me an old smoothy. Despite regular applications of Suave, the shampoo for people who desire smooth relationships, my life was still bumpy. I couldn't understand it.

So, in an effort to strike up smooth relationships with people who bumped me, I switched to Head and Shoulders shampoo. According to TV commercials, persons who don't use Head and Shoulders continually scratch their heads, which offends people who bump into them and causes these people to turn around and run away. So I figured if I used Head and Shoulders, I would be able to keep my fingers out of my hair, and people who bumped me would stick around out of curiosity to see what I did instead of scratch my head when I'm perplexed, which is often.

One thing perplexing me is President Reagan's hair. No matter how old he gets, his hair stays exactly the same. I saw him twice on TV the other night, 72 years old in the 11 o'clock news and 53 in a midnight movie called "The Killers." In 19 years, his perfectly trained pompadour didn't gray, thin or muss even slightly. I don't think Reagan has to comb his hair. He commands it, like a pet dog.

On the other hand, Reagan's 1964 co-star was Angie Dickinson and not only has her hair changed through the years, so has her nose. It has shrunk considerably. So one person loses part of a nose in 19 years while another person doesn't lose even one strand of hair trained to fetch newspapers. If that's not perplexing, it's at least politics.

Anyway, I'm no longer perplexed by why Suave shampoo didn't make me smooth, or Head and Shoulders didn't make me stop scratching my head when I see President Reagan's hair sit up. I discovered my wife was watering my shampoo.

I used to marvel at how long a bottle of shampoo lasted me. Shampoo isn't like razor blades; you can't keep using the last drop over and over until you remember to buy a new bottle. But I always thought it was remarkable how very seldom I had to buy shampoo. I was reminded of the Bible story where Jesus blessed the wine bottles so they kept pouring and never emptied, which impressed me more than unlimited loaves and fishes.

However, it also seemed remarkable that my shampoo changed its texture inside the bottle all by itself, without being touched by human beings. At first, the shampoo was globby and easy to pour onto my hand and rub into my skull. But later it got thinner and much of it trickled between my fingers. And later yet the shampoo became so thin I had to purse my hand to hold it and swoop it swiftly onto my head before it evaporated from sheer lack of substance.

And all during this startling metamorphosis, the miraculous bottle remained almost full while the shampoo produced less and less suds. I finally asked my wife what was going on and she said she read in a magazine that a good way to save money was to extend the life of shampoo by adding water.

A quick investigation revealed that she didn't add water to her shampoo, which is different from mine because it's for golden, lustrous hair. Mine is for dirty, greasy hair. She explained she didn't water her shampoo because she didn't want to save too much money for fear it would pile up around the house and block the passageway used by visitors who come to get a sunburn from sitting near her hair.

So now I understand why no one called me an old smoothy and I scratched my head when I saw Ronald Reagan's pompadour roll over for Angie Dickinson . My hair appeal was terminally diluted by my wife.

Life was a lot simpler before I got so clean. When I was a boy, the only reason I played school sports was so I could tell my mother I took a shower in the locker room. And I told my teammates I showered at home. I thought that was suave. ■

Candlelight photography
is just too much trouble

June 17, 1983

In TV commercials, Kodak is currently promoting a new film that will "take pictures by the light of a candle." It's not for me.

In the beginning, pictures were taken by the light of the sun. The photographer always was careful to have the sun at his back. If he were taking a photo of people, the way he measured whether there was enough sunlight to get a good reproduction was to ask his subjects to stop squinting. If they couldn't stop, there was enough sunlight.

If the old-fashioned photographer were taking a picture of an inanimate object, such as a building, he didn't have to tell it to stop squinting — or to stand still or smile, either. That is why, even today, regardless of the many improvements made in photo technology during the past 100 years, it still isn't necessary for architectural photographers to know how to talk, and it's a rare building that knows how to say cheese.

I became a professional photographer around the same time flashbulbs became a popular substitute for the sun. In between sunlight and flashbulbs there was a period when photographers created phony sunlight by exploding gunpowder to produce a sudden flash of light. This was done mainly in early James Cagney movies.

Anyway, there still are several people alive today who will laugh and slap their fat ugly thighs when they learn that I described myself as a onetime professional photographer. It may be true that I've lived much of my life slightly out of focus. But I did get paid to take pictures, and there's no question that reimbursement is the crucial criterion that distinguishes the professional from the amateur. If I won the photographers' race in the 1984 Olympics, I would have to give back my gold medal as soon as some jealous loser revealed that I was once paid money to take photos of high school football games.

My main job was writing about the games, but the newspaper that employed me couldn't afford to employ anyone else. So, along with my pencil and notebook, I also carried a 150-pound Speed Graphic camera and a bag full of film slides and flashbulbs as I ran along the sidelines. Ninety-nine percent of my photos died a deserved death in the darkroom, but that didn't matter. It was night football and I learned early in my journalistic career that all pictures of night football games look alike. So if I didn't get a decent photo of one game, I simply substituted a photo taken of an earlier game. One season I illustrated five different game stories with the same photo of a touchdown-scoring halfback who'd graduated two years earlier.

In those days, my main problem was that the high school didn't want used flashbulbs discarded on its athletic field, so I put them back in the bag. And then I couldn't tell the used bulbs from the new bulbs, so I frequently took photos that looked as if they were snapped during the United Coal Mine League playoffs.

Today, instead of sunshine, sophisticated photographers use light generated by a battery concealed somewhere inside the camera. And whenever a grandchild falls into a bowl of frosting, the battery is dead. But I don't care. I quit taking photos several years ago, right after the laughter died down. The laughter erupted when I asked a friend why a Polaroid Land Camera couldn't be used at sea, and he said it was invented by Edwin Land.

I certainly never intend to use the new Kodak film that takes pictures by the light of a candle. Sure, there would be no reason for the person I was photographing to squint. And I wouldn't have to worry about using used flashbulbs. But even if I remembered the candle, I'd forget the matches. ∎

If you're in high dungeon, you're sure to be gormless

July 1, 1983

A typically anonymous note from Dave Rood, editor of The Delta Reporter in Gladstone, Mich., said: "A historical marker denoting the place where Jim Fitzgerald was held in high dungeon is entirely out of order," according to Louise Bolitho, chairwoman of the Northern Michigan Society of Semantics. She was in high dudgeon when she said this. "That smart aleck should remember that stone walls do not a prism make," she added. "If he keeps that up I might even cancel my prescription when it perspires."

Even though there was no signature on the sneaky note, I knew it came from Rood because I recognized his rigid cowardice and limp wit. Rood was responding to a recent column in which I wrote that untrue charges made against me by my much older sister, Terrible Jean, put me in such "high dungeon" that I wouldn't dignify them with a reply. Rood was struck by my use of the word "dungeon" instead of "dudgeon."

He was not alone. Alice Peterson of Rochester, Mich., wrote: "Instead of sanctimoniously praising yourself for refusing to reply to Terrible Jean's accusations, you should fall down on your knees and give thanks that she did not call you a gormless dunderhead! Not only do you use dungeon in place of dudgeon on June 25, you drag that damned dungeon through the rest of your column, skipping gaily from the wrong word to a metaphor — or pun or whatever — of the wrong word, and back again."

Gormless dunderhead? I'm not surprised at Dave Rood's lack of sophistication, which is well-known throughout the Upper Peninsula, but I am surprised that someone who knows what gormless means wasn't smart enough to recognize that my use of dungeon was completely appropriate and not a pun or metaphor. ("Gormless" means unaware, dull or stupid. You read it here first, I'm sure.)

There was also a letter addressed to Terrible Jean from an old (what else?) and obviously demented friend of hers, Bill Arnold of Detroit, which said: "My memory of you is one of an intelligent, witty, charming and articulate person, whose cross to bear is that of the sister to an insensitive lout, a lout who has great need of a

57

dictionary so he can understand the difference between 'dudgeon' and 'dungeon.' Being the sniveling wimp that he is, he probably will blame the proofreader, typesetter or whoever it is that who tries to protect the public from his numerous and most obvious errors."

Arnold went on to say that he has "a friend with a dog which frequently has elimination difficulties. When this occurs, my friend solves it by giving the dog an issue of the Free Press which has Jim's column. The dog without assistance locates the column, separates it from the other sections, and promptly finds relief. Please tell brother Jim he is free to use this testimonial."

But enough of these scurrilous attacks upon my journalistic ability. They are completely without validity and the only reason I publish such malicious insults is to make Bob Talbert jealous.

According to most any dictionary, to be dungeoned is to be "shut up in or as if in a dungeon." Terrible Jean shut me up when she called me a worthless rat, a cheapskate and a creepo. I was left speechless by the injustice of her accusations, so I did not dignify them with a reply.

Emily Dickinson wrote: "Dungeoned in the human breast doubtless secrets lie." One of my secrets is whether I believe the Tower of London contains a high dudgeon or a prism cell. The answer would be a true measure of my gormness, which is confidential.

Here's looking at you — and that guy's dog. ∎

Someone's missed the cue in ignoring lofty pool shooters

July 30, 1983

It may be too late for a poolroom-behavior specialist to conduct a study aimed at discovering the possible effects of great heights on pool players.

Too bad. There are not many important questions left unanswered in this curious world. For instance, a British animal-behavior specialist recently conducted a study which finally answered a question that has puzzled people for years — should or shouldn't John McEnroe grunt when he serves tennis balls?

He shouldn't. Dr. Dennis Lendrem of Nottingham University studied McEnroe's serves at Wimbledon and published the results in New Scientist magazine. Dr. Lendrem discovered McEnroe's opponents were less able to return his ungrunted serves. Thank God that's settled.

Another example of how our intellectual community leaves no crucial mystery unsolved was recently supplied by Stephen Worchel, a social psychologist at the University of Virginia. His study revealed that people stand closer together while waiting in line for an X-rated movie than for a G-rated movie.

I always suspected that, but couldn't prove it. Now, thanks to the University of Virginia, I have the documented evidence needed to persuade my wife to let down the full hem on my raincoat, thus preventing the person behind me from stepping on my heels.

Ironically, I feel guilty about my gratitude to the universities and professors who discover the answers to questions pertaining to such cosmic subjects as tennis grunts and porno fans. That's because it may be my fault if the world never learns the difference between playing pool on the ground and in the air.

Several years ago I made a dream come true. I bought a full-size pool table for my basement. It cost too much, but I blunted my wife's objections by pointing out that the table brought us closer together. Before I got it, she had to phone me at a tavern. Now all she had to do was holler down the clothes chute.

At first, the dream purchase was a success. I enjoyed pool in my basement even more than when I played in poolrooms and bars.

59

There were no problems worthy of university study until we sold our house and moved into a 26th-floor apartment.

My wife was sure the pool table would have to be left behind. But I said we could knock out a wall between two bedrooms, creating ample space for the pool table. When grandchildren visited, they could sleep under the table and, in case of a tornado, be the best-protected kids in town. Did she want her sweet grandchildren injured by a tornado? What kind of a grandmother was she?

The moving cost, added to the expense of remodeling the apartment, brought tears to my checkbook. But what the heck. All my life I wanted just an ordinary pool table, but now, by God, I owned the highest pool table in Detroit — perhaps in the world. What fun!

Except I quit playing pool. That huge table sat there filling up two rooms for six years and I didn't use it six times. My wife sometimes used it for cutting sewing patterns and diapering grandchildren. I couldn't look at it without wishing for a tornado so I wouldn't feel so dumb.

Why did I suddenly lose interest in pool? I don't know. I suspect the reason has much to do with playing 26 floors in the air as compared to in the basement. I think an animal-behavior specialist from the University of Michigan should study this cosmic question and furnish a definitive answer.

Unfortunately, no psychologist can study pool players using my table on high. Last month I sold it. It seemed the only way to stop my wife from wishing aloud that we still lived in our old house so she could stuff my wasteful, non-pool-playing carcass down the clothes chute.

Barring an unexpected scientific breakthrough, I may have to live the rest of my life knowing what grunts do to tennis balls but not what heights do to pool players. It's enough to make a man trip on his own raincoat. ▰

Some people milk one mistake for all it's worth

For Labor Day, I was requested to wear "something in pastel colors or soft patterns." Appearance is important. That's why, if my wife hadn't already broke her foot stepping in a hole, she could break it kicking Victoria Principal in the fanny.

But there is more to appearance than the right clothes and a taut body. Besides not wanting to look fat and unfashionable, I also don't want to appear dumb. That is often a problem.

For instance, I purchased a half-gallon carton of milk at the grocery store and brought took it home with me. That isn't dumb; it's my job. My wife gave it to me and, if you'll excuse the immodesty, I do it rather well. I also am skilled at buying bread and bringing it home. You might say bread and milk are my life. At least, they're all my wife and I ever talk to each other about on the phone. She says bring milk and bread home and, by God, I always get the job done.

But I can't do everything well. I have my limitations and usually don't attempt to exceed them, for fear of appearing dumb. Until the other day, I never tried to do too much with milk. I simply put the carton on the kitchen counter and walked away from it. I didn't try to put it where it belongs.

It was because of my wife's broken foot that I went too far with milk and allowed it to make me look dumb. Since it's been difficult for her to get around, I have nobly taken over many of her household chores, such as making my side of the bed and putting my used paper plate in the waste basket. She is no longer on crutches, or even using a cane, and her limp is barely noticeable, but she still hasn't decreed that it is no longer necessary for me to treat her like the Queen of the World. I may become the first person in medical history to die from someone else's broken bone.

Anyway, it was in my role as handmaiden to the queen that I put the milk in the refrigerator. I even remembered to first put the carton in the plastic holder with the big handle that makes it easy to pour a half-gallon container with one hand when you need the other hand to hold your crutch. I was quite proud of myself. My dumb act had been committed, but it was not immediately evident.

Dinner time was dumb time. My wife forgot to serve my customary glass of milk and I offered, like a gentleman, to get up and fetch my own after she sweetly said it was either that or go without. Naturally I had trouble opening the new carton, but that's not what made me appear dumb. Safecrackers have trouble opening milk cartons. Where it says "Open Here," it should say "Open Here If You Have Iron Fingers, Otherwise It's Easier to Drive to a Farm and Milk a Cow."

It was when I attempted to pour the milk that I appeared dumb. When I'd put the milk in the plastic holder, I'd neglected to situate the carton spout directly opposite the holder handle. Instead, the spout was to the immediate right of the handle. If the carton were tipped forward in the normal manner, the milk would pour out the side, missing the glass by several inches. In golfing terms, the milk would be shanked.

"You probably think I put the carton in the holder this strange way so I could pour milk around a corner," I said, trying not to appear dumb in the queen's eyes. "Actually, I did it because I always like to know what time it is. When I pour milk sideways with my left hand, I can see my wristwatch at the same time."

But I know she didn't believe me. Despite my correct clothing and taut body from doing Victoria Principal exercises, I appeared dumb. Hoping to regain her esteem, I explained that Channel 2 had requested me to wear pastel colors or soft patterns on Labor Day because they televise best and I was scheduled to appear smart on the Jerry Lewis Telethon.

"I will tell all my friends to watch for you," she said. "I'll tell them you'll be the man looking into the camera with his ear." ■

Art dealers, have I
got a lamp for you!

November 26, 1983

My wife bought an amazing hanging lamp from Sears for $40. I think I can sell it to the Detroit Institute of Arts (DIA) for at least $100,000.

At an art auction, the DIA recently paid $67,000 for a 1939, black-and-white photograph of locomotive wheels. I looked at that picture for a long time, in my most sophisticated art-gallery manner. I squinted and then opened my eyes wide; I held the photo close to my nose, and then looked at it from across the room. I asked myself what the photo said to me, and what I wanted to say back to it.

But I couldn't figure out why it's worth $67,000. It may be worth $63,452, but not $67,000.

A spokesman for the auction house that saw the DIA coming explained that the photo "epitomizes the Industrial Age." Oh.

But what that $67,000 photo said to me was: "Here are a couple of locomotive wheels that pulled many freight cars in 1939." And what I wanted to say back to it was: "You are a nice enough photo but the locomotive wheels appear to be working properly, which doesn't epitomize the Industrial Age to me, unless it took from 1939 until now to get the photograph developed because the drugstore mislaid the film."

My wife's lamp does a better job of epitomizing the Industrial Age because of the astonishing things it can do that a candle or kerosene lamp could never do. Locomotive wheels transport freight and people, but so did stagecoaches and canal boats. The amazing lamp from Sears does more than merely improve upon the light provided by fire. It also mystifies and spooks, and causes grown people to cry like babies.

This lamp hangs on a chain in my old poolroom that is now the family room. My wife bought it so as not to waste the hook in the ceiling from which my Budweiser pool-table lamp used to hang. She simply could have removed the hook, but that wouldn't have cost $40 and caused grown people to cry like babies, so naturally she didn't do it. She has a reputation to maintain.

The first thing I noticed about the lamp is it has no switch. There

63

is no visible means of turning it on and off. It is the same as a candle with no match and no pursed lips to blow. How can that be?

"Just touch it on the base," my wife said smugly. Sure enough. First touch for dim, second for medium, third for bright, and fourth for back to darkness. Wow.

I have no idea how that touch system works, or why Sears substituted it for the ordinary on-off switch. Frankly, I've mistrusted Sears ever since it unexplainedly pushed Roebuck into such a subordinate role. What happened there, anyway? Was Roebuck too old-fashioned to go along with an Industrial Age catalog that tears out its own pages whenever the privy door is touched?

At first, the mystifying lamp was fun. I used it to demonstrate my magic powers to Emily, the two-year-old granddaughter. She laughed and acted suitably amazed, but not for long. Two days after Emily left the room, I was still playing with the magic lamp, and hollering out the window for people to come see what I had.

However, one night my wife and I were returning home and noticed a light in our window. We never leave any lights on. "It might be a burglar," she said.

"It could be worse," I said. "Our son could be back in town."

None of the above. The lamp has now taken on a life of its own. It turns itself on and off at will, no touch required. In fact, it no longer responds to touches or even squeezes. I think it's frigid.

The lamp most often turns itself off when I am reading by it, which causes me to sob, and turns itself on when no one is home, which causes me to suspect that Sears owns the Edison company.

That frustrating lamp epitomizes the Industrial Age. It should hang in the Detroit Institute of Arts, preferably over the $67,000 locomotive photo. I want $100,000, but I'll take $40.50. ■

I can be sockless, but
not bubbly, for a fortune

February 17, 1984

Beneath my calm exterior boils a definite conflict of interests. I am extremely interested in winning thousands of dollars worth of valuable merchandise for my wife. But I'm not at all interested in being bubbly. In fact, just the thought of being bubbly makes my socks shrivel.

Some people like to call attention to themselves. That's why entertainer Michael Jackson wears only one glove, which is more eye-catching than only one earring but not nearly as effective as only one shoe.

I remember returning home from the third grade wearing only one shoe, leaving its mate stuck forever in a muddy field. This brought me a great deal of immediate attention from my parents. It is possible to overlook that a boy is wearing only one glove, but a boy wearing only one shoe tends to list, either to the right or left, and it is difficult for him to walk into view without being noticed. If I were a rock singer today, yearning to be more noticed than Michael Jackson, I would never wear more than one shoe at a time.

When I grew older and wiser, I realized I could have masked the list caused by my lost shoe simply by shortening the sideburn on the side of my head corresponding with the shoeless foot. And that is what I'll do if I ever lose another shoe. As an adult, I don't want to be noticed for listing any more than, as a child, I wanted to be noticed for losing a shoe that cost my father $1.25. (He made me hop to school until the following winter.)

I don't want to be noticed for bubbling, either. Which brings us back — finally — to my conflict of interests. There is a TV game show called "Wheel of Fortune" on every weeknight. I hate the show, but I love to play the game because I'm good at it.

This schizoid problem is neatly solved by the remote-control device — the greatest invention since yelling — that enables me to control the TV set without leaving my chair. "Wheel of Fortune" is a 30-minute program containing 15 minutes of advertisements for sponsors and firms providing prizes, eight minutes of blathering between the host and contestants (speaking of shriveling socks), two minutes for two plastic persons to draw that day's winners in the state lottery, and only five minutes of actual game-playing. Everything except the game is tuned out by the almighty ruler of a remote kingdom.

The winner of the game is the contestant who requires the least letters of the alphabet to figure out what well-known phrase, title or name is being spelled out on a billboard. Because my head is full of useless information, I am often the first to shout out the correct answer. But I am never a contestant, and I never win any of the valuable merchandise prizes my wife covets.

"What good are you to me sitting there?" she always asks. And her aggression increased the other night when it was revealed that "Wheel of Fortune" is running out of contestants in the Hollywood area and is scouring the nation in search of fresh fortune-seekers: "There's your chance; go for it," she demanded.

I can't. The man on TV said the most important qualification for people auditioning to be "Wheel of Fortune" contestants is "they must be bubbly." That means they must jump, scream, clap hands and otherwise call attention to themselves in public. I am constitutionally unable to do that.

TV game shows discriminate against aspiring contestants who can't behave like idiots. The Federal Communications Commission should provide equal time for people who aren't Bozo the Clown. I want to play "Wheel of Fortune" through the mail and pick up my prizes at a post office box.

I will go this far: As long as I can keep both shoes on, I'll wear only one sock to the post office. I figure I won't list enough to be noticed because the sock surely will be shriveled. ■

You keep the llama;
I'll stick with vodka

June 29, 1984

Every evening when I get home from work, I want a drink — vodka, beer or something similarly relaxing. I'm not particular, except I don't want a llama.

The New York Times recently quoted a Montana llama breeder as saying: "They have a very tranquil, almost sedative effect on people. We sell a lot to lawyers and doctors. Instead of having a drink when they get home from work, they'll sit with their llamas and come away with a better view of the world."

No matter what you see on TV, doctors and lawyers really don't suffer all the stress in the world. Some of the rest of us also have tough days at the office. Newspaper writers, for instance, also need tranquilizers when they get home to help them forget what a jungle it is out there.

But I worry about what my wife would say if I flopped wearily into my favorite chair and asked her to bring me a llama. "It's not a jungle in here," she would say.

The New York Times described llamas as "sure-footed, innocent-eyed, sociable and relatively odorless." That's nice. But does a llama make a gentle clinking sound when slowly swished counter-clock-wise? Can a llama unparch a throat and restore a pulse beat? Will a llama fit in the average-sized coaster?

Odorless relative to what? I worry about things like that, and I want to leave my worries at the office. Ironically, one of the worries I don't bring home concerns Lee Iacocca.

It's ironical because our llama breeders are seeking government protection from imported llamas. The breeders could use someone like Iacocca to persuade Congress that llama import quotas should be imposed until the domestic production of llamas exceeds the number of doctors and lawyers who can afford coasters large enough to keep a llama from leaving paw tracks on a coffee table.

I worry about Iacocca's health because of what he said many times while plugging his book, "Iacocca: An Autobiography." He said that when he was president of Ford, "350,000 people reported directly to me."

I don't know how often they reported, but if it were only once a year, that's still almost 1,000 people a day, seven days a week. And Iacocca said they reported directly to him, not to his assistants. If he worked an 18-hour day, he could devote around one minute to receiving each report. That's too much work for a man who also must spend many days striding through TV commercials and refusing to live in the White House.

I'm assuming, of course, that Iacocca works as hard for Chrysler as he did for Ford. I assume that because on a recent hot, humid Saturday afternoon, I sat near Iacocca in Tiger Stadium. He and two associates were wearing three-piece suits with neckties. Every other person in the stadium was in shirt-sleeves or less. Obviously, Iacocca must at all times be dressed to receive a business report.

Anyway, for 40 years, North American ports were closed to South American llamas because of the risk of foot-and-mouth disease. But recently the Agriculture Department approved the importation of 350 llamas from Chile. This angered U.S. breeders who fear the competition will lower the price of adult llamas, which currently sell here for as much as $10,000 each.

Most llama investors buy them to shear and sell their fleece, which makes nice cloth. Only doctors and lawyers buy llamas to replace before-dinner cocktails. But whatever the reason for the llama business, no loyal citizen wants the profits to go to Chile simply because Chilean llamas grow fleece faster and don't pay UAW dues.

Although I prefer vodka to llamas, I sympathize with our llama breeders. It's too bad Iacocca can't help them fight imports, but a man so busy he wears a three-piece suit to the baseball game on Saturday afternoon certainly doesn't have time to llobby for llamas in Congress, even if he lloves them. ■

Laugh
if you can

If FBI restores deletions,
I'll accept the apology

May 18, 1976

Director Clarence Kelley has apologized for what the FBI did to me, but I am not going to accept until he tells me how they did it.

"We are truly sorry we were responsible for instances which now are subject to such criticism," Kelley said in a Missouri speech. "Some of those activities were clearly wrong and quite indefensible."

He put the blame on J. Edgar Hoover, probably because Efrem Zimbalist Jr. is still alive. Kelly admitted Hoover harassed and discredited thousands of Americans simply because he opposed their politics.

But it happened only "in the twilight" of Hoover's career, Kelley claimed. Never before has night been so long getting here.

The law now requires the FBI to tell a citizen if he or she ever has been investigated by the bureau, and why. So a year ago I wrote to Kelley, asking for the contents of my FBI file, if any. This started a fascinating correspondence which may result in the discovery of perpetual motion.

Kelley's first letter said there'd be a delay in answering my letter. A month later he said he'd send the file for $33 to cover office expenses.

I sent the dough and he wrote again saying I'd have to write again and this time have a notary public witness my signature. This was done.

Finally, after about six months, Kelley allowed me a slight peek under the curtain. I learned one reason I'm in the FBI files is because of something I wrote about the flag and J. Edgar Hoover in 1967.

That was when some Vietnam war protesters were burning the flag, remember? And Hoover was bombarding newspapers with "official bulletins" saying flag burners were nasty people who should be ashamed of themselves. I wrote a column saying flag burners were stupid but not criminals, as long as they owned the flags they burned.

I said the flag burning didn't do the burners any good. And to make my point, I suggested readers who disagreed with me should burn the column, which wouldn't do them any good. It turned out it

71

didn't do me any good, either. Several readers mailed me their ashes which made a mess of my desk.

Coincidentally, flag burning was back in the news recently, enabling a baseball player named Rick Monday to become a national hero. Two clowns tried to burn the U.S. flag in Monday's center field and he snatched it away from them before the blaze could be set.

This is the type of action the American public loves, especially when it is photographed. Monday received instant adulation, plus some plaques. Alert politicians said he could play on their team any day, and Monday may become the first baseball player to get an off-season job as secretary of defense.

All of which is OK with me. I'm as patriotic as the next outfielder, and those clowns had no business disrupting a ball game. But if they owned the flag, and burned it in a consenting adult's trash can, I'd give them the same tag that made Hoover yelp when I pinned it on the 1967 burners. They are dumb, but not criminal, and hardly worth the attention of the FBI chief who should quit harassing left-wing Boy Scouts and start catching crooks.

Statements such as that helped put the FBI on my tail, Kelley said, but he admitted he wasn't revealing my entire file. He said the law allowed him to withhold "information that is related solely to the internal personnel rules and practices of an agency, and intra-agency memoranda not available through discovery proceedings during litigation."

It is difficult to be certain what the gobbledygook means, but I think Kelley is refusing to reveal how his agents went about investigating me. Do "personnel rules" cover bugging my phone or opening my mail or telling my wife lies about me? Did they ever consider suggesting I kill myself?

Kelley's last letter said: "Enclosed are the documents from our files concerning you which are subject to disclosure. Deletions have been made and one document has been withheld ... "

In answer to Director Kelley's apology, I am sending him a deleted envelope full of withheld documents. ■

Simple letter took the stuffing out of his shirt

May 20, 1976

I don't care if his after-dinner speeches sound like organ music. Dr. Clifford Wharton Jr., president of Michigan State University, is not a stuffed shirt.

He wrote me a letter proving it.

The letter arrived several months ago, but I was reminded of it anew when Dr. Wharton spoke at the Detroit Press Club. He was there to explain why he couldn't explain what happened when the lights went out in the locker room.

When I hear Dr. Wharton talk about sports, I know why Joe Garagiola doesn't talk about nuclear fission. To each his own. Dr. Wharton looks dumb in a football helmet. When he speaks about putting things in "proper perspective," you know he means a man of his intelligence shouldn't have to waste his time defending dumb jocks who can't play games without cheating.

But there's a huge, wealthy alumni out there, and Dr. Wharton must play cheerleader in a business suit. The fans and sportswriters want to know how come a halfback used a credit card belonging to a rich alumnus. And Dr. Wharton says he cannot reveal a specific jersey number for fear of jeopardizing an ongoing investigation into alleged recruiting infractions involving a Yugoslavian placekicker from New Jersey.

But the MSU prez is not really as stiff as his public orations might indicate.

Last summer, in the middle of the football investigation, I received a letter bearing Wharton's signature. It addressed me as a "Spartan Supporter" which sounds like a hernia preventative. The letter was a stuffy attempt to explain why Wharton had forbidden all MSU employes to make any comment to nosy reporters on the scent of the scandal. It was full of educational gobbledygook, such as:

"The tendency of the media to report the allegations and conduct their own investigation undermines a procedure designed to protect the rights of persons charged and the objectivity of the investigation."

Translated, that meant the lousy news reporters were trying to

73

report news instead of performing a responsible journalistic function, such as selling shoes.

I answered Wharton's letter with a simple question: How could he write such crap? But to lessen the sting, I admitted athletic coaches and university presidents were not the world's only imperfect inhabitants. Even newspaper reporters can be suspect. To prove it, I cited the case of Furman Bisher, sports editor of the Atlanta Journal.

Georgia Tech awarded an athletic scholarship to Bisher's son, who is not an athlete. I thought this might interest Dr. Wharton, who was unhappy with the way MSU was being treated by the press. I added that my non-athlete son would graduate from high school this June and would love to attend MSU if he could only afford it.

Wharton's answering letter proved he could write plain English. He denied writing the first letter, blaming it on an ex-newspaperman, and added:

"We want all kinds of good students, even if they don't know the difference between a jockstrap and a pair of ear muffs. The trouble is that people won't shell out $7 a head to watch them study on Saturday afternoon. That means we haven't the dough to offer them IBM directorships to come here.

"But why don't you use the enclosed dollar and take your son out for a Big Mac and some fries?" Dr. Wharton continued. "Hype him up on MSU. We would like to have him become a Spartan Supporter even if he isn't a jock."

And as a precautionary afterthought, Dr. Wharton enclosed a second dollar, explaining: "Here's another buck for a Big Mac and some fries for your son's girlfriend ... The Department of Health, Education and Welfare swings a two-headed axe. Their thing right now is equal opportunity for women. We would be hung from the tallest tree in Washington if we tried to recruit your son as a Spartan Supporter without giving equal effort to recruiting another Spartan Supporteress. Or is it Spartanette Supporter? Spartanette Supporteress? Oh hell, you get the idea."

At the close of his speech Monday, Dr. Wharton asked if his $2 investment in recruiting had paid off.

I told him the responsibility for that decision has been delegated to my wife, and no announcement can be made at this time for fear of jeopardizing an ongoing investigation into alleged infractions which could undermine the procedure designed to protect the objectivity of the investigation. ■

O'Hair may not hear prayers, but God will

May 25, 1976

There are risks involved in investigative reporting. But I shrugged them off with my best Robert Redford shrug. There was a job to be done.

I was eavesdropping on a group accused of violating the U.S. Constitution.

I wanted to peak through the transom while standing on Deep Throat's shoulders. But I was alone, and there was no transom. Besides, the door was open. It was obviously the old purloined letter trick. If you really want to hide something, put it where everyone can see it.

I leaned in the doorway and pretended I din't see the five middle-aged people — four women and one man — huddled over a table in the middle of the room. They couldn't see me because I stood in the shadow of my enigmatic smile.

The people at the table were talking softly about love. "Let's all love one another," one woman said. "Yes," said the lone man. Sure.

Another woman, apparently the group leader, read from a mysterious-looking book. The words made sense to me, but I wasn't fooled. I knew it must be a code because, after she finished reading, the leader asked if her listeners knew what the words really meant. They said they did, which seemed to please her greatly.

The time was noon. The scene was a courtroom in the Detroit City-County Building. My assignment was to uncover the truth, no matter where it led me, never forgetting to retain all movie rights.

When the meeting broke up, the leader left the room through my door. We almost touched.

"Who turned out the lights?" she asked.

She was passing through the shadow of my enigmatic smile.

I frowned some light upon the situation, thus blowing my cover. I didn't care. I had decided upon an open investigation, which sometimes is necessary in the newspaper game.

Unlike government snoops, reporters can't get court orders to cut their own transoms. Sometimes we must stoop to non-stealth.

I asked the leader who she was and what she was doing. She said

75

she was Margery Junod, a clerk from the nearby Bureau of Taxation, and she was praying.

It sounded like a confession to me.

Madalyn O'Hair, the nation's most famous atheist, insists that it is unconstitutional to pray on government property. Her Society of Separationists (SOS) has filed suit to stop Margery and her friends from spilling Bible verses all over the public's clean floor.

Mrs. O'Hair's contention is that non-Christians are taxpayers and should not be forced to subsidize Christian prayer meetings in City Hall. If the Christians want to pray during lunch hour, they should go say grace under a golden arch. There should be no picking up of sandwich crumbs while genuflecting in the mayor's office.

Mrs. O'Hair used this argument to win a Supreme Court ban against prayer in public schools in 1963. Now she wants to stop the weekly prayer sessions that a handful of Protestants (Wednesdays) and Catholics (Thursdays) have been holding in public courtrooms for 23 years. She can probably do it.

The separation of church and state has been a sacred (excuse the word) principle here ever since it was painted on the bow of the Mayflower. If the atheists make enough noise and spend enough money on legal fees, they can probably force Margery Junod and her group to confine their Bible reading to the catacombs under Hamtramck.

By making light of a serious subject, I mean no disrespect to anyone's religious — or non-religious — beliefs. Steady readers (Mother and Aunt Madeline, to their dismay) know I have often razzed Christians for doing dumb things in the name of God. But this time it is the atheists who are jerks.

The greatest thing about praying, if you believe in it, is that no one can tell if you are saying a silent "Our Father" in your head or reviewing a dirty book. If you can think, you can pray to God for whatever, whenever, even while working for the taxpayers. And there isn't a damn thing Madalyn O'Hair can do about it. She can vacate courtrooms but not minds.

She may see me through the shadow of my enigmatic smile, but she will never know what I am smiling about. ∎

Shields are society's way
of punishing good guys

July 27, 1976

The East Detroit City Council has erected a six-foot chain-link fence around a picnic shelter in a park. There is no gate. No one can get inside.

The problem is that neighbors complained about the noise being made by people using the shelter. They also complained about the copulation, the smoking and the drinking.

So the City Council solved the problem by sealing up the shelter. Now, no one can have a picnic there. — with or without.

This is just the latest example of how our brilliant society forces the bad guys to behave by wrapping barricades and restrictions around the good guys.

I checked into Howard Johnson's in Port Huron the other night. The room clerk was sitting in the middle of a glass box. I expected goldfish to swim by his head.

"This reminds me of the penny arcade," I told him through a screened hole in his bulletproof shield. "There should be two handles sticking out of your case and a claw on the inside. For 25 cents I would get one minute to pick you up in the claw and drop you through the credit card slot. If you shook loose, I would still get a bubble gum ball."

Old-timers might remember when taxi drivers got out of the car and opened the back door for customers. Today, a big-city cabbie is so scared he won't get out of his car until it is parked in his bedroom with the blanket pulled up over the hood.

The shield between cabbie and customers always aches my chintzy nature. The idea of the wall is so I can't rob him. But what if the fare is $3 and all I have is a $5 bill? When I slip the $5 through the money slot, will he think I'm tipping him $2?

How do I tell him I'm not a big spender? Send him a postcard? I wouldn't dare pound on the shield. I think that would automatically fill the backseat with tear gas and set off an all-points alarm in Kojak's lollipop.

The ultimate in complicated security is the setup designed by a Detroit man for dry cleaners.

77

Clothes are bulky. You can't slip an overcoat through a money slot. So this guy constructed an acrylic cage with double doors. The customer opens his door and inserts the clothes in a closet. He then shuts his door which makes it possible for the clerk to open another door on the other side of the closet and snatch the clothes. Or vice versa. Both doors cannot be opened at the same time.

Beautiful. Who says people need people? After a hard day's work the dry cleaner clerk goes home and sleeps in an empty toothbrush tube.

The purpose of shields, of course, is to assure that nobody touches nobody no way. If a man can't shake your hand or pinch your bottom, he also can't break your face or grab your purse.

There may be some of us who think the game is worth the risk. Touching another person is supposed to be good for you. Many ministers encourage it during Sunday services. Psychiatrists use touching in group therapy and charge $50 an hour for teaching adults to play ring-around-the-rosy.

But there is nothing therapeutic about a stranger's touch at midnight in Central Park. A mugged man quickly learns to distrust the world.

And, there is more than one way to erect a shield against trouble. Instead of using glass or chain-link fence, you can simple remove the temptation.

Thus our Legislature is considering a law which would require customers to pay their newsboys by check, by mail. This is because so many paperboys are getting slugged and robbed. The lawmakers figure if the kids don't carry money, no one will rob them.

This is the same marvelous logic that has gas station attendants sticking cash through slots into underground vaults that can't be opened until noon the next day, with the sheriff watching.

This is the type of anti-crime thinking that has taken cash away from bus drivers so they can't change a dollar.

The way to stop the thieves is to forbid innocent citizens from owning anything worth stealing.

The next logical step will be to stop murders by making it against the law to die.

In a few years there probably will be portable shields for walking through ghettos or on campus. Double doors will be located strategically so that eating and the opposite will be similar to making a deposit at a drive-in bank.

But a shielded life isn't funny. It's the saddest damn thing I ever heard of. ∎

He didn't reform me, but
he made my skin prickle

August 24, 1976

A man stood up during Sunday services in Cliff Haskins' church and said that maybe God doesn't exist in a human form but rather is a mass of electricity.

I nudged my wife and whispered, "Is our Edison bill paid?"

Another man said he believes in God but has a hang-up on Jesus Christ. The resurrection is a lot of malarkey, he said, and Easter is just another Sunday, except that he is always careful to wear a clean shirt to church.

And a young woman told the congregation she knew God was alive because she had conversations with Him regularly, usually at home.

All this happened many Easters ago, and I am recalling it now only so that you'll know how Cliff Haskins runs his church. He encourages people to stand up and say whatever is on their minds.

Cliff is pastor of the First Presbyterian Church in Lapeer, the little town where I used to be editor. I left my job there about five months ago. Cliff is leaving his job next month.

There is no connection between the two departures. There is no truth to the rumor he is leaving because he has lost his greatest challenge — trying to get me inside his church.

Cliff has been a fine minister to my family. But in 15 years, he probably saw me on 15 Sundays. He accomplished this by staging events at which my attendance was mandatory under commandments outlined in the Gospel according to Ann Landers.

These commandments say that when a father's son is playing a mute shepherd in the Christmas play, the father shall be present to slouch in embarrassment when the dumb kid trips over his staff. Or when a father's daughter's child is baptized, the grandfather shall be present to hear his fair share of the howling.

So it is a gross understatement to say that I never was one of Cliff's more visible supporters. The most religious thing I've done in 25 years is baby-sit while my wife went to choir practice. But none of this can be blamed on Cliff. I had soured on church long before he came on the scene.

Longtime readers of this nonsense may recall a column I wrote entitled "My Church Is Inside." My mother is still sore about it. It was in response to a reader who asked why I didn't go to church every Sunday.

I told him. I said I was turned off by preachers who constantly were quoting the Bible and counting heads and raising funds to build magnificent, tax-free churches that were really country clubs.

I said too many preachers were speechless on the real moral issues — such as racial injustice — and too many congregations refused to listen to any minister who dared promote true Christianity as it was taught by Jesus Christ.

I am not trying to revive that old hassle. Reader response at the time established firmly that I am either a sacrilegious sap or a fine fellow — take your pick.

Some people think preachers should stick to their pulpits. My gang thinks preachers should go to wherever the good fight needs fighting, be it city hall or the county jail, even if it means canceling the 7 p.m. prayer meeting, for goodness sakes.

To each his own, as it is tattooed over my indigestion.

But, these many years later, I would be remiss if I didn't admit things are looking better as judged by the standards of a guy whose "church is inside."

Organized religion still can depress me terribly, such as last Christmas when a Midwestern city ran a Hindu sect out of town simply because it wasn't Christian. That didn't sound like Jesus Christ to me.

However, ministers like Cliff Haskins make me feel better.

For instance, he doesn't think it is enough for Presbyterian kids to go to Presbyterian Sunday School. He has the kids visit other churches — Jewish, Quaker, Christian Science, the whole list — in rich areas and in minority groups.

Many years ago, Cliff started joint Lenten services, perhaps the first in Michigan or anywhere. Catholic and Protestant congregations worship together.

The most splendid sight I've seen is Catholic priests and nuns in a Protestant church, singing loudly. It made my skin prickle, and I felt good. When I was a kid, a bolt of lightning would have flattened the church.

Cliff Haskins is switching to a church in Burlington, Iowa. As part of a going-away gift, his Lapeer congregation is giving him a scrapbook.

This column is for the scrapbook. I just wanted Cliff to know that he got inside my church a lot more than I got inside his. ∎

It was easier when I could talk back to bigots

September 9, 1976

When it comes to racism, I liked myself better 30 years ago, before my manners improved.

I used to talk back when someone said "nigger" or "kike" to me. There was even one time in the Army when I took a poke at a sergeant who made lousy remarks about my best friend because he was an Indian. It was the closest I came to earning a Purple Heart. The sergeant whipped me good.

A couple of years later I was in college in Port Huron. A black classmate and I went into a soda fountain. The clerk gave me my ice cream in a dish. The Negro got his ice cream in a paper cup.

He dropped his ice cream on the floor and walked out. I threw my ice cream on the clerk's apron and walked out.

My little display of temper didn't do the black guy one bit of good. But hot damn, it sure made me feel good to testify.

I don't feel that good any more.

The other night I met a fancy guy in a fancy restaurant. Noting that I'm now working in Detroit, he smirked and asked "How do you like it in niggerville?"

No matter how often I hear them, remarks like that pain my stomach and make my nerve ends twitch. It certainly isn't that they surprise me. I know the world is full of bigots.

But I am angered that these bigots take it for granted I won't be offended by their stupid remarks.

It happens all the time, usually at polite parties where rich people meet to tell each other how poor they are. Someone says it's raining and someone else blames it on bused Negroes in Detroit or mouthy Jews in Miami.

Years ago I would argue back, usually gaining attention by revealing that my mother was Jewish and my father was black and my skin had turned white from the crawling caused by the smirking racists I met at church suppers.

I don't do that anymore. My wife pointed out I wasn't winning any arguments or changing any minds, but I certainly was ruining a lot of parties.

So now I just calmly walk away, or bury my nose in ice cubes, when the bigots start spewing their crud. When that jerk made his "niggerville" remark, I simply pretended I didn't hear him.

But inside my pointed head I was wishing I was 20 years old again, and we were in an army barracks instead of a plush saloon full of my mother's friends.

Granted, there is room in this world, and at that cocktail party, for more than one opinion. But where does the white bigot get off assuming only black people are stung when some idiot condemns the entire black race because one Negro stole his aunt's purse?

Before you ask, the answer is yes, I know all bigots aren't white.

Last year my daughter was walking alone on the campus of Western Michigan University. Three black girls pushed her off the sidewalk.

"Get your white honky ass out of the way," one of the girls said while the other two laughed.

What does the great white liberal father tell his daughter? Lena Horne would never act that way? Henry Aaron hit more home runs than Babe Ruth? George Washington Carver did more than Jimmy Carter for the peanut?

I told my daughter to never forget that those three black girls proved bullies come in all colors. They didn't prove all blacks are bullies.

Street gangs are scaring the hell out of everyone in Detroit. This provides juicy fodder for the white bigots who almost joyfully identify the problem as complexion, not crime. I hear a lot of this nonsense because I'm the nut who wants to live downtown.

I politely remind these jerks that most of the victims of these crimes are black. And the most frightened people in Detroit are blacks who can't move to Bloomfield Hills.

I suck them in with the story about my friend from New York City. He's working in downtown Detroit now and he is afraid. He says he felt safer after dark walking in New York's Central Park.

And my listeners will say something sweet like: "I don't blame him. The niggers are trying to run the whites out of Detroit."

Then I tell them my scared friend from New York is black.

But I don't make much of an impression on the bigots. The trouble is my good manners. I don't pound the bar and rattle the silverware the way I used to.

I don't throw ice cream on the clerk's apron. I don't really testify.

I liked myself a lot better before I got so damned polite. ■

We cheer the cheaters, but we all pay in the long run

March 11, 1977

A movie currently showing around town is only so-so as entertainment but it is a great example of the modern morality play. It is "Fun with Dick and Jane" with Jane Fonda and George Segal.

Dick loses his well-paid job, so he and Jane become armed robbers to pay the bills. I watched in a crowded theater, and the people cheered and applauded every time Dick and Jane held up a liquor store or otherwise broke the law and escaped the police.

Times change, and you may quote me on that. My parents did not bring me up to cheer for bank robbers. If I had ever rooted for the crook to beat up on Ken Maynard, the kids sitting near me would have thrown me out of the theater.

Dick and Jane bear no resemblance to Robin Hood. They do not steal from the rich to feed the poor. They do it so they can afford to hire a man to clean their swimming pool every week. And audiences wish them success and Godspeed.

So what is going on here? Why do today's movie fans laugh when Clint Eastwood insults a man's virility simply because the poor man was dumb enough to become president of General Motors? Why do movie producers pander to this anti-hero attitude?

I don't know for sure. But I suspect Detroit Edison.

Dick and Jane draw the most audience approval when they rob the phone company. In our theater there was yelling and stomping and whistling. People are delighted when a public utility gets ripped off. Screwing the electric company is as acceptable as cheating on your income tax.

Recently I wrote about my Edison bill. It was $43 for 28 days when it shouldn't have been half that much. When first approached on the subject, Edison agreed a mistake might have been made in estimating my bill. But Edison suggested I pay the $43 anyway, and they would give it back to me someday if the mistake could be verified.

I said nuts. I refused to let Edison operate on my money while they searched for bugs in their computer. I figured Edison has more money than I have, and they made the mistake, so let them hold the chit.

You readers responded to my anti-Edison pronouncements with great huzzahing. The mail and the phone brought me dozens of horror stories from people who had wrestled in vain with the Edison billing department. I was urged to fight to the last kilowatt, and to never pay those greedy moneybags.

I also heard from a nice man at Edison. He was much friendlier than the Edison woman who fielded my original complaint. But she hadn't known I was a nasty newspaper columnist. She thought I was just another dumb customer.

The Edison man first heard of my gripe when he read it in his morning newspaper, which is an awful way to start the day, especially if your job is polishing the corporate image. My new friend at Edison moved quickly to make me happy and whole again.

Within a few hours I had Edison's admission that my bill shouldn't have been $43. I owed only $13.13. A computer was responsible for the outrageous estimating. Sorry.

The apology was accepted and the suddenly swift service was appreciated. But what about the unhappy customer who does not write a newspaper column?

He would have griped hopelessly and then paid the $43. And if he had enough money left, he might have gone to the movies and rooted for Dick and Jane to castrate the Establishment.

The similarity is not exact. Dick and Jane broke the law. I didn't. There is nothing unlawful about refusing to let the Edison use my money. But it is easy to see why readers would cheer me on in the same manner they would applaud Dick and Jane's holdup at the phone company.

The average guy feels helpless and hopeless fighting the utilities. He can't understand their complicated procedures, and he can't take his business elsewhere. He feels screwed.

So he will run out on his Edison bill without a twinge of conscience. He'll gyp the phone company and brag about it. He'll root loudly for Dick and Jane.

It is all part of the new morality. And it is easy to say the Establishment is getting only what it deserves. But the cheering fans should remember who pays for all the stealing in the long run:

Dick and Jane, and you and me. ■

MSU may have good doctors, but they don't play ball

April 6, 1977

Ron Karle insists it was wrong of me to write that Michigan State and many other huge universities measure their prestige by the size of their jockstraps.

Karle is editor of the MSU Alumni Magazine. In the current issue he devotes a page to an article headlined, "I Don't Believe It, Fitz." He says MSU alumni can be proud of their school for a lot of reasons that don't smell like dirty sweat socks. He says I would realize this if I only would visit the campus and talk to someone besides locker room attendants.

I do visit the MSU campus, several times a year. I like to walk through the long lobby in the university hotel and listen to the basketball coaches urging seven-foot-tall boys to enroll at MSU because the literature department needs tall poets.

During the same week that Karle told me sports aren't that important at MSU, I received a second communication from the university. This one was sent by Jack Kinney, who is executive director of the MSU Alumni Association.

Besides seeking my membership, Kinney also enclosed a fancy brochure which offered to sell me a table lamp that looks exactly like an "authentic-size Spartan football helmet and face guard, $34.50."

The alumni association also is selling a radio in a Spartan helmet, a book detailing 80 years of Spartan football, and beer mugs with Spartan helmets on them in green baked enamel.

It is probably just an oversight that the brochure didn't advertise a lamp shaped exactly like the brown fedora worn by the MSU botany professor who was the first person to pollinate a rose artificially.

But that's enough frivolity. I know that Karle is correct about the non-athletic accomplishments at MSU. The first vaccine to control a cancerous disorder was discovered at MSU. Karle could give hundreds more examples, and I probably wouldn't argue with one of them.

It should be recalled how this argument started. A year ago a sportswriter wrote that MSU students and alumni were ashamed of their school because some football coaches had paid some players more than the prevailing wage. I said I was one alumnus who wasn't ashamed.

Varsity athletes at MSU and similar universities are professionals — paid entertainers. They are on the payroll because they can produce a service that is profitable to the university.

I would not be ashamed if MSU paid more to get better teachers or better janitors. The same goes for split ends and seven-foot forwards. That's enterprise. It is cheating only when you get caught breaking the rules.

Universities join together and establish league rules that are reviewed regularly and weakened at meetings held in Florida or Hawaii. This must be done to control sports and to give faculty representatives somewhere to be representative.

The only inflexible rule is that if a coach is dumb enough to get caught cheating, he must be declared completely innocent after an extensive investigation, then fired. A committee of faculty representatives then is appointed to hire a better cheater.

That's how I feel about big-college sports. But it was never intended that my cynicism slop out of the stadium and stain the entire university. I know MSU produces more doctors than fullbacks.

I also know that the alumni don't return to campus on fall Saturdays to watch experiments in the chemistry lab. Old grads don't stand around the fraternity bar and talk about how many National Merit scholars have been recruited to study in the library next season.

That's why the alumni association doesn't sell lamps made in the shape of a botany professor's hat. And that's why everyone knows MSU coaches got caught cheating but only Ron Karle knows MSU produced five Rhodes Scholars in six years.

That's life in these United States. I don't make the rules; I just try to keep score. ■

86

Early bird gets the worm;
lazy bird gets the dream

June 25, 1977

It is probably fitting that the Wall Street Journal should confirm what I've always suspected — I am never going to be rich.

A Journal article said most high-powered executives get that way by saving minutes. You know . . .

They dictate into recorders while flying. They shave and read stock reports while being chauffeured along freeways. They eat lunch at their desks — or with clients while scribbling $1 million figures on the tablecloth.

Time is money; don't waste it.

The Journal told about a Detroit physician who used to have a tank of tropical fish in his office. He got rid of the fish because he was wasting too much time talking about them with his patients. Joe Sick would come in and say, "What kind of fish is that red one?" instead of immediately plopping his broken leg on the table. The doctor had to answer, and there went two minutes, or $200.

The Journal also described a new stand-up desk popular with Big Business. It has a perch seat "so the executive will remain more alert and will be able to walk his visitors to the door without being trapped in a desk situation."

Oh me. I would not lie and tell you I wouldn't like to have a million bucks. I realize money doesn't buy happiness, but it certainly buys a lot of marvelous things that make me happy. I can be as ambitious and greedy as the next guy. Unless the guy is one of those go-go minute counters described in the Journal.

Poor as I am, I feel sorry for a millionaire who hasn't got time to share his goldfish with a customer.

It was in 1973 that the New York Times described the typical day of a top White House aide: "Up before 7 o'clock, at his desk before 8, back home 12 hours later, he is the epitome of the nose-to-the-grindstone man the president likes, admires and appoints."

That White House aide's name was H.R. Haldeman.

What this country needs is more sloth in the White House. If guys like Haldeman ever start working 24 hours a day, the Republic may not survive.

Give me a White House aide who sometimes doesn't get back from lunch because of an exciting game of eight ball. A guy who goes home at 5 p.m. every evening and yells at his kids to stop watching TV and come to dinner. A guy who does no constructive work on Saturday but instead goes to baseball games or simply sits in the woods and watches the squirrels squirrel around.

I am sick of reading about congressmen who chin themselves 1,456 times before breakfast and then skip lunch so they can go to a gym and make their muscles sore.

It was easy to stifle a sob when I heard about the sweat-suited senator who was mugged while jogging through a Washington slum. What did the turkey expect? Rose petals strewn in his path?

If God had intended man to swim or sink, He wouldn't have invented Ivory soap. The big shots should learn to float with the tide, coast in neutral and walk on the grass.

Relax. Sure, the fastest runner will get free TV time to explain his shortcuts. But what does it profit a man if he wins the sweepstakes but loses his place in line at the Laurel and Hardy Film Festival?

This nation rewards — and elects — men who never waste a second. Men who buy sex from their secretaries to save on mileage, and then go home and take a Dictaphone to bed. This nation rejects men who loiter around pretty girls in the park, and waste lunch hours looking for old Fats Waller records in crummy secondhand shops.

It should be the other way around. The ambitious men, with rowing machines and cots in their offices, have made a terrible mess of things. They have forgotten that noses weren't created for grindstones. Noses were created to smell a flower or nuzzle a little kid.

A lazy man knows about noses. And he knows that sometimes the greatest thing to do is to do nothing at all. Just sit and watch and remember nice things. Go fishing without a pole. Go walking without a sweat suit.

Don't tell anyone, but I often let the phone ring on weekends. I realize it might be someone offering me gold. But they should call back on Monday.

No, I'll never be rich by Wall Street standards. I'll never make the White House except on guided tour. I don't have time.

Life is a goldfish, and I must watch closely how it glitters and splashes before it slips away. ■

Award-winning mourning
is too laughable to be sad

August 24, 1977

There has been no hint that Groucho Marx died from a drug overdose. If you are a show biz celebrity, there is something to be said for waiting 86 years to die, and I just said it.

When someone like Elvis Presley dies, two races immediately are begun.

In the first, newspapers race to uncover the secret autopsy which proves the star did not die from cancer. The real cause of death was acute perforation resulting from an unnatural relationship between the star and his guitar pick.

In the second race, the star's bereaved fans compete for sorrow honors. Who loved the lost star more? Some heartless people might measure this adoration by the number of albums bought or concerts attended while the star still shone. But this is too commercial. Money can't buy everything, including a sincere lump in the throat.

What counts is not economic investment in the star's memorial T-shirts. What counts is how loud a fan wails when first informed of the death. How far will the fan travel to throw his or her firstborn under the wheels of the star's hearse?

Ingenuity counts. Not everyone can get to the funeral. Thousands of Elvis fans were left moaning in airports by Memphis-bound airplanes which didn't have room for one more case of hysteria. But that doesn't mean the first prize for Magnificent Mourning can't be awarded to a mourner who never even sees the cortege.

Personally, in the case of Elvis, I was most impressed by the employes of Texas Instruments Inc., a factory in Midland, Texas, hundreds of miles from Memphis. They proved that if your sorrow is real, it is not necessary to see the corpse to get sick.

A few hours after Presley's death was announced, a Texas Instruments worker fainted. Within the next 30 minutes, four other workers keeled over. Plant officials, fearing some toxic gas, ordered employes evacuated to a parking lot where 100 others said they felt faint.

Inspection of the factory uncovered no organic cause for the contagion. But a Dallas professor, Dr. Heinz Eichenwald, blamed it on mass anxiety caused by the death of Elvis Presley.

"We see this often in the death of public figures with whom people identify or admire," Dr. Eichenwald said.

No other factory, in Texas or anywhere, reported an increase in faintings after Presley's death. Certainly this indicates that Texas Instruments workers loved Elvis more than anyone else did, at least under the group plan. You can expect that these people will receive the recognition they deserve when the Magnificent Mourning trophy is awarded in the mass sorrow category.

I was never a Presley fan, but that was my fault, not his. It was not Elvis' fault that he started singing in 1954 when I couldn't hear him. I was still in seclusion, recovering from the death of Glenn Miller.

I wonder how Presley's fans would like it if his body were lost somewhere outside Memphis? That's what happened to Miller during World War II. His airplane disappeared and there has been no word since. For Miller fans, this has meant over 30 years of anguished uncertainty and Tex Beneke.

I mention the loss of Glenn Miller only so you Presley mourners will realize we old crocks also have known real sorrow. And now many of us are knowing it anew, due to the demise of Groucho Marx.

The death of Presley received much more publicity than the death of Groucho. The worldwide wailing for Elvis was much louder. This is not because Elvis was more talented than Groucho. Don't be ridiculous, please.

The thing is that Groucho outlived his greatest fans. And the lingering death of an 86-year-old man leaves behind no cocaine-dusted mystery to titillate the public. If Elvis had been 86 when he died, there would have been no fainting at Texas Instruments.

All of which doesn't mean Groucho's death attracted no competitors for the Magnificent Mourner award. There was George Jessel who was angered because he wasn't invited to Groucho's memorial service.

"I was closer to him than anybody," Jessel told newsmen. "I was the only person who could make him laugh in the last six months."

Magnificent Mourners make a lot of people laugh. You might as well laugh at them. The big saps are never going to go away anyway. ■

How do you underestimate intelligence of a TV clod?

November 25, 1977

One TV commentator said Anwar Sadat's visit to Israel was more important than man's first landing on the moon.

One TV watcher said: "Tell them to take that bleeping camel jockey off my set."

Critics often warn TV executives not to underestimate the intelligence of their audience. Today's question is: Can it be underestimated?

Is there enough intelligence present to be underestimated or measured in any way? It is difficult to put a tape measure to the inseam of a gnat.

Sadat's arrival in Israel knocked the Michigan-Ohio State game off TV for six minutes. Thousands of football fans were furious. Many of them phoned Channel 7 and the Free Press to voice their beefs. Several of these complaints were recorded, word for word so that they later might be examined closely for traces of intelligence.

The "camel jockey" quote mentioned earlier was one of those complaints. It came from a woman who didn't really say "bleeping." She used the vulgarity most commonly heard when fun in bed is discussed. This vulgarity has not yet won wide acceptance in family newspapers, but stick around.

Here are some more illuminating opinions from TV viewers who would like to have seen Woody Hayes sock Anwar Sadat:

"It's terrible for us to kiss this Arabian guy's butt. Football is America. We don't want this jerk on. We got to watch some bleeping greaseball with a goatee trying to control things. Missing the game doesn't bother me as much as this guy. This is kowtowing to these Arabs. These Arabians will just go down to City Hall in droves tomorrow to say they own the world."

"Boy, it bleeps me off. I don't give a damn about Arabs and Jews anymore. I think the network executives are Jews."

"I think this is ridiculous that all three networks put this program on TV and I hope they get the FCC or whoever is responsible. They schedule the NASA moon shots when there is nothing else on."

"I think it's terrible that the broadcast executives can force us to watch this. It really opens your eyes to how much freedom we have in America."

"I think the president of ABC is the winner of the jackass of the year award."

End of quotes. I ask you, can the intelligence of those viewers be underestimated?

Sure it can. And I'll tell you how the TV executives will do it.

The essence of the complaints is that the Sadat news replaced an entertainment show, in this case a football game. To avoid this problem some TV producer soon will integrate the news into the entertainment so viewers won't notice it.

In the middle of a beer-swimming contest, Laverne will say to Shirley: "Hey, Shirl, I just heard that Russia and the United States have agreed on a pact to stop the proliferation of nuclear power."

And Shirley will say: "Yeah, there'll probably be film at eleven."

TV executives also will extend their clout as it pertains to the timing of newsworthy events. They told Michigan and Ohio State when to start playing. So why didn't they tell Sadat to land in Israel during halftime?

If Walter Cronkite had asked him, I think Sadat would have landed in Ann Arbor.

TV soon will realize its full power, at which time it will demand that all world leaders schedule news events for 5 o'clock Sunday mornings when Laverne and Shirley are sleeping.

Perhaps the most disturbing complaining came from the football fan who accused TV of forcing him to watch Sadat, thus interfering with freedom in America.

In its continuing effort to underestimate viewers' intelligence, TV will blunt this criticism by preceding every news special with this disclaimer:

"The following program contains news of worldwide importance. Viewer discretion is advised. There will be no footballs bouncing and no braless detectives jiggling. Correct grammar may be used. You may not want your family to see this program. You are free to turn off your set and leave the house without fear of penalty."

Onward and Upward. ■

Surely God must smile
on the barroom mass

December 30, 1977

All drinkers were cut off for an hour in a Detroit saloon the other evening, while a Catholic priest said mass. He also administered the sacraments of Confession and Holy Communion to all bar patrons who wanted to receive them.

The priest was in familiar surroundings and had no trouble fashioning an altar around the beer spigots and whisky bottles. He used to be a bartender there.

"Please don't print my name or the name of the bar," the priest asked me. "You could get me in trouble with Cardinal Dearden."

The owner of the saloon said: "Just write that the father and I work together. I corrupt souls and he saves them."

All of which proves again that if a smart-aleck columnist lives long enough, he will see his wildest exaggerations come true. I was only kidding, three years ago, when I wrote that Milwaukee saloon keepers should ordain their bartenders.

The Wisconsin Tavernkeepers' Association had threatened legal action against eight Catholic churches which had applied for unlimited licenses to sell beer. The saloon owners said it would be unfair competition for the churches to put a potential sinner and the devil's brew together so near to the confessional. The middleman faced elimination.

I suggested the bar owners could save money by skipping the lawyers and fighting the churches with the flip side of the argument. They could put priests behind their bars. This line of defense was something I called the "Alibi Scheme."

The Alibi Scheme was formulated at the close of World War II by some young veterans who had trouble getting to mass on Sunday. Please recall this was 33 years ago, before priests started saying Sunday mass on Saturday afternoon.

In 1945, if you missed mass on Sunday, you faced eternal burning in hell. Even worse, your mother might find out.

Many mothers quizzed their sons at Sunday dinner. "What was the sermon about?" "Did your cousin sing a solo?" "Did Father McCormick announce when the KofC picnic will be?"

93

These were hard questions to answer if, for medical reasons, the son had been forced to skip mass and limp to the Alibi Bar. But never fear, John the bartender soon would be here.

John always went to mass and he had a marvelous memory. John could recite the sermon and sing the anthem. He knew whose uncle took up the collection and whose aunt fainted from the heat.

John's recitations saved the skins of many sons who took notes on the inside of matchbook covers.

However, there came a time when the sons sickened of the Sunday sham. They tired of living a lie. They decided they should really attend mass. John should become a priest!

A collection was taken up to send John to the seminary and a glorious "Goodby, Father John" party was organized. There was even a pilgrimage to neighboring shrines. It seemed like a marvelous idea at the time.

But when everyone woke up the next morning, it was discovered that the seminary money had been spent on the goodby party. John returned to the bar, and the sons returned to the sham.

And I figured there never would be a bartender saying mass in a saloon. But 33 years later, Detroit's bartender-turned-priest proved me wrong. God bless him.

"After they've been away for a long time, many people find it difficult to return to the church and the sacraments," he explained, "so we take the mass to where they are."

"If we help one person, it's worth all the trouble," the saloon owner said.

It's expected there'll be another saloon mass near Easter. They are usually advertised by word of mouth, from bar to bar, but if you want to know the name of the saloon, phone me.

If you're Cardinal Dearden, I'll hang up. God knows I don't want to get a priest in trouble. And I figure if God knows, it's OK if the cardinal doesn't. ■

Too many simps get
in the way of the ERA

March 3, 1978

Marabel Morgan, my favorite simp, has written another book. It is called "Total Joy." Her first book was "Total Woman." Marabel is plugging her new book on TV talk shows and I have my TV throw-up pot ready for total use. Don't tell me I can switch channels. It is part of my job to watch people like Marabel parade their nonsense. As a responsible columnist, I must observe even the most nauseating phenomena and then report back to you. Otherwise you might not know important things, such as the fact that Marabel Morgan is a simp.

Marabel does more than write books and simper on TV. She and her apostles also hold seminars at which they preach that a woman can have a perfect marriage if she encourages her husband to be the complete boss in all matters, even when he is wrong. And when it comes to sexual relations, Marabel says a good wife doesn't tell her husband she is too tired until two weeks after she is dead.

Which reminds me of another simp. Anita Bryant recently said if government protects the civil rights of men who have sex with men, and women who have sex with women, it should do the same for "people who have sex with dead people and St. Bernards."

Anita really said that, in Washington, at a news conference before a National Association of Religious Broadcasters meeting. Her remarks were published in newspapers where anyone could read them, including St. Bernards, who have feelings, too.

I don't pretend to have Anita's expertise. I know St. Bernards are often good for a drink, but I had no idea their hospitality extended so far beyond offering a helping paw to people stuck in snowbanks.

As for live people having sex with dead people — that's a real shocker. How does Anita know such things happen? Probably her husband told her.

But enough about Anita. My mission today is to tell you about that other simp, Marabel.

At her seminars, Marabel says a woman must do three things to have a happy marriage: 1. Be nice to her husband, compliment him,

95

tell him he is great. 2. Stop nagging at him and trying to change him. 3. Understand and try to fulfill his sexual needs.

I guess the husband does his part by accepting all this sweetness without once complaining, even if the wife should accidentally slobber on his shoe while kissing his foot.

I know a lot of husbands who aren't great. They're not even semi-nice. These jerks shouldn't be told they are great, and they shouldn't be nagged, either. They should be traded in on St. Bernards.

These hopeless husbands have a wide variety of bad habits. Some of them hang around saloons and grab at waitresses.

Some of them hurry home from work so they won't be late for crabbing about the housework their wives didn't do because they were too busy taking care of the kids and working full-time at the neighborhood foundry.

Some husband smile at their wives only when the neighbors are looking. They touch their wives only on Saturday nights during brief encounters which, for the romantic husbands, serve a function similar to sneezing.

This is only a partial list. There are many more types of rotten husbands that only a Barbie doll like Marabel could appreciate. I mention their individual differences only to underscore the one thing all these jerk husbands have in common: They all agree with Marabel.

Most of these husbands never heard of Marabel Morgan, but they subscribe wholeheartedly to her philosophy, which they learned as boys at the knee of the neighborhood wife-beater. These guys really believe that wives exist solely for the glorification and satisfaction of husbands.

That's sad, but it's not the ultimate crusher. The ultimate is the fact that millions of wives also agree with Marabel.

These demented women really believe it's a wife's chief duty to understand and fulfill her great husband's sexual needs, even if she has to wear a keg of brandy around her neck.

It is little wonder that enlightened women can't get the Equal Rights Amendment ratified. There are too many Marabel simps out there who don't want equal rights. Their total ambition is to become total simpletons. ■

With friends like this, who needs to swallow a ring?

June 5, 1978

My friend Ralph has a new hero — U.S. Sen. Herman Talmadge, the Georgia Democrat millionaire. Ralph's old hero was Peter Lazaros, the Oakland County liar who died with a pacemaker in his chest and a diamond ring in his stomach.

"It is our ring. It had no place in his stomach," said the lawyer for a New York jewelry store, thus rendering a sharp disservice to his client.

It is not usual for a man to wear a diamond ring in his stomach, so Peter Lazaros' ring received extensive publicity. It could have started a fad, something like swallowing goldfish.

It could have become fashionable to plight a troth, or seal a seduction, by ingesting a diamond ring. This would have been great for the jewelry business. People who like to be seen wearing diamond rings would also want to be seen eating them.

But then comes a lawyer, employed by a jewelry store, and he tells the newspapers that diamond rings have no place in stomachs. Such a dumb lawyer would work for Right Guard and tell the world one armpit is enough.

Anyway, it was charged that Lazaros swallowed the ring so police wouldn't find it when they locked him up on a fraud charge. But he died while still in custody and the ring was discovered during the autopsy. The jewelry store immediately claimed Lazaros had swiped it while diamond shopping a few months earlier.

No one claimed the pacemaker, indicating Lazaros didn't mix business with medicine. Blue Cross probably paid for it.

Peter Lazaros was one of Michigan's most infamous characters. His name was connected with several magnificent frauds. At one time he claimed to have paid Mafia money to several government officials, including the mayor of Detroit. He was asked to prove this charge and was convicted of perjury.

At his funeral, Lazaros was eulogized by Father Saterios Gouvellis: "He did things some of us dreamt about but never dared to do. He always wanted to be first-class, and he tried."

My friend Ralph agreed with Father Gouvellis. "They say Lazaros

97

had to swallow that diamond ring several times to keep it hidden all the time he was in jail. I might dream of doing something like that, but I'd never dare do it. That's a first-class accomplishment," Ralph said.

"It's a good thing he didn't steal a bowling ball," I said.

As indicated earlier, Ralph is fickle about his heroes. Peter Lazaros was No. 1 for only a few weeks, and then Ralph read about Sen. Talmadge's pocket money.

The senator admits he's worth maybe $4 million. He also admits he depends on gifts for his walking around money.

"My out-of-pocket expenses come from donations friends give me — $5, a $10 bill, sometimes $15 or $20," he said in a Washington Star interview. "They come up and say they know I have a lot of expenses back in Washington and they want to help me."

The details of Talmadge's financial affairs surfaced during the settlement of his recent divorce. According to court records, in six years he spent only $600 of his own money on his personal expenses. Most of his day-to-day bills were paid with "small gifts of cash."

As chance would have it, it isn't necessary to list gifts of pocket money as income on tax returns. So the senator's benefactors are anonymous, and all his suits probably have 122 pockets.

"Here's a millionaire who walks down the street and people walk up and give him money, and he takes it," Ralph said admiringly. "When Senator Talmadge dies, they should get Father Gouvellis to give his eulogy.

"The senator has done things that most of us can only dream about but never dare do."

I couldn't argue with Ralph. Sen. Talmadge is living proof that if a man's dedication is strong enough, and his pockets are big enough, he'll never have to swallow a bowling ball.　■

Bigot deserves our bad manners, not our complacency

June 12, 1978

Call him Motormouth. That's what the guys at the club call him when he can't hear them.

"Here comes Motormouth," they say when they see his car turn into the driveway. This is a warning to sensitive souls who might want to run and hide. Some people, on some days, simply don't feel strong enough to listen to Motormouth, whose major fault is that he knows everything. Everything.

One of the things he knows the most about is Detroit. He hasn't been inside the city limits in 15 years. "You couldn't pay me to go there. I don't want to get my head bashed in," Motormouth likes to say.

But Motormouth doesn't require eyeball experience in forming his golden opinions. He doesn't have to live there, or work there, or even visit there to know that Detroit is a jungle. And he knows why.

"It's the niggers," he explains. Motormouth is white. But you guessed that.

In fact, you might well think you know Motormouth. You probably do. The Motormouth at my club is not an exclusive. Detroit is surrounded by Motormouths. Other big cities have the same problem.

My particular Motormouth is a high roller. He plays gin rummy for big stakes and he flies to Vegas regularly "for the real action." He is loaded with bucks and he wants everyone to know it.

But wealth is not a requirement to be a Motormouth. He doesn't have to belong to a fancy club. I once stood behind a Motormouth in an unemployment line. And I heard another Motormouth spout his crud at a church supper.

Wherever they might be found, Motormouths are easy to identify. They are always talking. They are always positive what they are saying is the absolute truth. And they always know what caused the trouble, whatever the trouble might be. It was caused by someone whose complexion and/or heritage is different from Motormouth's.

Thus the white Motormouth who lives 100 miles away knows

blacks have made Detroit unsafe for human habitation. He tells this to everyone within earshot. And no one tells him to shut up.

Certainly some of his listeners agree with Motormouth. He is their cheerleader and they are his echo. They would like to be Motormouths themselves but they do not have their leader's eloquence. They have not yet learned how to talk clearly with their mouths full of crap.

But the world is Motormouth's podium, so he is heard by many who know he is wrong. They know he is a jerk who would rather hate than think. But they do not argue with Motormouth. They don't want to start a fuss.

That's what bugs me. Everyone is too damn polite.

Motormouth goes unanswered, and that's how his number multiplies. His unsure listeners, often children, figure Motormouth must be flying right because no one is shooting him down. So they accept his prejudices as fact, and they repeat them. That's how little Motormouths are born.

Sometimes Motormouth gets into print. A suburban newspaper publishes a column which contains readers' opinions, phoned in anonymously. Motormouth called a while back and said:

"If people are dissatisfied with our local police department, they should have to deal with Detroit police. They won't even try to help the white person. They are afraid of the ghetto and won't go there."

That's a lot of hooey, of course. A stupid lie. But Motormouth said it, and thousands of people read it — and believed it.

It is ridiculous to say Detroit police refuse to help white people. Motormouth couldn't begin to document such an outrageous charge. But he doesn't have to.

Motormouth is never required to prove his poison. No one wants to argue with him for fear of upsetting the hostess who worked for hours on her seating arrangement.

Maybe it's a price that must be paid by those who want to live in a genteel society. But the price is too steep. Motormouth deserves more dissent than simply running and hiding from him.

No matter what the social setting, church or saloon, Motormouth should be told he is an idiot. There is something to be said for bad manners, and I just said it. ■

Carrier trashed letters, and it wasn't even junk mail

August 4, 1978

It now costs 15 cents to mail a letter. The cost is the same whether the letter is delivered to the address on the envelope, or is dumped in a garbage can by the mail carrier.

You may think that's a silly thing for me to write. That's because you don't live in Detroit's Michigan-Livernois area. Several people who live around that intersection saw mail delivered to garbage cans recently. At first, they couldn't believe what they were seeing.

It happened several times, always in the middle of the afternoon and always the same mail carrier — a woman. She would park her little jeep near the large trash containers at Zieger Osteopathic Hospital. She would get out of her jeep and dump what appeared to be handfuls of mail into the trash.

Could such a thing be? Was the United States mail being discarded in broad daylight, in a crowded neighborhood, in full view of anyone who wanted to watch, by an employe of the U.S. Postal Service?

Or has the clever government devised a piggyback delivery system in which municipal garbage trucks are tricked into doing most of the work?

The man who told me about the garbaged mail asked that his name not be published. He is apparently afraid the neighborhood Postal Service might be offended and take revenge. He doesn't want his mail delivered through his plumbing, so I'll call him Sam.

"I talked to a woman who watched through her window while the carrier dumped mail into the dumpster behind a Coney Island restaurant," Sam said. "I guess the hospital containers were full that day.

"I went out and looked at what she had dumped. It was regular mail. I even saw one pension check. That really made me mad. There are a lot of poor people in that neighborhood. I wondered if someone was going hungry while waiting for a check that was thrown in the garbage."

Sam phoned postal authorities. A postal inspector, wearing a gun and long rubber gloves, came out to paw through the garbage. He found lots of mail.

That same afternoon, Sam said, the inspector peeked while the mail carrier made her daily dump.

The postal inspector is Gordon Moore. I phoned and asked him for the details on the dumped mail. He said he couldn't tell me. He said I should ask the assistant inspector in charge, a man named Gene Potter.

So I talked to Potter. He said he didn't know anything about the case but he would ask Moore about it and then call me back and tell me what Moore said.

As a taxpayer, you might think that was an unnecessarily slow way for the public to get public information from public employes. You might think it would have been simpler for Moore to talk to me directly. You probably want your mail delivered on time, too, you dummy.

Anyway, Potter did call me back. He identified the mail carrier in question as Deandra Harris, a temporary employe who had been delivering mail since June 26.

Potter confirmed that Inspector Moore had indeed seen her dump mail into the garbage. Potter said Deandra Harris had been fired immediately and charges are pending while the investigation continues.

Why did she throw the mail in the garbage?

"She said it was because she didn't have time to deliver it," Potter said.

This month the National Association of Letter Carriers is voting on whether to ratify a tentative contract with the Postal Service. The vote is being conducted by mail. Results should be known by Christmas, except in those areas where garbage collectors are on strike. ∎

There must be a lesson
in this — right, teacher?

October 3, 1979

The circulation department of my favorite newspaper advertised for teachers to deliver papers before going to school in the morning.

The ad urged teachers to "earn cash and take advantage of your free time" by delivering the Free Press "in a way that won't interfere with your classes and will carry through your vacation periods."

Many teachers were stung at the suggestion that they should stoop to putting newspapers on stoops. One angered teacher wrote to the newspaper: "Where do you figure teachers have so much free time? . . . To a teacher doing his job, free time seldom exists. Your ad was a tactless insult."

Teachers think they are too good to deliver newspapers in their spare time. They don't deny they could use extra income, and they can't deny they get longer vacations than anyone except state legislators. But teachers feel it would be demeaning for them to accept employment at a job traditionally done by little boys on bicycles.

Some of you might say it's a good thing teachers don't want to deliver newspapers. In view of high school graduates who can't spell their names, you might fear teachers would be as good at delivering newspapers as they are at teaching, which would force subscribers to read January's newspapers in August.

You might even say it is deliciously ironic that newspapers need teachers to deliver papers because little boys no longer can handle the job because they don't learn enough from their teachers.

There could be truth in what you say. I once had agonizing experiences with a paperboy who usually missed my house once a week but still billed me for seven days because he didn't have the slightest idea how to subtract one day's charge from the weekly charge. And it took him 40 minutes to make change for a $10 bill, with his mittens off. He certainly was a lousy advertisement for his arithmetic teacher.

But it wouldn't be true to say teachers are being invited into the newspaper delivery field strictly because today's little boys lack the education required for the job. There are bigger reasons for this

103

change in the circulation for newspapers, and the biggest reason probably is the change in the size of the individual newspapers themselves.

Today, the average little boy can't lift more than 10 average Sunday newspapers at the same time. If he delivers the Sunday New York Times, he needs a moving van for each issue. He no longer has to worry about catching his pants in his bicycle chain, but few little boys are licensed to drive moving vans.

As newspapers have grown fatter with advertising supplements that used to be junk mail, little boys have been forced to shift their increasingly heavy load onto their parents, who have rebelled quickly at playing chauffeur in snowstorms. These parents now are saving money on gasoline by paying their sons not to deliver newspapers.

So circulation managers have turned to teachers for help, tempting them with added income and the therapeutic joy of outdoor exercise. But the teachers are insulted.

What's the answer? It's obvious. The job of delivering newspapers must be made more creative and thus stimulating to the teacher's intellects. They should not be required to stoop to stooping on stoops.

It is a bore to trudge up and down porch steps to flop today's bloated newspapers in front of doors. When I was a newsboy, the papers were thin enough to be folded into compact squares which could be thrown great distances onto porches. They could be sailed around corners, and, in rough weather, a good newsboy had to know how to play the wind.

My route was along a riverbank where a poor throw literally could be blown out of the country. Canada was on the opposite shore. On bad days, some of my customers had to pass through customs to find their newspapers.

I think teachers would respond to the challenge of throwing thin newspapers, especially onto today's porches, which, conversely, are shrinking as swiftly as newspapers are bloating. Those teachers who missed porches would only be continuing in the tradition of their craft. Johnny can't read because he can't find his newspaper.

The only problem is how to shrink the size of newspapers. I asked teacher for a solution, and he suggested the newspapers start by eliminating all stupid columnists like me. ■

I would gladly have sat
for a Cavanagh briefing

November 30, 1979

"I can't make up my mind whether you are completely anti-social or just anti-celebrity," my friend Ralph said. It seems a question worth pondering, especially during the week Jerry Cavanagh died.

Ralph had just learned I rejected an invitation to attend a briefing and reception at the White House. Jimmy Carter wanted to brief me and some other honored invitees on SALT II. Ralph couldn't believe I didn't want to be briefed by the president of the United States.

"Just look at this," Ralph demanded, showing me a newspaper article about Beverly Payne, the TV-2 anchorwoman who was invited to the same White House briefing. She wanted to attend, with a camera crew, but her bosses balked. They said "public relations puffery" by the White House wasn't worth the trip. So Bev Payne said she would take a vacation day and pay her own way to Washington.

"She has a sense of history," Ralph said. "She probably realizes the president won't say anything terribly important, but she also realizes it is a great honor to be invited to hear him say it. She will tell her grandchildren about it someday. You're so old you could tell your grandchildren about it today. What is wrong with you?"

What is wrong with me? I'm always rejecting invitations to attend large parties where I could watch celebrities juggle hors d'oeuvres and cocktails. I realize most invitations are extended only because I'm a newspaper columnist and the hostess wants me to write about all the famous people who keep hanging around her home, telling her what a darling person she is. But that's not why I'd rather stay home and shoot pool. I don't want to be loved for myself alone. If I did, I wouldn't always carry my press card in my nose.

Besides, Ralph conceded, it isn't only celebrity parties that give me a severe case of previous engagements. I shy away from all large gatherings that require guests to slice roast beef on their laps, even when those guests are so unknown they must peek at their own name tags before introducing themselves.

And it isn't only presidents and famous statesmen I don't like briefing me. I've hidden behind doors to escape briefings from

105

township zoning administrators. It has been my experience that briefings from whatever source are never brief enough, and the persons being briefed usually would be better off if they stayed home and played Crazy Eights with their children.

All this doesn't mean I'm a recluse. Few people go to more movies, stage plays and restaurants than I do. And there are several piano players who will testify I won't go home until after the bartender is tucked safely into bed. I enjoy talking to people, one or two at a time.

So I deny Ralph's suggestion that I might be anti-social. I simply am anti-roast-beef-on-my-lap. And I couldn't be anti-celebrity. If I were, how could I have enjoyed being with Jerry Cavanagh so much?

As the ex-boy mayor of Detroit, and a highly visible candidate for governor and U.S. senator, Jerry Cavanagh was one of the biggest celebrities in Michigan. Certainly he was recognized wherever he went in Detroit and, amazingly, he seemed to recognize everyone he saw, and he always had time to chat with them. Once I sat next to him at a banquet and, by actual count, 43 people stopped to shake his hand in 15 minutes. He introduced them all to me and never flubbed a name.

I knew Cavanagh for only the last three years of his life. We met a couple of times on purpose, for lunch, and several more times by accident, for drinks. We talked about my nephew, son of Terrible Jean, who lived with the Cavanagh family while attending law school. Or we talked about how much pleasure Jerry was getting out of his new baby daughter who, he always pointed out, was younger than my grandchildren.

Jerry usually said something that made me feel good. The last time we were together, we lost track of time, and he said his wife would forgive him for getting home late when he told her he was with me. My wife felt the same way about him. What more can two good Irishmen do for each other?

There was a time when many informed politicians thought Jerry Cavanagh someday would be president of the United States. I would have gone to his briefings. ■

There's something rotten
in Anita Bryant's orange juice

May 30, 1980

By her own admission, Anita Bryant soon will become a divorcee. I don't hate her for that, but I am worried she might recruit our children into divorcement. She shouldn't be allowed to teach school or lead scout troops.

For many years, Anita has crusaded against the disintegration of the traditional American family. A lot of old-fashioned people think divorce has a disintegrating effect upon the traditional family. For some of these people, Anita's getting a divorce is as shocking as Norman Vincent Peale's giving up the ship because he doesn't believe in shores.

Is Anita Bryant a phony? Has she been drinking screwdrivers in those TV commercials? I hate to make that judgment. At last report, her husband had written an open letter begging Anita to "return as my wife and the mother of our children." She had gone into seclusion to study the Bible. Perhaps she will read something to lead her back onto the path of unsundered orange juice.

But if there is no reconciliation, it should be remembered what Anita Bryant often said about gay people: "Homosexuals cannot reproduce, so they must recruit. And to freshen their ranks, they must recruit the youth of America."

This type of preaching put many citizens on guard against gay recruiting stations in post office buildings. Parents instructed their children to refuse to freshen all ranks, even if a recruiter promised to teach them a trade and station them in Honolulu.

More specifically, Anita formed an organization in 1977 to fight an ordinance forbidding discrimination against gays in Miami, Fla. Her organization was called "Save Our Children," thus spawning an acronym just close enough to "SOS" to save local children from mass sinking by gay school-crossing guards. Thanks to SOC's victory, Miami children can swim across the street with nothing to worry about except heterosexual sharks.

Because of her well-publicized crusade, many people admire Anita Bryant as a morally upright person who lives by the Bible. If divorce were disintegrating to the traditional family, Anita Bryant certainly wouldn't get one, would she? It is something to think about. Such a persuasive and attractive divorcee could give asundered orange juice a good name.

However, the Bryant followers who followed her into divorcement soon would have a problem in their ranks: how to freshen them. Morally upright, Bible-reading divorced people don't reproduce much more than homosexuals do. The only way to avoid stale ranks would be through recruiting drives.

If Anita Bryant were proselytizing for divorce, would you want her helping your children across the street everyday? Would you want her teaching them biology? Those are questions each person would have to answer for himself or herself, perhaps in the voting booth.

Of course, some people would claim it is possible for a divorced person to teach children without influencing them to fly to Las Vegas for a divorce. This is similar to the argument made by people who say a homosexual can be a scout leader without leading the troop into a gay camporee. Certainly this is an argument that should be considered by anyone who feels compassion for Anita Bryant as she faces the ridicule and other problems her new life-style will create for her.

But do we really want to risk having our children divorced before they're out of junior high? Do we want the traditional American family disintegrated almost before it is integrated? Is it safe to ignore what the Bible says about the sacred bonds of matrimony?

I don't think so. If Anita Bryant goes through with the divorce, she should be banned from occupying a position of authority over children. Otherwise she will become a threat to all parents who want their children to cross the street to school without getting divorced.

Moral: Let no man put asunder his orange juice, lest the vodka be discovered, and he be stabbed by his own screwdriver. ■

Some random thoughts
for the animal in us

October 13, 1980

The following paragraphs, concerning animals, may appear to be unrelated, but actually they have a thin thread running through them. You're invited to follow the thread . . .

• For 10 cents you can buy a goldfish in a Dearborn Heights pet shop and watch it be eaten alive by piranhas and other carnivorous fish from South America. Some spectators are so fascinated by cannibalism they spend $5 in one visit.

• A big bear recently mutilated a small bear at the Detroit Zoo while the public watched. One man was so angered he wrote my very favorite letter to the editor: "I will never take kids to the Detroit Zoo again after witnessing the revolting carnage . . . The zoo attendants just watched. Is this what we pay them to do? The Detroit Zoo will never get my money again. I would like to see that large bear stoned to death."

• Influenced by her radical parents, a young woman vowed long ago never to buy a coat made from the fur of an animal killed just to keep her warm and stylish. But last month she bought a used mink coat. Her explanation is that General Motors would make Cadillacs even if there weren't a market for previously owned cars.

• A dedicated outdoorsman, fighting to keep oil drillers out of a state forest, explained he needs the forest for training his dogs to run bear and raccoons. A true sportsman, he explained that during training season he doesn't shoot the animals, he just chases and trees them. Naturally, this is nice for the bear and raccoons, who probably sit up in the trees and thank God they don't have to worry about oil slicks.

• The New York Times published an article about a hog farmer who economizes by raising his product in tight, confining quarters. This prompted Anne Xanthippe George of Westland to write the Times: "I have an even better idea . . . Why not stand the hogs on their heads, side by side, thereby saving even more space and money. So what, if these living, breathing creatures are agonized and uncomfortable? Makes no difference, they face slaughter anyway. When death is inevitable, suffering is immaterial."

• News item: "Hercules the Bear, a 560-pound grizzly who makes

109

$45,000 a year doing toilet paper commercials in England, has been missing since he decided to go for a swim off the coast of Scotland last month." Sudden thought: Maybe Hercules discovered he didn't need $45,000 any more than he needed toilet paper.

• A University of Texas researcher fed marijuana to male mice to prove it lowers their sexual desire. I learned from a private source that this important study was financed by the Dallas Health Department in an effort to lower the incidence of male mice in singles bars.

• My favorite outdoor writer, in defending the trapping of animals, expressed exaggeration over anti-trappers who protest by evoking the image of Bambi and charging that cruel treatment of animals leads directly to cruel treatment of human beings. "How 'antis' can equate the feelings and sensitivities of wild animals with those of humans is beyond me," he wrote. "A childhood spent at the knee of Walt Disney, probably."

End of thin thread. So where are we? I don't know about you, but I'm up a tree with a slightly used, $45,000-a-year bear, fleeing oil slicks and clapping my paws in glee at the thought of the man who was so angered by the sight of violence at the zoo that he wants to see a bear stoned to death. But who should throw the first stone at a stoned mouse?

My trouble, obviously, is I can equate the feelings and sensitivities of wild animals with those of humans. I really don't know how I got this way, because I never saw a Walt Disney movie that didn't make me wish I were anywhere else. But I hereby promise to change my foolish attitude on the same day a raccoon tells me it enjoys being chased up a tree by a dog.

Speaking of dogs, if it costs 10 cents to watch a piranha eat a goldfish, how much does it cost to watch a dog eat a cat? ∎

Phyllis Schlafly's license plate should read 'DUM'

May 8, 1981

Phyllis Schlafly would be pleased to learn Michigan is leery about issuing auto license plates that say YES.

"It could be offensive to women's groups," said a spokesman for the Secretary of State's Office, explaining that "yes" could have a double meaning. He is afraid of "had" for the same reason.

Certainly. As Schlafly recently told a U.S. Senate committee, "Men hardly ever ask sexual favors of women from whom the certain answer is 'no.' "

She was referring to pedestrian woman. "When a woman walks across the room, she speaks with a universal body language that most men intuitively understand," Schlafly said. Her theory is walking women who are sexually harassed usually get what they're looking for. She disapproves of these women who use body language to ask for pinches and propositions from men.

I'm sure she also would disapprove of motorist women who willingly drive across town with YES on their license plates. After all, what purpose could such a plate have, other than to tell male motorists that the woman at the wheel wants to be pulled over and ravaged?

Sure, there are those fanatic women's libbers who would suggest a woman has YES on her license plate because her name is Yolanda Estelle Smith or because she is a loan officer at a bank where all loans are guaranteed by the federal government or because she is trying to stamp out negativism.

Nonsense, of course. Such explanations of an obvious attempt to have curbside sex are as weak as saying a certain woman walks with her shoulders back and her chest out because she learned good posture when she was a Girl Scout. Everyone knows a woman who walks like that is selling more than cookies. Virtuous women slouch. A recent survey of shoe repair shops proved conclusively that women with round shoulders have round heels.

Naturally, a woman who wiggles when she walks will welcome a YES plate on her car, especially when she can't find a parking place and get out and wiggle. Such rolling advertising will give her instant

111

rapport with intuitive men who use cars in their never-ending search for women to sexually harass. But what about women like Phyllis Schlafly?

That is what's worrying the Secretary of State's Office. By 1983, Michigan auto plates will have three letters, including vowels for the first time, along with three numbers. The secretary's office is scrutinizing those three-letter combinations, such as ASS, SAP, HAD and YES, that might have unacceptable connotations. Plates are sold haphazardly, so unless a scrutinizer rules otherwise, it will be possible for a round-shouldered woman to have YES on her license plate.

To counteract the universal language on her plate, she will have to drive with her head out the window, shouting "no." And you can bet some extremely intuitive man will shout back: "Your lips tell me 'no, no,' but there's 'yes, yes,' on your plate." And as quickly as that, an innocent woman will be sexually harassed without even getting a chance to get out of her car and prove her virtue by slouching.

Or what if one of Schlafly's shuffling followers gets a HAD plate? The poor woman will have to keep shouting out her car window that she hasn't been had. She can hardly be more explicit without risking her virtue, no matter how badly she slumps while shouting. Such an oblique message hardly can be expected to dissuade men who operate on intuition alone.

Obviously, license plates containing such blatantly sexually suggestive words as "yes" and "had" would cause terrible trauma for female drivers with virtue. It is to be hoped that Michigan's secretary of state, a man, will ban these two words. Such a wise action would prove that Michigan protects virtuous women who are forced to hide their sluggish hips from public view while driving.

It also would prove a person doesn't have to be female to be as monumentally silly as Phyllis Schlafly. ■

May the birds of bondage trickle down on Reagan

July 3, 1981

President Reagan keeps sending me letters asking for money. It must be humiliating for him to have to do that. He should be emancipated from the bondage of depending upon me for financial support. He should be free at last.

In his latest letter, the president said the Republicans' No. 1 priority is to win control of the House of Representatives from the Democrats in the next election.

"I believe the key to electing a Republican majority by 1982 is to implement the National Republican Congressional Committee's comprehensive GOP Victory Plan now," Reagan wrote. "I hope, at this crucial time, you will strongly consider sending a $15, $25, $50 or even $100 contribution to the committee."

By a fortunate coincidence, before I'd decided how generously to respond to the president's letter, I read what he said in a speech to the national convention of the NAACP in Denver. That speech inspired me to totally reject Reagan's request for my money, for his own good. After he thinks about it, I'm sure he will understand my refusal, and someday he will thank me for it.

Reagan told the NAACP that major slashes in food stamp, welfare and Medicaid spending offer blacks "an emancipation" from dependence on government handouts, which he called "a new kind of bondage."

Certainly. Two hundred years from now, someone will write a book describing how, in 1981, black people began the terrible struggle to free their children from the slavery of eating tax-funded lunches at school and set them on the path toward becoming presidents of corporations that escape paying taxes by threatening to move their factories to a Sun Belt on the moon. Instead of being called "Roots," this book will be called "Boats."

Boats are important because of Reagan's trickle-down theory of economics. According to him, when big corporations make buckets of money, some of it overflows and trickles down to where poor people live with empty pails. This trickle ultimately becomes "a rising tide (that) lifts all boats." All poor people have to do to become rich is sit

113

in their boats. If they can't afford boats, they float on their backs.

Some skeptics ask what the poor people do until the trickle becomes a stream, and the tide comes in. They sit on the beach and protect their sand castles from trampling by volleyball players. That's a lot more fun than going to the post office and waiting in line to buy food stamps.

The marvelous thing about a poor man rising with the tide, instead of using Medicaid to stay alive, is the great feeling of independence it gives him to be able to refuse welfare and thus release public funds for more important use, such as subsidizing the tobacco industry or building gymnasiums for congressmen.

It is my contention that President Reagan and the GOP Victory Plan should not be denied this great feeling of independently rising with the tide. Certainly it must be as degrading for Reagan to ask me for $15 or $100 as it is for a poor person to ask the government for a cheap lunch, or cut-rate surgery. So I'm sending the president an emancipation proclamation instead of money. He can quit writing "gimme" letters, shake off the bonds of begging, launch a boat in his rose garden and sit in it until it floats.

My only regret is that because I didn't donate to the GOP Victory Fund, I won't receive the "special memento of President Reagan's inauguration" that his letter promised to contributors. The memento wasn't described, and I'm curious to know if its what I think it is.

I think it's a lapel button picturing a black woman, pushed off ADC, doing the backstroke in a stream full of sharks. Below the picture it says: "Free at last, God Almighty, free at last." ■

Maybe a nice, long bath
would help Reagan think

August 24, 1981

President Ronald Reagan wrote a personal letter to the Wayne County Neighborhood Legal Services. It began with this warm salutation: "Dear Mr. Neighborhood:"

That's a mistake, of course, probably due to offhandedness. According to news reports, the president sometimes says the wrong thing when he speaks offhand, and maybe that fault has crept into his writing.

White House officials have threatened to bar reporters from picture-taking sessions with Reagan if they don't stop asking questions. Reporters are supposed to attend such "photo opportunities" only as observers, but some of them ask the president questions anyway. This upsets presidential aides who worry that Reagan will be caught off guard and say the wrong thing.

"We don't think the way to make policy is by offhand comment," one top Reagan aide told Newsweek magazine.

Once I was present during a presidential photo opportunity in the White House. What happens is that dozens of photographers are uncaged and allowed to swoop into a prescribed area and take all the pictures they can in, say, three minutes. A high-level official counts off the seconds and speaks sharply to any photographer who dares linger beyond the time limit.

As a newcomer to such organized disorganization, I was stunned by the loud click-clacking-whirring of the cameras and the noisy shoving of the photographers as they vied for better angles. If President Reagan can be heard making policy under such circumstances, he can't be speaking offhand. More likely he is shooting from the hip, which is the same thing, except gun control nuts are sometimes offended.

People who talk offhand or shoot from the hip are speaking before thinking. No one wants a president who makes policy before thinking, so it is probably good that Reagan's aides are determined to protect him from having to answer questions and pose for pictures at the same time. If President Gerald Ford had had similar protection, the world never would have learned that he couldn't wear a helmet and play football at the same time.

However, it is poor publicity for a White House aide to admit to Newsweek that the president can't be trusted to answer questions offhand. It would be much better for Reagan's image if he could find answers in his head instead of on his hand. The way to stop speaking offhand, of course, is to rehearse in private before speaking in public. It isn't easy to do this when you don't know what some pushy reporter might ask you while cameras are clicking. But perhaps the president could take a tip from his wife, who speaks to herself in the bathtub, which is not a photo opportunity.

Nancy Reagan told Family Circle magazine she gets into the tub and has long, imaginary conversations. "And I am absolutely sensational! Really, just wonderful! All the right words came to me, and I say exactly what I think," she said.

If President Reagan took a long bath every day, and practiced answering aloud every question his aides could think of and slip under the bathroom door, he might never have to make policy offhand again, and he would be spared the embarrassment of having to segregate reporters from photographers.

The next step should be to stop the president from writing letters offhand. His "Dear Mr. Neighborhood" letter to the Wayne County Neighborhood Legal Services solicited cash contributions to help elect Congress members who support the Reagan program. One aim of that program is to eliminate federal funding for neighborhood legal services, which provide free civil legal services for poor people.

Perhaps Mr. Neighborhood responded to Reagan's letter by mailing him an empty envelope addressed to Mr. White House. The president could spare himself such embarrassment, plus postage, if he didn't write a letter until after taking a long bath and figuring out how poor people can squeeze legal advice out of a stone policy made offhand. ■

What's this? No Izod
shirts in the bread line?

September 19, 1981

Certainly it was a terrible week for Lech Walesa, head of Poland's Solidarity labor union. It was bad enough when the Communist Party Politburo, warning of possible bloodshed, said it would use all means necessary to prevent the union from gaining political power.

But then, God help the Poles, People magazine delivered a more fearsome blow by including Walesa on its list of worst-dressed people.

It is not known if Walesa still retains enough respect from Solidarity members to continue as an effective leader. These are anxious days for Polish workers. Solidarity has just defied Russia by calling for free elections. There are important battles to be fought, and it can't be easy to follow the leadership of a man who has neither an alligator on his shirt nor a designer label on his butt.

Walesa might plead poverty, which certainly can't be denied in a nation where people must stand in line for hours to pay a week's salary for a loaf of unsliced bread. What laborer can afford to buy fancy clothes?

But such an excuse won't wash. Money does not make a man well-dressed. For proof, please note that Wayne Newton was also on People's worst-dressed list. Newton is a Las Vegas entertainer who makes millions of dollars every week. If he wanted alligators on his shirts, he could buy Florida and drain the Everglades.

No, you can't buy sartorial excellence any more than you can buy good taste. Some men simply know enough to be offended by the sight of brown shoes and blue socks in a bread line, and some don't. From what I've seen of Walesa, I suspect he got on People's list by wearing a long-sleeved sweater under his suit coat. A man doesn't have to be wealthy to know better than that.

The problem is the multiple sleeves. When you put a suit coat on over a long-sleeved sweater, two things can happen and both are bad:

• The sweater sleeves stick to the inside of the coat sleeves and bunch up above the elbows. This makes your arms appear bulky and proletarian. And when you try to take the coat off, the bunched-up sweater sleeves cause your arms to become stuck inside the coat

117

sleeves terribly, and the next time you wear the sweater, you trip over its cuffs.

• When putting the coat on over the sweater, you are smart enough to hang on to the cuffs of the sweater sleeves, to prevent bunching inside the coat sleeves. But you hang on to the left sweater cuff with your right hand, and vice versa, which forces you to put both arms into the same coat sleeve. This prompts Truman Capote to call you a trend setter, and your picture appears in People magazine, but not in the best-dressed department.

Defenders of Lech Walesa's clothing may claim he must wear a long-sleeved sweater under his coat in the winter because there is no central heating in bread lines. That's an alarming excuse. For the sake of correct appearance, women wear open-toed shoes in snow-drifts. If a man isn't strong enough to freeze for fashion, how can he be strong enough to stand firm when 100,000 Soviet soldiers conduct military maneuvers near the Polish border?

People magazine performed a public service for all Poland by revealing that Lech Walesa doesn't dress any better than Wayne Newton. The last time I saw Newton he was wearing tire chains around his neck. No labor union should be led by a man who has been put in the same dressing room with Wayne Newton. Does Douglas Fraser wear tire chains?

Incidentally, People magazine also did something for the United States. It revealed that Secretary of State Alexander Haig is one of the best-dressed men in the world. He never will embarrass our country by appearing at a summit meeting in proletarian sleeves.

Well-dressed leaders such as Haig are one guarantee that this nation will forever remain free for all citizens, and such an important institution as People magazine will never be hindered in its never-ending efforts to attain new heights in bubble-headed vacuity. ■

Doctors who keep us waiting are all wet

April 21, 1982

When it comes to doctors, what I want is revenge, and I'm not ashamed to admit it. I don't like to get mad, because anger messes up my good times, but I do like to get even. I recently did something dumb at the car wash that I want to do in a doctor's examination room.

Before I went to the car wash, I showed up five minutes early for a 1 p.m. appointment at the Kresge Eye Institute. I finally saw a doctor's assistant at 2:15. I didn't see a doctor until 2:45. Why do doctors think their time is more valuable than their patients' time?

This is a sad song I've wailed several times before. And, each time I rap doctors for being inconsiderate and arrogant, I hear from dozens of patients who say amen, amen, jab the thoughtless jerks again. But I also hear from a few patients, and doctors, who insist that not all doctors overbook appointments to make certain no moment passes unmilked of money.

That is true. So I hereby qualify today's remarks to except those doctors who don't waste their patients' time in the name of greed. I only wish those innocent doctors advertised in the Yellow Pages. Something like: "Free Office Calls for All Patients Required to Wait More Than 20 Minutes Beyond Appointment Time."

Incredibly, some doctors try to establish personal innocence by hanging the guilt on their hired help. When criticized for making 2 p.m. appointments with 15 different patients, they say they're sorry but they didn't do it, their receptionist did. That brand of baloney reminds me of something J.P. McCarthy, my favorite disc jockey, proclaimed the other morning.

McCarthy righteously named entrepreneur Mark McCormack "loser of the day" because he is committing the terrible sacrilege of marketing Pope John Paul II's coming visit to London, selling papal T-shirts and other holy souvenirs for filthy lucre. But McCormack simply is doing the job he was hired to do for the pope, the same way he does it for Muhammad Ali and Arnold Palmer. The loser is Pope John for allowing McCormack to be hired.

And the loser in the overbooked doctor's office isn't the woman who makes the appointments, it's the doctor who hired her. What the doctor loses is the love of weary-from-waiting patients, many of whom are loath to complain to the person holding the scalpel over their good health. And the only thing the doctor receives to compensate for that terrible loss of affection is enough money to buy every drugstore within 1,800 miles of his prescriptions.

Doctors who keep patients waiting endlessly usually use the "emergency" excuse. They say they often can't keep an appointment with one patient because another patient needs them more. The answer, of course, is if these emergencies occur so regularly, the doctors should regularly leave gaps for them in their schedules. If, God forbid, a gap should ever remain unfilled, without a shivering patient waiting in every examination cubicle, the despondent doctor could spend his idle time kicking himself for neglecting his investments.

While waiting until 2:15 for my 1 p.m. appointment with the eye doctor, I kept thinking about the work I could have been doing in my office if the doctor hadn't invited me to his office 75 minutes before he could see me. And I kept wondering what I could do to get even with him.

I didn't think of the proper revenge until later when, at Paul's Car Wash, I left my car at the first cleaning station and strolled to the end of the wash line. Soon an employe was running around frantically, questioning people. He wanted to know who'd taken the keys out of the silver Oldsmobile. It was blocking the line and stalling profits. Who was the big dummy who absent-mindedly locked his car and walked away with the keys in his pocket?

Me! I was plugging the production line and costing management money.

Now all I have to do is make an appointment for my eye doctor to examine my headlights. I'll park the Olds in front of his eye charts and eat the keys. ∎

Patients of these eye doctors are seeing nothing but red

May 3, 1982

Two doctors' wives insisted their hard-working husbands are well worth waiting for. And Dr. James R. Smith of Petoskey wrote: "I'm quite sure patients crap on their doctors far more than the other way around. If I were your doctor, I would sever our relationship and let you go elsewhere. I'm not sure you even deserve care."

That was the negative reaction, in total, to my column rapping those doctors who overbook appointments and keep patients waiting for hours, making it clear they think their time is much more valuable than their patients' time.

The positive reaction was much larger. There are a lot of people out there still waiting at 3 p.m. for 2 p.m. appointments, and they are angry about it. I even heard from several doctors mad at other doctors for keeping them waiting. The most damning testimony came from an employe of a suburban eye clinic. Her name is withheld to protect her job but, believe me, she is real. Listen to her:

"Our senior ophthalmologist decided to group his patients by certain days: new patients only on one day, post-operatives only on another day, etc. There is no thought of the needs of the patients as to whether their particular complaints fit into that day or whether a patient's day off fits into the doctor's schedule. Patients often wait three hours for an examination to be completed.

"The younger ophthalmologist often keeps patients waiting, too. An emergency case needing immediate attention? No. He and his assistant are closeted in one of the examination rooms discussing their love lives. When they finish this important medical function, they'll get around to the patients.

"God help you if you have the first appointment of the afternoon with either optometrist and have taken part of your lunch hour. You may be docked for taking extra time off work, but you won't be examined until they finish the backgammon game they're playing in their office.

"The taxpayers have decided to fund medical care for the poor on the theory that if poor people are healthy, they might have a chance of being cured of poverty as well as illnesses. In many medical

121

facilities, patients are not identified to the doctor as to whether they are fee-paying, privately insured or on Medicaid. That information is handled by the business office alone. But in our clinic the daily schedule contains the insurance code beside the patients' names. The doctor is able to decide whether the Medicaid patient deserves as much time as the fee-paying patient.

"The junior ophthalmologist sees most of the Medicaid patients and is booked two to three months ahead, so if you are poor and can't see, you'll just have to wait. The optometrists won't see Medicaid patients at all. That would affect the patient-profit ratio of their cost center, and their salary increases would not be as large.

"The senior ophthalmologist won't see retarded patients, most of whom are on Medicaid. The junior ophthalmologist doesn't examine these patients as carefully as "normal" patients because "they are retarded and don't need to see as well." The bill to Medicaid (taxpayers) is not lowered in these cases, of course. The taxpayers pay full price for little or no care for retarded patients who need to see better if they are to learn.

"If a doctor doesn't feel like working hard on a certain day, he yells at the receptionist for booking him too heavily. If he is in the mood to work, he yells at her for not booking heavy enough. Usually there are the same number of patients each day. He doesn't plan ahead for vacations. He just decides to take off and tells the receptionist to phone two or three weeks' of appointments and cancel them . . . "

End of quotations from clinic receptionist. She had more to say, but there's no more room. I will return to her the next time a doctor tells me that patients crap on their doctors far more than the other way around. ■

Is that the same thing as dog catchers breeding pups?

August 30, 1982

A state agency says one way to cut the cost of health care is to cut the number of doctors selling it. That angers my friend Tom, who sells groceries.

"In the food business, competition is good for the customer because the more grocery stores there are in a neighborhood, the lower the prices are," Tom said. "Why doesn't it work the same way in the medical business?"

"Because it's difficult for the A&P to convince Jane Customer that she must eat a $5 lamb chop, after consultations with two other grocery stores, or she'll die," I said. "Also, Blue Cross won't pay for the lamb chop."

But seriously, folks. State health officials recommended that the number of students entering Michigan's four medical schools be cut by about 100 in 1983. Michigan had 17,000 doctors at the beginning of 1980. That's 545 optimum patients per doctor but, according to the state Office of Health and Medical Affairs, each doctor should have 725 patients, with optimum or any other disease.

It wasn't disclosed exactly how that higher figure was reached, but I suspect it resulted from an architectural space-efficiency study which determined that 725 patients can be squeezed into the average doctor's waiting room for a 10 a.m. appointment.

Tom the grocer conceded most people probably wait longer in checkout lines than in medical offices. "That's because supermarket cashiers don't make phony appointments to ring up 725 sales at the same time," he said, "but I don't care about that stuff.

"What I care about is the sad fact that the more doctors there are per patient, the more the cost of health care goes up. That means when the number of doctors increases, more people get sick. If the grocery business worked that way, I could open 100 new stores and more people would get fat."

Tom was being unfair, of course. There is a big difference between selling food and selling medical care. For one thing, grocers don't have the grave responsibility of filling empty hospital beds.

Dozens of American cities have more hospital beds than patients.

123

These beds were purchased in anticipation of more people getting sick enough to go to the hospital. But many people don't know they should be hospitalized. It is the doctors' responsibility to tell these people how much they need to go to the hospital and how much their medical insurance will cover. Otherwise, busybody cost-cutters will convert empty hospital beds into prison bunks, leaving displaced doctors with no free place to conduct business and causing thousands of laid-off nurses to discover they can make more money bagging groceries for my friend Tom.

Another important difference between the food and the doctoring businesses concerns customer acceptance of professional diagnoses. When Jane Customer goes to the supermarket, she pretty much knows what and how much she wants to eat. She may be somewhat influenced by attractive labels, point-of-purchase advertising and newspaper coupons. But if a produce clerk says Jane looks wan and should take two heads of cabbage every night before going to bed, she is liable to tell him to go jump in the lettuce bin.

On the other hand, when Jane goes to the doctor, she has no idea what she needs. She knows everything about cabbage and nothing about brain surgery. If the doctor prescribes a heart bypass, she has it. She thinks the doctor is trying to save her life. She never suspects him of being desperate to make money because there are too many doctors in town and he has only 545 patients when he should have 725.

"The cost of health care wouldn't be so outrageous if doctors had to compete for customers by lowering prices, the same way I do," Tom the grocer said. "Doctors who create work for themselves are the same as firemen who set fires."

Tom was really steamed. To make him feel better, the next time I went into his store, I refused to buy any groceries without first getting a second opinion. ■

I can't trust someone who lost JCPenney's periods

The first sentence of the letter read: "On August 5th, you'll be celebrating something special — your 57th birthday."

How nice, I thought. It was three weeks until my birthday, and already a friend was sending me best wishes.

But then I read a succeeding sentence: "Mr.*Fitzgerald,*of course I don't know whether you're married or single, or whether or not you have children."

Of course? The writer knew my age and birth date, but not whether I'm married or have children? What kind of a friend was that to be wishing me a happy birthday?

The signature said my birthday greeter was R. Michael Howard, president of the JCPenney Life Insurance Company. I noted that R. Michael Howard has a period after his first initial and a space between that initial and his middle name and also between his middle name and his last name. And I wondered whatever happened to the periods and spaces that used to clearly distinguish JCPenney from a typographical mishmash.

James Cash Penney founded the J.C. Penney empire in 1902 and remained active in its operation almost until his death, at the age of 95, in 1971. He and I go back a long way together.

When I was a small boy, my father bought the family clothing from J.C. Penney. He bought life insurance from Harry Hickey who was best man at my parents' wedding. J.C. Penney wasn't even invited to the church, let alone the reception.

When I was a teenager, I swept floors at a J.C. Penney store. I remember they were creaky wooden floors and required regular oiling. Also, before each sweeping I had to spread kitty litter on the floor to keep the dust off the merchandise. This was done each morning without benefit of an environmental impact study.

Later, when I sold and wrote newspaper advertising, my best customer was a J.C. Penney store. And if I'd ever left the periods and spaces out of J.C. Penney's name, the store manager wouldn't have paid for the ad.

Back in any of those old days, I would have been thrilled to receive birthday greetings from James Cash Penney. I always admired him because he was a firm believer in newspaper advertising and never competed with Harry Hickey. It is not thrilling to have R. Michael Howard remember my birthday.

For one thing, he said if I don't buy $5,000 worth of JCPenney life insurance by Aug. 5, it will cost me more on Aug. 6 and forever after. I hate deadlines, and I especially hate a deadline that coincides with what is supposed to be a happy occasion. Thanks to R. Michael Howard, I can spend my birthday feeling dumb for blowing forever the chance to buy $5,000 worth of life insurance for $20.70 a month.

Speaking of dumb, the birthday card from R. Michael Howard said I would be allowed to "EXAMINE YOUR POLICY FOR 30 FULL DAYS AT NO RISK TO YOU." (The capital letters are R. Michael Howard's; he probably got them from the same place he's hiding JCPenney's periods and spaces.)

Now, I realize there's not much a doddering old fool of 57 can do to amuse himself in the twilight of his insurable years. But spend 30 full days reading one insurance policy? Is R. Michael Howard sure I can stand the excitement?

When asked, I usually answer that I don't want anything for my birthday. But this year I do. I want, please God, to be taken off the mailing list of every clothing firm that sells insurance, and every gasoline company that sells shoes. I want never again to receive a stupid letter from a friendly corporation that warmly inserts my name into the middle of each paragraph to show that it really knows all about me — except it doesn't know I died five years ago.

And I want each of you who receives birthday greetings from the JCPenney Insurance Company to use its postage-paid return envelope to send this column to the "attention of RMHoward." Add a note asking if he knows how to keep the dust off his insurance.■

Cars with long names are better at Russian roulette

October 31, 1983

The auto business is now officially recovered. I just bought a 1984 Oldsmobile Cutlass Ciera Brougham Detroiter. That's not a Hertz fleet, it's one car. Now, more than ever, I will be hearing the dismaying sound of my wife tearing along the perforated line.

All of the above is a writer's gimmick, designed to keep you reading in anticipation of possibly discovering what the devil the intrepid columnist is expounding upon today. I'm rather anxious to find out myself, so let's get on with it.

I don't often buy a car. The previous one was a 1977 Oldsmobile Delta 88. I'm not sure why, each succeeding year, manufacturers attach more different chrome names to one model car. It surely can't have anything to do with justifying an unjustified price hike, so it must be to give car-wash employes added opportunities to snag their rags.

Anyway, the Delta covered more than 108,000 miles without an inch of trouble, and I was prepared to keep driving it until it made me mad. For me, a car is not an object of romance or ego gratification; it's transportation. If I don't have to get somewhere quickly, I'd rather walk. And if I don't have to get there at all, I stand at a city bus stop.

Unfortunately, my wife feels otherwise, and she drives the family car much more than I do. There were times when we were a two-car or three-car family; I'm probably the only person extant who owned two AMC Pacers, speaking of extinct, at the same time. But now the children are grown and gone, and I walk to work, so it makes absolutely no sense to buy insurance and parking space for two cars.

That's what I thought until two things happened. First, my wife persuaded me that only a latent wife-beater would force his wife to play "Russian roulette" (she has a mean way with words) on the freeway in a 100,000-mile-plus car. She was afraid the old Olds would make her mad, which would be a terrible tragedy, before it made me mad, which would serve me right.

Second, the dealer who sold me the 1984 Olds with five names said my 1977 Olds was worth practically nothing as a trade-in. Maybe $100. Good Lord! I'm not sentimental about cars, but I'm practical.

127

That old Olds is worth 20 times $100 to me, even if I drive it only once more. Just as long as I drive it to pick up my wife after she loses at Russian roulette in the fancy Oldsmobile Cutlass Cierra Brougham Detroiter she made me buy. When I pull up alongside her, stranded on the side of the freeway, I will smirk my tires.

I hate to sound bitter, but a person who waited seven years to buy a new car quickly learns the meaning of "sticker shock." Back when I bought cars with only one or two names, I was able to pay cash. But this time, as the grievously shocked stuckee, I couldn't swing a cash deal without liquidating my stock envelope (Henry Ford II has a portfolio) and selling my entire family to Kunta Kinte (now starring in the splendid "Master Harold and the Boys" at the Birmingham Theatre).

So two-thirds of the monstrous amount had to be financed and now, for the first time in 20 years, I'm making monthly car payments. That is, my wife is making them. She spends most of her time at the family desk because she writes thank-you notes to people to thank them for sending her thank-you notes, and she knows many people who do the same thing. So it was only practical, long ago, to designate her the family check-writer.

Her job is to pay $1,000 worth of bills with the $800 I deposited and have enough left over for dinner and drinks at Peg Leg's. My job is to sit across the room and keep from sobbing as the distinctive, bumpy-rip sound of checks being torn along the perforated line mounts to a crescendo and I realize she isn't going to make it again.

Onward and Upward, and keep an eye out for smirk marks on the freeway. ■

I told you 16 years ago
J. Edgar was no hero

November 25, 1983

In 1967, after the nation received a stupid sermon about war protesters from J. Edgar Hoover, I wrote: "If he hasn't anything better to do, Hoover should read that portion of the Warren Report which states clearly what a lousy job the FBI did in protecting John Kennedy from Lee Harvey Oswald. He might also prepare a message explaining why every cop in the country knows there is a nationwide crime syndicate (Mafia) but the FBI never does anything about it."

In 1970, after reading a Life magazine article describing the FBI in action, I wrote: "Law enforcement has made great strides in this country since the vulgar old days when G-men gunned downed George Raft. There may even be some truth to the gossip that J. Edgar Hoover is now doing Pat Nixon's hair."

In 1975, through the Freedom of Information Act, I learned the FBI investigated me for writing all of the above plus other equally uninspired words critical of J. Edgar and his merry band of dark suits. For $33 I obtained a copy of my FBI file which revealed I was a country newspaper editor with a limited audience that paid no attention to my radical ravings.

The reason for rehashing my old troubles with the FBI is NBC-TV's recent miniseries, "Kennedy," which depicted J. Edgar Hoover as a bigoted, blackmailing, window-peeping creep. As portrayed in foreboding shadows by actor Vincent Gardenia, Hoover came across as Adolf Hitler's evil stepbrother.

It is amazing what a difference 16 years can make. For more than 40 years, Hoover was one of this nation's greatest heroes. According to the news media, movies and radio and TV shows, he could do no wrong. In 1967, it wasn't at all surprising that the FBI was alerted when I dared to throw a dinky dart at its sacrosanct director.

At that time, my righteously indignant objection was merely that Hoover regularly spent taxpayers' money to bombard the country with reprints and broadcasts of his stuffy tirades against such dangerous criminals as apple-pie haters and Vietnam war protesters.

"I think it is splendid that J. Edgar Hoover has such high-flown opinions on all controversial issues. It is also OK if he wants to tell the

129

world that his mother brought him up right. But, by God, he should buy his own postage stamps," I wrote, speaking of stuffy tirades.

The aforementioned Life article included photos of an FBI agent helping Martha Mitchell, wife of the then-U.S. attorney general, solve a crucial problem of state. Martha needed a dress ironed, and an unidentified FBI man did the job for her.

"The FBI is made up of selfless men who want no personal glory for their marvelous achievements. They want only to protect you taxpayers, you people who pay their salaries, from wrinkled dresses," I wrote. "If an ordinary, glory-mad maid had been pictured ironing that dress, she would probably have demanded that Life print her name. But there was no maid around that day. She was probably out fighting the Mafia. Somebody has to."

That was the type of wimpy criticism that got a writer investigated by the FBI in 1970. Things began to change a few years later, after Hoover's death, when his successor, L. Patrick Gray, admitted under oath that he lied to aid the Watergate cover-up.

"I was warm and hot all over, almost like a woman in menopause, because I had told a lie," Gray said.

So I wrote: "The explosion you heard was J. Edgar Hoover cracking through his gravestone headfirst. He devoted his life to fighting the Red Menace and earning respect for the FBI, and now he is betrayed by a replacement who forgot to take his estrogen pills."

Now, on national TV, Hoover has been pictured with clay feet up to his eyebrows. And there will be no FBI investigation.

Onward and Upward. The next director of the FBI may be Rodney Dangerfield. ■

Naked lady, moving piano
make a deadly sandwich

March 12, 1984

On Nov. 25, 1983, a Detroit Free Press headline said: "Bar's boss suffocates atop nude on piano." That headline, one of my all-time favorites, is a splendid example of how even the most negative news can be presented in a positive light. Mayor Coleman Young surely would approve.

It happened in San Francisco. According to the story below the headline, 38-year-old James (Jimmy the Beard) Ferrozzo, manager of a topless bar called the Condor Club, was accidentally killed when a mobile grand piano was inadvertently activated while he was on top of it. It was after regular business hours, and Jimmy the Beard was alone except for a 23-year-old woman who escaped serious injury.

The piano, usually used by a dancer for grand entrances and exits, was hoisted electrically to an opening in the ceiling when Ferrozzo's foot apparently brushed a control switch, police said. Because Ferrozzo was too far from the center of the piano top, he missed the opening and was pressed against the ceiling.

The headline could have said: "Bar's boss squashed to death between piano and ceiling." But that would have been negative reporting. It would have made San Francisco look like a city where it isn't safe to ride a piano.

Instead, noting that Ferrozzo's companion was between him and the piano top when he died — probably to keep warm, as she was wearing no clothing — the headline writer generously put the grisly news in a perspective not too damaging to the mobile piano business in San Francisco.

"Bar's boss suffocates atop nude on piano." Notice how much more positive "suffocates" sounds than "squashed to death." People are seldom squashed to death by hugs and kisses, but it is well-known that people are often suffocated by love while being smothered in affection.

Also, the headline writer's adroit use of "atop nude" took the onus off the piano. To suffocate atop a nude is obviously a more positive way to die than to be squashed to death atop a piano. Such a positive headline gave the mobile piano manufacturers of San Francisco

131

almost as much protection as they'd have had if a sign atop the Condor Club piano had said: "Please keep your onus off the piano."

The headline writer obviously took a positive cue from the reporter who wrote the suffocation article. The first paragraph said: "The night manager at one of America's best-known topless bars was killed when he was sandwiched between the club's ceiling and a nude woman atop a moving piano."

Sandwiched. I ask you, is that more positive than squashed, or what? Readers received the impression that Jimmy the Beard was pastrami and a mobile piano was as harmless as a slice of whole wheat bread. That paragraph couldn't have been written more positively by the public relations director of the San Francisco Association of Mobile Piano Manufacturers.

That is the type of positive reporting Mayor Coleman Young yearns for when he complains about the news media's using negative reporting to give Detroit a dismal image. Take the turkeys, for example.

Last October, 1,200 frozen turkeys rotted when the refrigeration system failed in a city-supervised warehouse. The turkeys were federally donated, and the city was supposed to distribute them to hungry people. The mayor said press reports of the wasted turkeys were overblown and unfairly implied that the city had done something terribly wrong.

He was right. Every article I read simply said the 1,200 turkeys rotted. How much more positive it would have been to read this headline: "City rescues 1,200 turkeys from being eaten."

And the lead paragraph could have explained: "Mayor Young announced today that, because of his compassion, 1,200 frozen turkeys earmarked for Thanksgiving dinners were spared from rude chewing by carnivorous people. Instead, the turkeys were allowed to melt peacefully in a warm warehouse."

Onward and Upward, and put no onus on the pastrami, please.■

That will teach him to use logic at breakfast

March 21, 1984

I would like to say you won't believe the following true story, but you will. And that is a painful commentary on the state of the world. It means we have come to expect human beings, individually and corporately, to remain stupidly rigid in the face of conclusive proof that they should quit acting loony tunes, for Lord's sake, and bend a little in the holy name of common sense.

Last Friday morning, Frank W. Brochert, a 41-year-old lawyer with offices in downtown Detroit, went to the Colonnade Cafeteria in the Penobscot Building for breakfast. He noted the menu sign said the breakfast special, for only 96 cents, was one egg, bacon or sausage, toast and coffee — no substitutions.

That sounded like a decent deal to Brochert, except he'd already had his morning cup of coffee. So he got a poached egg, bacon and rye toast. Nothing to drink.

"That will be $1.25," the cashier said.

"I told her it should be one dollar — 96 cents plus four cents tax," Brochert told me. "She said no, that because I didn't take coffee, my breakfast was a la carte and cost $1.25.

"I asked her if I took a cup of coffee and poured it out, what would the cost be, and she said one dollar. I decided it was ridiculous to waste a cup of coffee and so I gave her a dollar and took the tray. And she said, 'Sir, you cannot do that; you must either pay another 25 cents or take a cup of coffee.' "

But Brochert did neither. He sat down to eat breakfast. The fun was just beginning.

"A man dressed in white kitchen clothes came to my table and said I owed another quarter," Brochert continued. "I explained I didn't want to waste the coffee and I thought it would be in the best interest of the restaurant to simply charge me a dollar and save the coffee which they could sell for 42 cents.

"The man insisted the restaurant policy of no substitutions or deletions had to be strictly adhered to. We went back and forth, I telling him the policy was ridiculous and it would not make sense for me

133

to get a cup of coffee and pour it out, and him insisting I pay a quarter or take the coffee.

"By this time I was getting a bit exasperated, so I told him to call a cop. He left and a few minutes later returned with a Penobscot security officer who politely told me to pay for my meal. But when I explained the circumstances, he said, 'I'm not getting involved in this' in a tone that indicated he thought the whole thing was as ridiculous as I did. And he left."

The debate continued. The Colonnade employe insisted the menu sign said no deletions from the breakfast special were allowed. Brochert said let's go look at it, which they did. The sign said nothing about deletions. The employe still insisted the lawyer pay 25 cents or take a cup of coffee.

By this time, Brochert was so irritated he invited the employe — even though he was bigger and younger — to step outside to settle the argument. At this point, the employe finally gave up and left — after warning Brochert never to return to the Colonnade.

"I was barred for trying to save the restaurant money!" Brochert exclaimed.

On Monday, I spoke with Janet McIntosh, the Colonnade manager. She confirmed that no deletions are allowed on the breakfast special ("they might lead to substitutions") and said the supervisor only was following policy when he confronted Brochert, who was "rather obnoxious." But she conceded it was "more than likely" the policy would be changed.

McIntosh also said "I won't appreciate" reading the Brochert story in the newspaper.

I don't blame her. But I have my duty to perform, in the holy name of common sense. ■

If AT&T stops writing me, I'll stop trying to call it

April 23, 1984

Lately the mail has brought me, in six different envelopes, six plastic phone-charge cards from AT&T. I don't want them. They worry me. I'm going nuts trying to figure out what to do with them.

Each of the cards has the same name and number on it. Each arrived attached to a handsome brochure that, on the cover, urges me to "Reach Out and Touch the Future." I don't want to do that. It is the future that scares me.

I have no idea why AT&T sent me six identical cards when one would have been too much. If I have any questions, the brochure says, I should dial 800 CALL ATT. Is that supposed to be clever? AT&T's customers have phone numbers. Why does AT&T have phone letters?

Because AT&T has taught people to dial numbers endlessly, it is awkward for them to dial letters. CALL ATT figures out to 2255 188. Why doesn't AT&T just come right out and say so? I resent being put to the trouble of translating letters to numbers, especially when 800 CALL ATT is usually busy anyway.

That's probably why AT&T disguises its numbers as letters. It really doesn't want anyone to call it because, as the world's largest phone company, AT&T is embarrassed that people can't get it on the phone. I dialed 800 CALL ATT 15 times in two days. Eight times the line buzzed busy. Seven times a taped voice said all the operators were busy and I was put on hold to listen to dentist-office music.

I don't know how long the music plays before a live operator comes on the line. I refuse to wait on hold to talk to the phone company. The people who sell phone service should answer their phones promptly, to demonstrate the convenience of their product. I also won't buy a car from a salesman who takes me for a demonstration ride and runs out of gas.

So, unable to communicate with the communications giant, I'm left to speculate on why AT&T sent me six identical charge cards attached to six identical brochures in six different envelopes addressed to six identical addresses. And I speculate the giant is sloppy but

135

doesn't care because it knows it's big enough to get someone else — you and me — to pay for the losses caused by its slop.

I've heard from several readers who also received multiple mailings of identical AT&T cards. I don't know the production cost of each card and brochure, but it has to total a few dollars. If I had to receive six cards, I don't know why AT&T didn't at least save postage by mailing them in one envelope.

All I know is now that AT&T and Michigan Bell have separated, long-distance rates will be cheaper. My wife spends most of her time talking long distance to our two daughters who live less than 100 miles away. From another colorful brochure, which AT&T sent me eight times so far, I learned that for me to benefit from lower long-distance rates, our daughters must move to Belgium.

But you want to know why I'm afraid of a future with six AT&T cards? Kathleen Vokes is why. She is the Howell woman who received phone bills totaling more than $60,000 last January and February. Ma Bell, promising to straighten things out, explained that some crooks charged thousands of calls to Vokes' card number. Two months later, Vokes told me AT&T had just billed her for $56,000 and sent her five new charge cards, four with a new number and the fifth with the old number the crooks use.

Faced with that type of corporate efficiency, I have six charge cards that could fall into crooked hands. I can't burn plastic without stinking up my apartment. I won't cut up the cards and throw them in the trash because a trash picker could glue them back together. I won't flush them down the toilet because a sewage plant worker might have daughters living in Belgium.

What can I do with them? According to the AT&T brochure, they are "state of the art" cards that I can "insert into new special public AT&T Card Caller phones."

I know where I'd like to insert them.   ■

FBI has slick scheme for a Ferrare called Cristina

September 17, 1984

Cristina DeLorean recently was hired as hostess of a talk show on KABC-TV in Los Angeles. At least, that's what she thinks.

Actually, the show is a sting operation. The only people who see it live are FBI agents looking into a KABC studio through a mirror. Tapes of the show won't be shown publicly until Cristina's trial begins in a federal courtroom now being constructed by Metro-Goldwyn-Mayer.

Mrs. DeLorean is using her professional name, Cristina Ferrare, for the TV show, which ties in neatly with the reason for the sting. She was Ferrare when she met and soon thereafter married John DeLorean, and the FBI is seeking evidence to convince a jury that the only reason DeLorean agreed to an initial blind date was that he thought Ferrare was an Italian sports car.

The government came up with the talk-show ploy in response to criticism from Hollywood set designers who said nasty things about the motel rooms usually used in FBI films.

"It isn't just the 40-watt light bulbs and the dreadful pictures on Holiday Inn walls," one designer complained. "Sometimes you can't hear the dialogue because the ice machine in the hallway is making so much noise, and when the FBI actors begin talking too fast, everyone in the audience knows it must be getting near checkout time."

Also, the switch to a TV studio gives the federal government a splendid opportunity to refute often-heard accusations that the agent in charge of FBI sting operations got all his film experience in the 1930s directing Richard Dix and Margaret Lindsay in spy movies usually shown as the third half of double features.

"You'll notice that the government always films in black and white instead of color," one movie critic wrote in her review of an FBI-Erotic release showing John DeLorean fondling cocaine. "That is just an underhanded attempt to visually slur the sting victim. Any person filmed squatting on a luggage rack, in grainy black and white, with a rumpled bed in the shadowy background, is bound to look guilty. If 'The Sound of Music' had been made in a Best Western motel, Julie Andrews would have been arrested for child molestation."

137

So the Cristina Ferrare talk show is being taped in full, glorious color. And every other precaution is being taken to fool her — fake newspaper reviews, fake fan mail, fake autograph seekers and fake celebrity guests to sit on her interview couch. (It is irrelevant but interesting to note that the FBI now is trying to figure out what in the hell to do with an agent who was hired only because he looked exactly like Truman Capote).

You may think it is farfetched to suggest that the government would go so far to prove that John DeLorean once mistook Ferrare for an Italian sports car (thus violating the Mann Act, which forbids the driving of a woman across state lines for transportation purposes).

But it recently was revealed that the U.S. Selective Service purchased (your tax dollars at work) the names of 113,093 boys who innocently registered for free birthday treats at the nationwide chain of Farrell's Ice Cream Parlors. If our government will use children's parties and singing waiters to find out when boys will be old enough to register for the draft, it will certainly fake a TV show to finally stick a sting on a DeLorean.

It is, indeed, getting near checkout time. ■

DeLorean can teach old panhandlers new tricks

November 16, 1984

Fortunately, because otherwise you wouldn't believe it, I have the clipping to prove that in the Feb. 3, 1978, issue of the Detroit Free Press, I had the incredible prescience to write: "There must be a cheaper way to get from the Free Press building to the London Chop House without risking confrontation with ambitious panhandlers who hire lawyers to help them beg."

I was referring specifically to John DeLorean, who, almost seven years later, became perhaps the most famous panhandler in the history of begging.

Those 1978 words were part of a column written in response to a DeLorean interview in which he complained about crime in Detroit streets. "You can't walk from your office to the London Chop House without getting the top of your head caved in," he told a Free Press reporter.

At the time, De Lorean was trying to get Detroit to build him a $15 billion factory so he could manufacture sports cars here. He said his factory would hire the crooks right off the street and give us all a safer town to walk in.

I agreed with DeLorean about the danger of being a pedestrian in downtown Detroit. "There is always the danger of bumping into one of the business magnates who lurk around the Chop House entrance," I wrote. "One of these magnates is liable to hit you on the hat if you refuse to build him a $15 billion factory on the riverfront."

That was early 1978. The city didn't come up with enough dollars to persuade DeLorean to locate here, one of the few times in recent history Detroit taxpayers could have been mugged, but weren't. The factory was built in Northern Ireland, and DeLorean mugged Great Britain instead.

And last week, in a $5,000 ad in the Los Angeles Herald Examiner, DeLorean lived up to the advance billing I gave him in 1978. He panhandled. He begged people to send him $5 to $100 each to help pay his legal bill. DeLorean owes $1 million to the lawyers who convinced a jury it's no crime to fondle cocaine in a movie if the movie was directed by Cecil B. FBI.

139

"It really has been tremendous," a public relations executive handling DeLorean's advertising campaign told reporters. "We've actually had people calling here asking for the number of the post office box so they can make contributions."

My wife says I have an irritating habit of always exclaiming "I don't believe it!" when I'm shocked by the news of the day. She's right. And I never exclaimed it louder than when I read that people are sending money to John DeLorean.

If you sent money to him, or if you know someone who did, or someone who knows someone who knows someone who did, please give me his or her name and address. I am willing to be persuaded, but until I'm put in touch with someone who actually contributed to the DeLorean defense fund, I can't believe it!

Another thing John DeLorean said in that 1978 Free Press interview was: "Money's not a motivation to me, it never has been. The real thing that turns me on is accomplishment."

According to that philosophy, maybe DeLorean doesn't want free money nearly as much as he wants to accomplish the tough job of persuading people to give it to him.

The next time a street panhandler asks me for 25 cents, I'll tell the lazy bum to hire a public relations consultant, put an ad in the newspaper and turn himself on to just how much a man can accomplish if he's not afraid to ask the public to build him a $15 billion doorway to sleep in. ∎

The joys of marriage

My ham prefers mustard
pickles to bruised tomato

January 5, 1977

Because I like mustard pickles on ham, my wife insisted I accompany her to the supermarket. Which is how I ended up in the great tomato race.

My mother always served mustard pickles with ham. So did my wife, in the early years of our marriage. But for several years now, I have been forced to eat ham without mustard pickles. This irks my palate and prompts me to scream a little.

"Screaming won't do any good," my wife always says. "The stores do not sell mustard pickles anymore."

I refused to believe all those huge supermarkets could not find room for a few jars of mustard pickles. Last week I finally accused her of sloppy shopping. This was not the smartest thing I have ever done.

The next thing I knew, I was inside the nearest Farmer Jack's. My wife sometimes moves so swiftly, I actually cannot feel the leash being attached. I always have been a corner-grocery person. When I was a boy, I went to the store and handed the man a list written by my mother. The grocer did all the work while I stood around and watched for opportunities to sneak something out of the candy jars. This is the intelligent way to buy food.

Supermarkets are too big. I never can find anything. Mostly, I never can find a clerk who will take my list and do my shopping for me. It probably is easier to swipe candy, but I never can find the jar of jawbreakers.

"I will find all the food," my wife explained this fateful afternoon in Farmer Jack's. "You have to look for only one thing — mustard pickles. If you find any, I will eat each pickle while standing on the checkout counter."

I spent 30 minutes in the pickle row. I relocated jars so I could see to the back of every shelf. I asked a clerk and he handed me some mustard relish which is not the same thing at all.

Real mustard pickles do not come minced for hot dogs. They are whole, like dill or sweet pickles, and they come swimming in a mustard sauce, accompanied by little round onions, red peppers and hunks of cauliflower.

I couldn't find any. There are dozens of other types of pickles, especially prepared for everything from cocktail parties to bar mitzvahs, but no mustard pickles.

I found my wife in Health Products, fondling antacids, and confessed my failure. She is not one of those gracious winners who will not say "I told you so."

"I told you so."

An hour later, still groveling, I helped her pile $50 worth of groceries before one of those friendly checkout women who call everyone "Sweetie."

"You do not want this tomato, Sweetie," she said, pointing out a large bruise my wife hadn't seen because she was so worried I would find some mustard pickles. "Your husband can take it back and get another tomato. I'll wait, but hurry."

More than half our pile had been rung up. There was a long line behind us. Those people might get unruly if forced to wait too long while I fumbled through the store looking for an unbruised tomato. It was more responsibility than I felt equipped to handle.

"I have never been in this store before. I have no idea where the tomatoes are. My experience has been limited to the pickle section," I told my wife, loud enough so Sweetie could hear me.

"Sweetie, the tomatoes are right over there," the checkout woman said, pointing toward Canada. "Just take a shortcut through that checkout lane, and hurry, Sweetie."

She was referring to the next checkout lane which was not being used at that time. My wife says most checkout lanes in Detroit supermarkets are not being used at any time. The same thing is true of teller windows in downtown banks. This is to promote everlasting friendliness. A town that stands in line together grows old together.

Anyway, there were "Closed" chains hanging across both ends of the checkout lane through which I had been dispatched. I stooped under the first chain and it caught my coat collar, almost forcing me to hit the floor with my face. So I leaped over the second chain and it caught my foot, this time putting my face even closer to the floor.

"I am a grown man. I cannot believe I am doing this," I said to myself. But I was. And after racing to the produce counter and switching tomatoes on the run, much like a relay man grabbing the baton, I was faced with those two chains again. To avoid that staggering delay, I tossed the tomato across the counter to my wife. A perfect throw.

But she did not catch it. We went home with a bruised tomato and no mustard pickles.

Onward and Upward, and every word is true, I swear to Sweetie. ■

All I did was tell the story about the mushrooms . . .

July 15, 1977

Several readers have asked if my wife ever gets angry about some of the things I write about her.

Yes.

For instance, she didn't like it when I made her famous with the publishers of the American Heritage Dictionary. It was a snaky tale.

She is so afraid of snakes she assigned our son to go through my new dictionary and put tape over every picture of a snake.

She said I wouldn't dare write a column about that because nobody would believe it. But I wrote it anyway, and she was right. Nobody believed it.

I resented this slur upon my credibility, so I kept writing. I invited people over to see the dictionary for themselves, warning them to beware of the dirty socks and dust balls in the bookcase. Consequently, some leading citizens were convinced and they testified publicly that yes, indeed, there is tape pasted over every picture of a snake in my American Heritage Dictionary.

Eventually, this incredible news reached the people who publish the dictionary. Thus began my extended correspondence between them and me, concerning my wife's peculiar behavior. I even sent them a photo of a pasted page, plus a photo of the unusual woman responsible for it.

They sent back the photo, with tape pasted over her face.

She was angry about my exposing her fear of snakes to public ridicule. But not as angry as the time I told the world about the mushroom in our shower.

I only did it because she bugged me one morning by saying, "It needs more grout."

Grout?

She said grout the same way I'd say potato. Everyone knows what a potato is. But what the devil is a grout?

She was trying to put me down. I knew that. Grout had something to do with the $400 tiling job a workman was currently doing in our shower.

She was cutely pointing out we had to pay him $400 because I was

145

too dumb to do the job myself. I was so dumb, in fact, I didn't even know what grout was.

I wouldn't give her the satisfaction. I simply nodded my head wisely and said, "Right, more grout is needed. Now more than ever."

Then I ran out of the house, jumped in the car, sped to work and grabbed a dictionary with untaped snakes. Grout is "a thin mortar used to fill cracks and crevices between masonry."

Now how did she know that? What did I marry, a bricklayer?

That night, at dinner, I casually remarked. "Remind me to check the grout in the shower. For $400 I want to make sure he doesn't miss any crevices."

"You looked it up in the dictionary,"she said.

It was simply one more snide remark in her continuing campaign to have Ann Landers declare me this nation's No. 1 Household Klutz. Deeply stung, I decided then to make the mushroom public knowledge.

The mushroom is how we discovered the shower walls were leaking and water was seeping everywhere. One morning I leaned over to wash between my toes and I saw a cute little mushroom growing between the tile crevices (that's where the grout goes, you know).

It looked just like the ones that grow on the golf course. Naturally, I was excited. After all, how many people do you know growing mushrooms in their shower?

"People are not going to believe this," I told my wife. "I must take a picture of that mushroom and put it in the newspaper. Our bathroom will become a tourist attraction. The kids can sell tickets and cotton candy."

"It is not a mushroom," she said, "it is a fungus; a dirty toadstool. It grew because the mortar behind the shower is always soaking wet. If you write anything about that awful thing, I will kill you. People would think I am the world's worst housekeeper."

In the face of such threats, I agreed to shut up about the mushroom. And I kept my word until she hit me with the grout. Then my journalistic integrity forced me to reveal my own wife was practicing agriculture in a residential zone.

At dinner the evening the mushroom column appeared, she used grouty words and pounded the table with her hard hat. I told her I had made her famous and she should thank me.

We were eating cauliflower. "If you grew this cauliflower in the washing machine, I probably can get the Maytag people to put you in a TV commercial," I said.

Yes, she does get angry sometimes. ∎

It's a sign of the times
when wives become escorts

October, 14, 1977

New life-styles create etiquette problems for corporations who mail out mass invitations to grand openings. American Motors recently invited me to come see its 1978 models and to bring along my "escort."

In more than 20 years of marriage, I never have regarded my wife as my escort. She has accompanied me, guarded me, even stalked me. But she never has escorted me.

Men are escorts; women are the escorted. Don't ask me why. I didn't make the world or write the dictionaries. I just work here.

"I guess American Motors doesn't want wives at its party," I told my wife. "I think I will ask Howard to go with me. All the girls say he is a fine escort."

Every man should have another man who always will meet him for lunch, even if it is past midnight and the place they meet never serves food, even at noon. Howard Bon Vivant is my man.

"I know you are kidding," my wife said.

It is customary that wives are not too fond of the men who are ever ready to meet husbands for lunch. Wives don't understand how it can take a man five minutes to eat lunch at home, but eight hours to eat it at a place that doesn't serve food. Wives always are inclined to blame their husbands' friends for this phenomenon, which really isn't fair.

In my case, I'll admit it was Howard who long ago decided it would be impolite to walk out of an establishment hungry without first giving the owner ample time to build a kitchen and hire a chef. But I didn't argue with him. In fact, it was I who pointed out Mahatma Gandhi, a holy man, went for days without eating lunch and there is no record of his wife ever getting angry about it.

But anyway, my wife was correct about the American Motors invitation. I was kidding. I knew American Motors didn't care if I took her to its party. It just didn't know for sure what to call her.

It would not have been practical to have the hundreds of engraved invitations printed individually. So American Motors came up with a politically adroit invitation which covered every possibility.

Many years ago, when an invitation was mailed to a business

147

address, it was possible to tell the invited person to bring his wife. If he weren't a he, or if he didn't have a wife, the mailman had made a mistake.

Women didn't have business addresses in those days. And bachelors, being automatically suspect in their personal habits, never reached the corporate level where they were allowed to receive mail at the office.

A few years ago, when women began to reach executive positions, it became wise to print invitations saying the invited person's "spouse" also would be welcome at the party. Otherwise, Women's Lib might report the party giver to the American Civil Liberties Union.

But this extension does not cover the swingers, male or female in whatever combination, who woke up together one day to find it socially acceptable for unmarried persons to live in the married state.

It no longer is a disgrace for a business executive to stretch a one-night stand into a 15-year encampment. The gossip no longer is fatal when a corporation president leaves his wife behind and introduces his companion as "the woman I live with."

So corporations must be careful when they have 2,000 invitations printed for distribution to influential people. If they invite the president of AT&P to bring his wife, and he is living with his secretary, whose name is Ralph . . . well, you can see the problem.

American Motors does not want to risk offending paramours, courtesans, homosexuals or people going steady. They all buy cars, too. So I was invited to bring my escort, and I brought my wife.

But I still am uncomfortable with that word. An escort has got to be masculine. I have heard of many bars that boost business on certain nights by advertising free drinks for "unescorted women." I have never heard of a bar offering such a freebie to unescorted men.

If I ever hear of such a place, Howard will have to lunch at home, and I will give the owner six weeks to build a kitchen and hire a chef. ■

Cats are good for one thing: they're good to hate

October 19, 1977

It was a depressing coincidence that Albumen gave birth to four kittens the same day I received medical assurance no cat is going to cure me of feeling depressed.

The depression began when I first learned Albumen was pregnant.

"You know I hate cats. I have always hated cats," I told my wife. "There is no way new cats are going to be born in my home."

"Our children have never owned a pregnant animal before. This will be their first chance to witness the miracle of birth," my wife said. "It will be a wonderful learning experience for them."

"Karen will really be thrilled," I said. Karen is our oldest daughter, and she was present at the birth of three human beings, all of whom now call her Mother. "She will probably be amazed to learn that kittens grow inside cats. She probably thought they grew inside saucers of milk that were allowed to curdle too long on back porches."

Our other two children, Ferd and Nerd, are aged 21 and 19. I like to think they also know all about the miracle of birth. Otherwise, I wasted a lot of money taking them to dirty movies when they were young and impressionable.

Before this goes any further, you probably want to know why the cat is named Albumen. I asked Ferd.

"Nerd named her that because he likes the white part of the egg best," Ferd explained.

Now you know why the cat isn't named Yolk. You also know why I don't bother asking intelligent questions around our home. It doesn't do any good.

For instance, you might ask why a pregnant cat named Albumen has been living in the home of a man who hates cats. The answer is there always has been a lousy cat of some sort living in my home, for more than 20 years now, despite the fact that cats are good for absolutely nothing except testing myths (is there really more than one way to skin one?).

My wife explained this phenomenon only a few days after we'd exchanged vows, and only a few hours before we began exchanging curses. It seems stray cats always have appeared at her door, no matter where she lives, and will never go away.

I suggested maybe this was because she always fed the stray cats. In all seriousness, she described her formula for handling stray cats:

"I don't really want them to stay, so the first two days I don't feed them. After that, I have to feed them, or they'll get so hungry they'll go away," she said. Honest, she said that.

What has always puzzled me is how all the cats in town learn about her two-day test. I suspect there's a Cat Newspaper that regularly carries full-page ads telling how to get to the Fitzgerald home and how to behave when you get there:

"Lick the kids' noses, snuggle in the lady's lap, avoid the old man and bring enough food for two days. After that, you're in."

That's how Albumen got in. Never mind how she got pregnant. Ferd and Nerd were ordered to get her fixed, but they rebelled. Lately they have come under the influence of something I wrote.

"If you can be against hunting and bullfighting, how can you be in favor of fixing?" Nerd asked me.

Before I could explain sterilization is more humane than a world full of stray cats too poor to subscribe to the Cat Newspaper to read where we live, it was too late. Albumen was bulging.

Obviously, abortion is not allowed at our home. On the 16th day of October, Albumen's miracle came to pass — four times.

This was the same day that I, deeply depressed, read about research at Ohio State University. The research indicates dogs make good psychotherapists for depressed persons who do not respond to two-legged doctors. Once a patient learns to trust a dog, the patient also will trust doctors who are nice to the dog.

Without being asked, the research director added that cats are not as useful. "They are not as warm. And it is the rare person for whom cats are as good as dogs," he said.

So my raging depression will continue unchecked — unless, speaking of rare persons, there are four someones out there who want a kitten. They are real cute — mostly black with white splotches, as though they'd been spattered with the white of an egg. ■

Once upon a time I spent
Saturdays as a bachelor

May 31, 1978

It happened several years ago. A phone rang from out of the distant past, reminding me I hadn't always been married, it just seemed that way.

The same call reminded my wife that she didn't actually marry me so much as she saved me.

She didn't wear a wedding veil, she wore a Salvation Army cape. Her dream, from the day we met, was to move with me into a vine-covered Rescue Mission we could call our own.

The phone call was from Jerry. He was two classes behind me in high school around 1940. After World War II, he was two drinks ahead of me at the Alibi Bar.

Jerry and I were members of a loosely knit group of veterans generally called, for lack of a more apt title, the Town Bums. Membership was varied and transient, numbering anywhere from 10 on bleary Sunday mornings to 25 on soggy Saturday nights when nobody could get a date.

Many of us attended college, if classes could be arranged so as not to interfere with the cocktail hour (3 p.m. to last call). Some of us looked for jobs ("I've been sitting on this stool all day and not one job has walked by"). All of us lived on public funds — unemployment pay, GI Bill, insurance rebate or mustering-out pay.

There was even one bum who still was a member of the military service. Archie was stationed at a nearby air base, but he spent all of his time on furlough. He was the only soldier I ever knew who was worried about getting drafted.

Some of the bums had been wounded in the war. Tom, my special buddy, left most of his index finger on Iwo Jima. He used to stick his finger stump up his nose and startle the devil out of innocent passersby.

Jerry phoned because he'd been in a minor collision while driving through my town. Police claimed he was drunk. They had put him in jail and what could I do about it?

It had been 15 years since I'd seen Jerry or heard one word about him.

151

"He has probably settled down to become a responsible citizen, just like me," I told my wife. "He has probably just had a bad break — the type of thing that could happen to any social drinker who bumps against a cop with a sensitive nose."

"He might be Public Enemy Number One," my wife said. "He might be the biggest souse in the state. This might be his 25th arrest this year. Are you going to run around trying to get some bum out of jail?"

"He's my friend," I explained, listening to the sound of bugles and drums. I felt like Pat O'Brien forgiving Jimmy Cagney for crippling Pat's grandmother. "Besides, I know Jerry's not the state's biggest souse. Don is. You remember Don. He stopped to use our john last year and fell in the bathtub."

So anyway, I didn't check Jerry's record. I simply bailed him out of jail and pointed him toward his hometown. This was on a Saturday morning.

That afternoon my wife and I attended an International Girl Scout fiesta at a huge fieldhouse. Our youngest daughter, klomping in wooden shoes, was somewhere among those thousands of squealing girls. As we searched and searched for her, I made a sudden observation.

"You know," I said, "I'm the only man in this place. I must be losing my mind."

"You used to spend Saturday afternoons in the Alibi Bar with Jerry and the other bums," my wife said, and I could hear her tambourine rattle. "Seeing your darling daughter at a Girl Scout party is better than hanging around a saloon, isn't it?"

Her question made me think, really think, about how marriage had enriched my life and changed my Saturdays. I could not give her a dishonest answer.

"No," I answered.

Onward and Upward. ■

My wife may be two steps back, but she's a finger up

September 23, 1978

Bill and Pat Gormally, a married couple from Providence, R.I., are walking 17,000 miles around the perimeter of the United States. She is walking a quarter-mile behind him.

"Each of us has his own pace," Bill Gormally explained to a newspaper reporter when the two backpackers strolled into Michigan the other day. "I usually wind up walking about a quarter-mile ahead of Pat after a couple of hours. But we never get much farther apart than that since we stop for a rest then."

He takes a 10-minute rest while she takes a five-minute rest and then closes the gap. When she catches up to him, they take off together again, and he quickly leaves her behind again.

Think about that. A husband and wife are hiking around the nation together, but not really. So far they've covered over 13,000 miles. She can't keep up with him, and he won't slow his pace to match hers. They communicate through hand signals.

My wife and I often meet downtown and then walk home together. It is a handicap walk. While I'm in my office, earning money, she is in stores, spending it. She buys large packages for me to carry home. The packages are my handicap.

They don't do the trick. No matter how many parcels I'm forced to carry, they still don't slow me down to her pace. This is not because she is a slow walker. It's because she can't pass anything without stopping to look at it or pet it or invite it to walk home with us and stay for a few days while I put it through college.

"Don't walk so fast," she hollers while I'm still within hearing distance. "It looks awful for me to be walking a block behind you. It looks like I'm your servant."

"If you were my servant, I wouldn't be carrying this bag of watermelons," I holler back. "And you wouldn't be a block behind if you hadn't stopped in the park to watch that little baby grow old enough to vote."

Like the Gormallys, when the gap grows too large for yelling, we communicate by hand signals. Actually, my wife uses her hands. Mine is more a finger signal.

153

My wife's principal objection to walking behind me is that Gloria Steinem disapproves. The rear position traditionally has been used to demean women. In some countries, even today, wives are required to walk several yards behind their husbands. This is regarded as an overt admission that men are born to lead and women are born to follow them.

My wife is not prepared to make such an admission, as a pedestrian or as a person. She suspects that I walk fast in an effort to establish my supremacy. She insists that when a husband and wife go walking together, they should do it side by side, not in single file.

If the wife walks in the husband's wake, passersby assume the wife is less than the husband's equal, even if he is carrying the watermelons. This makes Gloria Steinem angry. That's what my wife says.

"When I told her about the Gormallys' mode of walking, for 17,000 miles, she was incredulous. She couldn't believe Mrs. Gormally would allow herself to be so grievously demeaned in full view of everyone who lives on the perimeter of the United States. She suggested that Mrs. Gormally should shoot her husband. In the back, of course.

"You are failing to understand a greater truth than the Equal Rights Amendment," I explained. "It is of supreme importance that each person should proceed through life at his or her own pace, unshackled. Some of us must march to the beat of a different drummer, and if the rest of you can't keep up with us, that's too bad. A man has to do what he has to do."

My wife's reply to my unassailable logic was flattering. It was the first indication she's ever given that she has been paying attention to me, and learning from me.

She has learned my finger signal.　　　　　　　　　■

154

Fondueing is a fishy way
for people to eat a meal

December 30, 1978

It should be noted that his wife always has shielded the husband from mankind's never-ending march backward, out of the kitchen. That's why he assumed the hunks of meat on his dinner plate were cooked, and subsequently spent several minutes chewing raw roast beef.

"This meat is really tough," he whispered to her. They were guests at a holiday party and he didn't want to offend the hostess who was perched on a nearby extension cord.

"You're not supposed to eat it until you fondue it," the wife said. "And please don't embarrass me by telling everyone you don't know what fondue is. People will think you live in a cave."

A little pot of liquid sat at each end of the table. The two pots were attached to the nearest wall by electric cord. In hushed tones, the wife explained that the husband should spear a hunk of meat with a skinny fork and then dip the meat in the nearest pot until it was cooked. Then he could eat it.

"If I lived in a cave, that's probably how I'd cook my dinner," the husband said. "These people have a big stove in their kitchen. Is it broken?"

The husband always has considered himself a totally reasonable man. And he always has considered it totally unreasonable for a man to equip a kitchen with $20,000 worth of cooking appliances and then go into his backyard and burn his hamburger over an open fire.

For more than 20 years, the husband has been crusading to keep cooking in the kitchen where it belongs, and out of places it doesn't belong, such as forests and beaches and porches. If people don't sleep in hammocks in kitchens, they shouldn't fry potatoes in patios. That's what the husband always says.

His wife is weary of hearing it. "People have been fondueing for many years. It's fun and it tastes good," she explained. "I would have told you about fondue a long time ago but I knew you would say dumb things about it. I get sick of hearing you say dumb things."

Properly chastised, the husband stuck a forkful of roast beef into the fondue pot at his end of the table. He noticed there were several other forks sticking out of the pot, all unattended. He was reminded of fishermen who prop their poles off the edge of the dock and sit back in the shade, waiting for a strike which is often signaled by bells attached to their lines.

"Will a bell ring when my meat is done?" he asked. "I warned you about saying dumb things," she said. "You're supposed to check your meat every once in a while, until it's the way you want it."

After a minute, the husband pulled out his fork. There was nothing on it.

"I think a shark got my roast beef," the husband said.

He promptly was criticized for not securing his roast beef more tightly to his fork. The wife dipped into the pot with a big spoon and dredged out his meat. The husband threatened to turn her into the game warden. She put his roast beef back on his fork and told him to be patient.

Five minutes later, at the other end of the table, the fondue pot was boiling noisily and the people were cramming hot food into their fat faces. But at the husband's end, the frustrated fishermen were expecting the hostess to tell them they should have been there last week.

"I think the chef should check our extension cord for a loose connection," the husband said. "If that doesn't work, we can always call an electrician to come bake us a cake."

It was finally decided that the pot was operational, but just a little slow. More patience was added to the menu. The wife said the delay only added to the fun, but she doubled the warning against her husband saying dumb things. It was no use.

He advised the hungry fork holders to move into the kitchen. "The fishing should be faster there," he said. "The microwave oven has been converted into an aquarium." ■

My love runs as deep as a full tank of gasoline

March 24, 1979

The husband and the wife were speeding down the freeway. "We need gas," she said.

The husband was driving. "From where you're sitting the gas gauge is deceptive," he said. "It looks to you like the needle is near empty, but it's not. We have lots of gas."

She leaned over and looked directly at the gauge. "We are going to run out of gas and be marooned on this freeway all night. I hate you," she said.

"You are honking the horn with your head," he said. "Lee Marvin is right. The depth of love can be measured on a gasoline gauge."

In court testimony, actor Marvin compared the shades of love to the fuel gauge on a car's dashboard. He said his feelings for his former live-in girlfriend, Michelle Triola Marvin, never got higher than the quarter-full mark.

From where she sat, it appeared to Michelle they had more gas.

"There are all degrees of love," Lee told the judge. "I think of a gas tank with the empty and full positions. There is young and frivolous love. There is childlike love. Then there is the other end of the scale which could be the love between people, a deep regard for the other person, truthfulness, loyalty, fidelity and a tremendous sense of selflessness toward the other person."

The judge went along with the analogy, saying that, when it came to Michelle, Lee's needle was apparently more to the left than the right side of the gas gauge.

The wife wasn't interested in rehashing the Marvin trial. "Why didn't you fill the tank before we left home?" she asked.

"Because my love for you is young and frivolous," the husband answered. "I'll get gas at the next exit."

He didn't. He drove right by the next exit, and the wife screamed for an explanation.

"That was a Texaco station and I don't have a Texaco credit card," he explained. "Besides, my love for you is childlike."

"It would be better to pay cash than to run out of gas on the freeway," she moaned.

"When I pay cash, there is no receipt and, at the end of the year, I forget to deduct the cost of the gas from my income tax," he said.

"Is this a business trip?"

"So far, it certainly hasn't been a pleasure trip."

The wife honked the horn with her head again. "The needle is below empty and it's 12 miles to the next exit. We'll never make it," she said.

"When the needle says empty, it never means it. It means you have enough gas to last 30 minutes," he said. "Especially if you're parked."

The wife began to sob. The first greatest fear of her life is snakes. Her second greatest fear is running out of gas on the freeway. She is convinced no one except motorcycle gangs with snakes in their leather pockets ever stops to talk to stranded motorists.

As usual, the husband was right. They made it to the next gas station.

"Need gas?" the station attendant asked.

"No," the husband answered. "I just drove in here to show my wife I have a deep regard and a tremendous sense of selflessness toward her."

"You're not funny, and neither is Lee Marvin," she said.

"My love for you has changed through the years. When we were first married, I loved you a bushel and a peck," he said. "Today I love you a gallon and a pint."

"From where I'm sitting, you should have your oil checked," she said. ■

Ending marital acrobatics
would be small price to pay

April 25, 1979

The husband was down on his hands and knees, looking under the bed. "I can't find it anywhere," he muttered.

"What did you lose?" the wife asked.

"Your consortium," he said.

According to the dictionary, a consortium is "any association, partnership or union." Six years ago, a Utica housewife named Barbara Osantowski broke the second toe on her left foot in a motorcycle-car accident. Last month, a jury awarded her husband, Roy, $180,000 to compensate him for the loss of Barbara's consortium.

The jury felt sorry for Mr. Osantowski because his wife's injured toe stops them from enjoying certain things together that made them happy before the accident. Although she doesn't even limp, Mrs. Osantowski says she is unable to hike, hunt and dance with her husband the way she used to.

Barring a successful appeal, the $180,000 apparently must be paid to Mr. Osantowski by the insurance company that insured the driver of the car that ran into his motorcycle when his wife was riding on the back. In an out-of-court settlement, an additional $20,000 was awarded to Mrs. Osantowski for her broken toe.

The husband explained the Osantowski case to his wife because she recently injured her left shoulder while reaching for a six-pack in a supermarket. It hurts so much, she can't hook her bra.

"We don't have as much fun together as we did before the accident," he said. "What I miss most is doing handsprings together."

"You wouldn't dare sue the supermarket," she said. "You have always blamed high insurance rates on greedy lawyers who convince soft-hearted juries to pay people millions of dollars in damages for 25 cents worth of suffering."

"This is different. This is handsprings in the park every Sunday afternoon," he said. "I deserve to be compensated for the loss of such important consortium."

"I'll admit it's uncomfortable for me to do handsprings with no

159

bra, but if anyone is going to collect a lot of money for my injury, it should be me, not you," she said. "Mrs. Osantowski suffered the pain of a broken toe but she got only $20,000 while her husband, who didn't feel any pain, got $180,000. Why is that?"

"I don't know for sure, but I can make a good guess. There's no denying that I do better handsprings than you do, even when you can snap your bra. So I am losing more when our handspringing is cut off. Maybe Mr. Osantowski is a better dancer, hunter and hiker than his wife was. It's a terrible thing for a champion to be forced to retire while his skills are still sharp. That's real pain."

"If I were the supermarket's lawyer, I would tell the jury you could do handsprings with someone else besides your wife," she said.

"No American jury would ever approve of a surrogate handspringer," he said. "It's too kinky."

"Why can't you do handsprings all by yourself?"

"That would fly in the face of togetherness. Every American jury knows happy married couples do everything together. If you can't go out handspringing with me, I will stay home with you. Instead of handspringing, we can spend our Sunday afternoons looking on high shelves and under chair cushions for your lost consortium."

"How much are you going to sue the supermarket for?"

"I've been thinking about that," he said. "The loss of hunting, hiking and dancing companionship was worth $180,000 to Roy Osantowski. I'll let a jury decide if handspringing was as important to our marriage as hunting, hiking and dancing was to the Osantowski marriage. It might have helped if we did cartwheels together, too."

"If you do win a lot of money," she said, "it means we never can be seen handspringing in public again, even if I do relearn how to hook my bra."

"It's a terrible price to pay, but no one ever said it was easy to become wealthy doing nothing." ■

Snoopy wife makes it hard to sneak a Snickers

October 17, 1979

"Where did this Milky Way wrapper come from?" the wife asked.

"I haven't eaten a Milky Way in at least five years," the husband said with innocent calm. But inside his head he was raging against himself. How could he possibly have been dumb enough to leave that balled-up wrapper on the table beside his chair where Mrs. Sherlock Holmes was sure to find it in the morning? His plan had been to burn it and flush the ashes down the toilet while she slept. How could he have forgotten?

It was true he hadn't eaten a Milky Way in several years. The balled-up wrapper was from a Snickers bar. She would discover this when she took the wrapper into her laboratory to check for fingerprints. He might as well confess and beg for mercy.

For several reasons, all fat, neither the husband nor the wife should eat candy. This is easier for her because she doesn't like candy as much as he does.

The husband believes a successful marriage must be built on trust. When his wife swore to eat no more candy, he believed her. He never searches her pockets for Heath bars. When he kisses her, he never sniffs for the smell of chocolate. He never grants their grandchildren immunity from prosecution if they will testify she bit from the same giant Hershey bar that spoiled their appetites.

He is a marvelous person who has implicit faith in the integrity of his spouse. He never would suggest she might fall victim to the overwhelming temptations that assault innocent people from every billboard and force even men as committed as St. Peter to three times eat a Three Musketeer bar.

On the other hand, the wife believes a successful marriage must be built on suspicion and good detective work. She believes a husband is guilty until an analysis of the contents of his stomach proves him innocent. She is ever alert for any clue the husband might be enjoying life more than she is.

For instance, there was a recent evening when the wife was out of town, visiting her mother. To take some of the pain out of the lonely hours without her, the husband and their son went to a jazz concert.

161

There was a photographer present and he snapped the heartwarming scene of a father and his son boogying down together. He later tried to sell the picture for a Saturday Evening Post cover, but Norman Rockwell hasn't been dead that long.

So the photographer mailed the photo to the husband's home, which is also the home of the wife. The husband thought it was a good picture. The son's red, shoulder-length hair shone brightly in the bar light, matching the husband's nose. The son had his paintings tucked neatly inside his bicycle clips, and the husband's socks drooped just enough to hide his rundown heels.

The wife put the photo under her microscope and said to the husband: "There is one glass in your hand and two more full glasses on the chair beside you. Why is that?"

"I ordered three drinks at once for fear the waitress was a mirage and I would die in Death Valley," the husband explained. "Karl Malden should warn people to never leave home without a canteen."

But back to candy. In the lower lobby of the husband's apartment building there is a vending machine which dispenses 10 cents worth of Snickers bar for 25 cents. Next to it there is a box which releases newspapers for 20 cents each. Around 10 o'clock the other night, the husband began his regular descent to buy a newspaper.

"I hear more than 20 cents jingling in your pocket," the wife called from three rooms away.

This hurt the husband, who only wants to be trusted by the person he loves most. When he returned with the newspapers, he anticipated a body search and left the Snickers bar out in the hallway, in a potted plant, to be retrieved after the wife went to bed. He'd teach her to mistrust him.

The scheme worked beautifully. But then he forgot to burn the candy wrapper and flush the ashes down the toilet. His honest confession gained him no mercy, which is exactly what the big dumbo deserved. ■

Guys, don't you just love my new shirt!

June 18, 1980

"Did anyone at work tell you that you looked nice today?" the wife asked the husband.

She is always asking him that. And he always has to answer that no one even noticed he was wearing a new suit. Where he works, the women always are telling each other they look nice, even when they're wearing denim overalls and spike-heel shoes. But no one ever admires the men's clothing out loud.

The husband has studied this phenomenon for many years and in several different locations. His conclusion is that one of the differences between male and female is that women are always saying "I just love your blouse" to each other, but no man alive ever has told another man his shirt is lovable.

This conclusion angers the wife. "You are saying women are more vain than men, and that's just another male chauvinist myth," she says. "Everyone knows men look in the mirror just as much as women do, and they spend more money in barbershops than women spend in beauty shops."

This type of anti-chauvinist argument irks the husband, not because it's specious, but because it's irrelevant. He doesn't claim men are less vain than women. He simply claims men don't tell each other they look nice, but women do.

The husband doesn't know why this is true, anymore than he knows why it's now fashionable for women to wear high heels with long or short pants. For him, it seems like yesterday that only the dumbest women in town wore high-heel shoes at the same time they wore slacks or shorts. He can remember his daughters covertly pointing at these unstylish women in the supermarket and giggling. He can remember when this type of costume was a foolproof way for prostitutes to advertise their profession.

But today, grandmothers go to church in Levis, tottering on spike heels. The husband says this is the same as a man wearing spats with his tennis shorts. Sometimes he says this to people who don't know what spats are, which sends the husband back to the rest home in search of warm milk.

163

Anyway, his research has revealed that a woman occasionally tells a man she likes his tie and that a man sometimes will tell a woman he likes her dress. But most usually the clothing compliments are strictly between females, never between males.

This doesn't bug the husband one bit. He has seen women spend entire evenings talking about nothing except their clothing. He doesn't think this makes them inferior to males, just different. With a dismaying lack of originality, the husband says vive la difference. He would hate to waste time talking about some guy's trousers when there are so many more important things to discuss in these troubled times, especially during the baseball season.

It is the wife who is bothered when no one compliments her husband's new outfit. When he returns home from work to report another day of no praise for his pants, she is distraught.

The husband doesn't mind that his wife has such a proprietary interest in his clothes. It's a price he's glad to pay, rather than go shopping without her. He is depressed by most men's stores, which offer all the verve and excitement of a funeral parlor. If left to make his own decisions, he buys the first thing the salesman shows him, just to get out of the place before they say the rosary.

And when he gets home, the wife never likes what he bought. It's much easier to take her along for large purchases that require the husband's body for fitting and to let her choose all the tie-shirt accessories while he waits in the poolroom. The only drawback is she becomes peeved when her selections don't get rave reviews from his peers, and she won't accept his explanation that men are different from women and don't gush over each other's lapels.

For the husband, it is a conundrum not yet solved. A conundrum is the problem faced by a man who always dresses for dinner, but has lost his spats, and his milk is getting cold. ■

Laugh at foibles if you
must, but love them, too

December 28, 1981

At a cocktail party in Grosse Pointe, a recently divorced woman said she and her ex-husband are "closer than we ever were."

Say what?

Change the scene: Back downtown, as I was hurrying out the door, my wife asked whether I would mail a letter for her. Sure.

"Just a minute," she said, then sat down and started writing the letter.

Another scene change: During a weekend in a Cincinnati motel, my wife suddenly groaned: "I've lost my gold bracelet, the one you gave me. It cost $100."

The loss didn't bother me, for two reasons. First, I'd never pay that much for a bracelet. Tight questioning revealed the actual cost was nearer $50. She used the higher figure because she estimated its value had appreciated that much since I bought it.

I said a 50 percent cut in the depth of her groaning would be equitable because the bracelet would never be worth $100 unless she sold it, and she'd never do that because of its sentimental value. She assigns sentimental value to everything she has owned for more than a year, and she will part with none of it, including the glop in 20 covered saucers in our refrigerator.

The second reason I didn't mourn the bracelet was I knew it wasn't really lost. She'd brought two multi-pocketed purses to Cincinnati, plus a traveling bag with more than a dozen separate compartments, and two suitcases. I assured her the bracelet was somewhere in her luggage and she would be delightfully surprised to find it someday when she was looking for something else, such as a strayed grandchild.

But she insisted she'd looked everywhere and the bracelet truly was missing. The last time she'd seen it was at the swimming pool where she remembered saying she would put the bracelet somewhere she'd be sure to find it. That's where she puts everything. Three Christmases ago, she brought home two wristwatches, purchased for grandchildren, and put them somewhere she'd be sure to find them. She hasn't found them yet.

165

So we searched the swimming pool area for the bracelet, with no success. She then reported the loss to the room clerk and alerted our Cincinnati relatives to be on the lookout for a gold bracelet with no arm through it. She scattered her sad story about indiscriminately, along with our address, and someday we will entertain strangers, visiting from Cincinnati, who didn't find the bracelet but figure we owe them food and lodging for all the days of their lives they spent searching for it in answer to my wife's urgent pleas.

You know the bracelet finally turned up, or I wouldn't be writing about it. A few days after we returned home, it was back on my wife's arm. One thing about me, I'm the type of person who always says "I told you so." After I said it, she grudgingly conceded she'd found the bracelet, but she absolutely refused to tell where. That really bugs me.

Which brings us back to the original scene, starring the woman who is closer to her ex-husband now that they're divorced. I figure they split because she did things that bugged him, or vice versa, or, most likely, both. But what could they do that would drive a spouse further up a wall than I travel when my wife asks me to mail a letter she hasn't written yet or sends out search parties to find something lost in her purse?

My wife's husband loves her madly, and she knows it. One of the reasons is I enjoy laughing at her foibles, once I come down off the wall. Another reason is motel pillows are never fat enough for me, so I always take along my own pillow, and then leave it on the motel bed. There's one in Cincinnati right now, where the bracelet isn't, and my wife laughs about it.

If I were Ann Landers, I'd say couples who are closer than ever once they're divorced didn't have much reason to split. Maybe they just didn't laugh enough when they were married. Too bad. Foibles are funny, and have sentimental value. ■

Mystery solved: Plug
a drain, save a hairpin

July 17, 1982

For many years of marriage, the husband puzzled over the mystery of the plug in the mouth of the drain in the bathroom sink. He didn't want to ask his wife to explain it. He wanted to figure it out for himself. It was the type of challenge he enjoyed, as opposed to Rubik's Cube or jogging three blocks.

The mystery was that he kept finding the plug in the drain, but no water in the sink. Think about it.

There are old-fashioned sinks with rubber plugs attached to chains, and modern sinks where flipped switches slide metal plugs into drain openings. But whatever the method of plugging, the purpose is the same — to keep water in the sink.

So why did the husband, while living in a succession of homes offering every variety of sink plug, frequently find an empty sink with the plug in the drain? What happened to the water? How did it get out of a plugged sink?

He plugs the sink to hold water for shaving in the morning and washing his hands before dinner in the evening. Many people don't use sink plugs for these purposes. They just run faucets to rinse razors and hands. The husband prefers sloshing, which might appear strange, because he also prefers showers. He hasn't taken a bath in 40 years.

His explanation for this apparent contradiction is primordial. He believes human beings evolved from a liquid environment and require a certain amount of harmless sloshing to keep from going insane and trying to swim to China. And he believes sink sloshing is sufficient to keep him sane. His wife prefers bathtub sloshing, up to her neck, which not only keeps her from paddling toward Hong Kong but also from venturing anywhere near a rubber wading pool. When they vacation on the oceanfront in Florida, she sits on the beach in Georgia.

In view of the wife's preference for bathing, it is interesting that the husband never once started to take a shower and found himself standing in an empty bathtub with the plug in the drain. The mystery of the disappearing water was confined to plugged sinks, a fact which only added to the puzzlement. If she plugged the sink without putting water in it, how come she didn't do the same thing in the bathtub? It certainly wouldn't make any difference in the water bill.

At first, he thought his wife simply forgot to unplug the sink after sloshing and the water eventually evaporated. This solution seemed particularly feasible during periods of high humidity in the bathroom. Another possibility was that she was such a sloppy slosher she splashed all the water out of the sink and there was no need to pull the plug.

But these theories had to be rejected when the husband stealthily entered the bathroom immediately after she left it.

There was no time for the water to evaporate, and no evidence of sloppy sloshing, but the plugged sink still was empty! There also were no soggy sponges or towels that might have been used to soak and wipe the sink bowl dry, perhaps in an effort to transport water across the bathroom without a pail.

The husband was going buggy trying to meet the challenge of the sink mystery. One day the frustration got so bad he found himself thinking about going jogging. That's when he realized how close he was to the brink of trying to swim to China. Badly frightened, he finally admitted there are some puzzles a husband never will solve, and he asked the wife why she put the plug in the sink but didn't turn on the water.

"Because everything falls as far as it can," she said in the same voice Moses used when dictating to his stone stenographer.

She meant when she combed her hair at the sink, hairpins sometimes fell out of her hair, but they never went down the drain. The mystery plug had prevented the loss of thousands of dollars' worth of hairpins.

Why didn't she unplug the drain after combing? What for? She put the rescued pins back in her hair. Why drain an empty sink?

The husband said he understood completely. He also said he should have married Rubik. ■

I can watch a sunset and
a thigh-slap in a glance

August 21, 1982

Every evening at the appropriate time, when we are home alone together, my wife pulls open the window drapes in our high-rise living room and says: "Look at that sunset."

She doesn't say: "Look at that sunset, Jim."

My wife almost never addresses me by name, and vice versa. It isn't necessary. I know I'm the one she's ordering to look at the sunset because there is no one else in the room for her to order around.

And, as I continue to read the newspaper or watch TV, it isn't necessary for me to mumble, "I saw the sunset yesterday, Pat." I can omit the "Pat" because she knows she is the only woman by that name married to a jerk who would rather read a newspaper or watch TV than look at a sunset.

It was in a newspaper that I read about some college students who play a drinking game while watching reruns of the old "The Bob Newhart Show" on TV. Every time Bob's wife calls him "Bob," or he calls her "Emily," the students chugalug some beer. To make yourself feel needed, please realize that this type of higher education probably wouldn't be possible if it weren't subsidized by taxpayers.

I love to watch Newhart reruns because Bob and Emily live across the hall from Howard Borden whose brother Gordon works for the U.S. Forest Service and is called Warden Gordon Borden. Also, I take a sip of buttermilk every time Emily slaps her thighs.

Way back when the series was first run, I noticed right away that Emily was an excessive thigh-slapper. I always urged Pat to watch for Emily's thigh-slaps, and I counted them out loud, always saying, "See, she did it again; what did I tell you?" Pat usually expressed her interest in my thigh-slap observations by screaming and jumping out the window. Fortunately, that was before we moved up nearer to sunsets.

But I didn't notice how excessively Bob and Emily called each other by name until it was called to my attention by those students in pursuit of higher education. Now I count name-calls instead of thigh-slaps. During one memorable 30-second scene, while Bob and Emily were home alone together, she called him "Bob" five times. She sat

169

right next to him and kept saying things like: "Bob, my thighs are sore, Bob."

"Married couples don't talk to each other that way in real life," I told my wife Pat. "I don't like it when TV isn't true-to-life. I like it when Robert Young gets arrested for trespassing."

"Look at the sunset," she said.

The funny thing is, I really do look at the sunset every time I'm ordered to. I don't mind looking away from the TV for a few seconds because I only watch reruns and I already know Barney Miller's lines better than he does. And if I'm reading the newspaper, I simply put my right index finger on the line I'm reading so I can quickly find my place again after I'm done looking at the sunset.

But my wife never believes I look at the sunset because my reaction falls far short of matching hers in enthusiasm and pure rapture.

"If you really looked at the sunset, you would exclaim how splendid it is," she said the other evening. "You would get out of your chair and run to the window to get a closer look at how swiftly the sun disappears behind Stroh's brewery. You would sigh deeply and be awed at the glorious colors our almighty God painted in the heavens. You would be so thrilled by the sunset you wouldn't care if you ever found your place in the newspaper again."

"People don't talk like that in real life," I exclaimed. "I must be on Walton's Mountain."

Later that same night, when my wife went to bed first, she leaned over my chair and I looked up from my newspaper to receive a goodnight kiss. While she kissed me, she reached down seductively and knocked my right index finger off my place in the newspaper.

"Onward and Upward , Jim," she said, slapping both her thighs.■

The problem with sign
language is mixed signals

September 11, 1982

The language of love requires no words. That's what the husband keeps telling himself as he remains ever alert for signs signaled by the wife. Often he misses the signs, or misreads them, and sometimes, when his mood reflects the dark side of the moon, he thinks if she really loved him, she would speak to him.

He owns two pairs of bedroom slippers, both Christmas gifts. He never wears one pair because they are slippery and have almost no backs on the heels and won't stay on his feet. The other pair he wears everywhere within a two-mile radius of the bedroom because they are soft, full-shoe slippers with a fuzzy lining that is pleasing to his toes.

He keeps both pairs of slippers under his side of the bed. He always slides the slippery slippers back against the wall at the head of the bed, behind the night table, where they can't be reached unless the reacher assumes the prone position and stretches mightily. He always puts the soft, toe-pleasing slippers under the part of the bed where his feet land when he begins to get out of the bed in the morning, and where he sits in the evening when he returns home from work to shed the burdens of the marketplace and the laced, wing tip shoes his daughters can't believe he still is wearing in 1982.

But lately when he reaches down and under for the soft slippers, he grabs the slippery slippers. To reach the soft slippers he must sprawl and stretch. Who is switching the locations of his slippers, and why? Have the dust balls under the bed been somehow energized into angry poltergeists? Is the wife doing it to drive him crazy so she can have him committed to an asylum and thereby gain control of his stuffed leather chair with the great footstool?

He asked her. She said she was switching the slippers as a sign to him that the soft slippers were all scuffed up and the slippery slippers looked much better on him, especially in the grocery store. As a reasonable man, he couldn't help wondering why she hadn't simply told him that, instead of sending signs, and saved him the sleep he lost because of nightmares about being attacked from below by angry dust balls.

And then there was the evening he was resting in his stuffed

171

leather chair and, without saying a word, she held a full-size grocery bag under his nose. Why was she doing that? The bag was open and half-full. He looked inside and saw trash. "That's nice-looking trash," he said.

She shook the bag. What sign was she giving him?

She pointed, and he finally got the message. Beside his chair is a small trash basket into which he regularly drops Snickers wrappers and mail from his congressman. She wanted him to empty his basket into her bag. Why didn't she simply say so?

"Why else would I put a bag of trash under your nose while you're sitting next to a trash basket?" she asked. He had no idea.

There was one sign he didn't ask her to translate into words until after they'd been married 27 years. He was afraid to. He'd seen this sign regularly in every home they'd lived in. It was a long-handled brush sticking horizontally out of a toilet, with the bristles just above the water and the handle held securely between the lowered seat and the bowl.

He figured she was telling him to scrub the toilet. But he gave up scrubbing toilets when he got out of the Army, so he always acted as though he never saw the brush. He used another bathroom, even when he had to go to the Mobil station on the corner.

But lately, under the influence of women's lib, he began to feel guilty. He didn't want anyone to think he married her to clean his toilets, even though she married him to change her tires. So he apologized for ignoring her sign of the protruding brush. And she said she didn't want him to scrub the toilet, she was simply letting the brush drain.

In the language of love, reading signs correctly means never having to run to a gas station. ■

I can't even commit
my dumbness in private

April 22, 1983

When you do something dumb, but no one else knows it, it's not so bad. No one likes to be razzed for being a klutz. A dumbo who operates in private is much less embarrassed than the baseball player who drops a pop fly on national TV.

This is being written on my 28th wedding anniversary. Naturally, there is a connection between my longtime marriage and a dumbo's desire for privacy. I'm always careful to establish connections between column paragraphs. That's because I'm deathly afraid of committing potpourri while someone is looking.

Some things have changed, and some haven't, since the day my intended and I eloped. Two of the changes involve stockings and the occasion of thoughtful sin. Fortunately, both of these changes are part of the same advertising campaigns, otherwise I would be skirting close to the edge of potpourri.

Lately I've noticed more and more gorgeous women wearing nothing much more than long woolen stockings with no feet in them. Usually, these women are well-known actresses — such as Victoria Principal — who stretch their slim, sexy bodies in TV and newspaper ads for exercise salons. It appears they have no reason whatsoever to pay some outfit to make them look better, and it also appears they should be able to afford complete stockings.

At first, these apparent contradictions puzzled me . But then I heard from a woman who was rejected by a well-known exercise salon because she was too fat. She was told she would scare away prospective customers who would regard her obese appearance as evidence the salon's slimming techniques didn't work. Which certainly makes as much sense as a hospital cutting its death rate by admitting healthy patients only.

I never did learn exactly why women skinny enough to be allowed inside exercise salons never walk in their stocking feet. But there certainly must be a connection between being slim and having no feet in your stockings, otherwise Vic Tanny would be guilty of potpourri, which sounds fattening.

Anyway, when I was a schoolboy, the nuns taught me to avoid sins of thought as well as sins of word and deed. A sexy, scantily-clad woman was occasion for a sin of thought. If an innocent male should stumble upon such a woman, in flesh or photo, the best way for him to think about something else was to do push-ups or other exercises.

That was yesterday. Today, in every newspaper and on every TV channel, the sexy women, so scantily-clad they don't even have feet in their stockings, are selling exercise. I can't touch my toes without bending at the waist and thinking of Victoria Principal. Ah, sweet irony of life — at last I've found you.

But, as mentioned earlier, some things haven't changed since I got married. For instance, I'm still the same mechanical klutz today I was then, and my wife still talks about it.

Recently, it was my intention to punch $100 out of an automatic bank teller machine. But I never punch those damn buttons right the first time. After fouling up my secret code number, I never punch enough zeroes. This time I punched $10 several times instead of $100 once. It was a dumb thing to do, but no one was looking, so I didn't care.

Except I threw the damning bank receipt in a waste basket at home and, as soon as she had a large audience, my wife read it aloud, asking why I punched $10, $10, $70 and $20, in that order (I can't add, either), on one trip to the bank. And she admitted she often picks through the trash for evidence of my dumbness.

That's the type of thing I've put up with for 28 years. You might wonder if there's a connection between a happy marriage and husband abuse. If it isn't potpourri, it must be love. ■

Dumbbell: Those beans
are made for pumping

April 27, 1983

In the living room, on the little table next to my chair, there was a can of yellow beans. Also a can of green beans. The two cans were full and unopened. Such an unusual juxtaposition would never occur in Alfred Taubman's home.

Why were the beans in the living room instead of in a kitchen cupboard? Where were the pad and pencil that should be on that table — in the refrigerator?

The beans hadn't been there the night before. There were no grandchildren visiting, so they couldn't be blamed. The apartment's only occupants for several days had been my wife and me, and I knew I hadn't put two cans of beans in the living room.

"It had to be you," I told her.

"Sing it," she said. "I also like 'The Nearness of You.'"

We have been very close lately, because of my surgery. I don't know what I'd do without her.

It was minor surgery, performed in five minutes by a dermatologist who kept me waiting only 50 minutes beyond my appointment time. If it had been major surgery, the wait might have been much longer. The seriousness of a person's illness can be measured by the number of hours he is willing to wait beyond appointment time before snarling something nasty to the receptionist and storming out of the waiting room.

My skin surgery was so insignificant I wouldn't have waited even 50 minutes except I was reading a New Yorker magazine, which is almost as mollifying as waiting in the bar for a restaurant table. But the tiny incision was made in the middle of my back, and suddenly I needed my wife more than ever.

"If my shirts buttoned up the back, it wouldn't have taken 28 years for me to fully appreciate you," I told her the first morning she changed the bandage on my wound. There was no one else to do it.

Also, there was no one else to put canned beans in the living room. At first, I didn't demand that she reveal why she did it. It was fascinating to guess. Did she bring the cans to my chair the night be-

175

fore so she could sit down and read the labels? Does she have trouble getting to sleep after reading those exciting ingredients?

Was she cutely reminding me to eat my vegetables? Had Andy Warhol or some other twit declared it fashionable to decorate living rooms with canned beans? Or was she using cans of beans as paper weights to keep my little table from blowing away when I sneezed?

Amazingly, that last guess was closest. Honest. My wife said anyone who knew anything could easily figure out why she had two cans of beans in the living room. I couldn't; how about you?

The answer is: The two cans of beans were ersatz dumbbells.

My wife uses them as weights, one in each hand, while exercising along with some muscle guy on TV every morning. Usually she remembers to return the cans to the kitchen before her husband, a real dumbbell, comes nosing around.

That's not what I call class.

What I call class is the way Alfred Taubman exercises. He's the real estate tycoon who recently made a few billion dollars by selling a spare hunk of California he had lying around the house. In a recent newspaper interview, Taubman said:

"I have a gentleman who comes to my home every morning at 6 o'clock. We do calisthenics, work on the light and heavy bags, then we spar three or four rounds."

Now that's class. What I need is a gentleman doctor who comes to my home every morning to change the bandage on my back. Then I wouldn't have to sing "It Had to Be You" to a woman who needs a gentleman grocer who comes to her home every morning to deliver ersatz dumbbells.

Otherwise, there always will be the danger that someday I'll be terribly embarrassed by a phone call notifying me my wife is lying on her back in the A&P, pumping beans. ∎

She doesn't need a magic wand; a spatula will do

June 11, 1983

The U.S. government is going nuts trying to figure out what to do with 4.8 billion unneeded gas-rationing coupons. The coupons should be given to my wife, who won't waste them because she is a Child of The Great Depression.

Although her given name is Pat, I often call her Wanda, which is short for Waste-Not-Want-Not Wanda. She never throws anything away because she grew up during the impoverished 1930s, watering her vegetable patch with month-old bath water.

Shortly after we were married, 28 years ago, Wanda bought a giant jar of peanut butter. She still has it. Every time I suggest there is not enough peanut butter left to cover my Saturday noon toast, Wanda says, "Waste not want not," and reaches for her rubber spatula.

This spatula makes the miracle of the loaves and fishes look like Mother Hubbard's cupboard. By simply scraping it around inside any empty container, Wanda magically, not to mention majestically, materializes enough food to feed a family of four for a week.

On a recent evening, after several minutes of shaking and pounding a 15-year-old ketchup bottle, I meekly sobbed that it might possibly be empty. "It's too bad your magic spatula won't fit inside a narrow ketchup bottle," I said.

Saving steps, Wanda immediately slid into the kitchen to get her newest anti-waste implement. It is a pencil-thin stick with several rubber prongs on one end. She bought it through the mail. Wanda buys everything through the mail so she can save the box it arrives in, in case she ever wants to send it back.

What you do is thrust the skinny spatula into the narrow bottle until it hits bottom and the rubber prongs, pointing upward, are pressed tightly against the interior of the bottle. Then you suddenly yank the skinny spatula out of the narrow bottle, causing the rubber prongs to emerge pointing downward.

This maneuver forces whatever is inside the bottle to burst out, no matter how badly it may want to stay inside, and fly through the air.

"My god, we are playing catch the ketchup," I said, completely awed.

177

"All you have to do now is wipe it off your face and put it on your potatoes," Wanda explained.

(The names and addresses of two independent witnesses will be furnished upon request.)

Now that you understand what Waste-Not-Want-Not Wanda is all about, you also will understand why she is the most logical depository of those 4.8 billion gas-rationing coupons. Our wealthy government paid $10 million to have them printed 10 years ago when the Arab oil embargo persuaded some top-level bureaucrats that gasoline rationing was inevitable.

Today, now that oil supplies are glutful, those same bureaucrats are busy building sky shelters for the inevitable return of Chicken Little. And taxpayers are paying $20,000 annually to store 2,000 tons of gas coupons in an Army depot in Colorado.

"I just want to get rid of the damn — darn — things," Ronald Winkler, a deputy assistant energy secretary, told a reporter.

It was suggested that the coupons simply be burned and that any complaining taxpayer be told to kiss our ashes. But the government, realizing that where there's smoke there's a smoking gun, is reluctant to be that publicly wasteful.

So give the 4.8 billion coupons to Wanda. As a true Child of The Great Depression, she will accept them simply so she can make sure they're not wasted. Storage will be no problem because she will put the coupons in her purse where they will immediately become lost.

For Wanda, losing is not the same as wasting, because she knows if she ever really has to find something that doesn't appear to be anywhere in her purse, she can always scrape it out with her magic spatula. ■

Breakfast, lunch and dinner
are served by Calamity Jim

July 23, 1983

In the olden days, pioneers going West often lived off the land, eating berries they picked and animals they killed, almost never going to the supermarket. In modern days, husbands going nuts should insist their families live off the kitchen, eating food purchased years earlier. This would thin out cupboard and refrigerator shelves, making it possible for husbands to find what they're looking for the same week they begin looking, and preventing them from sobbing and pounding the Formica with their heads.

I can't cook beans, but I could learn to be a gourmet chef quicker than I can find a can of beans in the kitchen my wife has stockpiled against the day the entire state of New Jersey unexpectedly drops in for lunch.

Normally, only my wife and I live in our home. Our son is a frequent boarder but it isn't necessary to provide food specifically for him. He always eats on his feet, while walking through the kitchen, and it is solely because of him that our garbage disposal hasn't been turned on in seven years.

That son, incidentally, is 25, but he hasn't been in our family as long as what I ate for dinner the other night. I ate frozen spaghetti that, to my astonishment, was packaged in a window envelope. When I first discovered it in the back of the freezer compartment, I thought it was a letter from Reader's Digest Sweepstakes

"You wouldn't be astonished by modern cooking methods if you were the kind of a husband who helps his wife in the kitchen," my wife said. "Just drop the envelope in boiling water."

I refused to respond to her unjustified attempt to identify our domestic situation with the Women's Lib movement which I support wholeheartedly, despite Bella Abzug's hats. There is no question that when both husband and wife work outside the home, they both also should work inside the kitchen. But my wife is a full-time homemaker, I'm a full-time hack, and there has never been any decent reason for me to learn how to boil water.

Until now. Because my wife stepped in a hole and broke her foot, and I lacked the foresight to marry a horse, she currently is

179

enthroned in the living room, with her injured extremity exaltedly elevated, from where she declaims instructions to her indentured servant in the kitchen.

"Make me a cup of coffee," she declaimed. "All you have to do is plug in that pot of water on the cupboard and when it begins to boil, pour it in a cup with a teaspoon of instant coffee."

Fifteen minutes later, the water still wasn't boiling. Intensive investigation, spurred on from the living room, finally revealed I had plugged in the electric can opener.

There is not only too much food in our kitchen, there is too damn much machinery trailing stupid look-alike cords.

"How about a cup of can opener?" I asked.

It also seemed reasonable to ask how a family of two possibly could leave so many leftovers in the refrigerator. "I was brought up to waste not, want not," she answered, evoking Herbert Hoover.

Why was there so much canned and jarred stuff in the cupboards? "It was on sale." Why is there dinosaur meat in the freezer? "It will come in handy when New Jersey drops by."

How could any innocent husband be expected to find a jar of peanut butter amidst such an overwhelmingly gigantic accumulation of foodstuffs? "Some husbands believe in the Equal Rights Amendment."

She said that the same evening I discovered it is dangerous to drink while cooking. I accidentally poured milk into a glass of vodka and tonic. I did not discover penicillin.

But the resulting sobs of anguish may have been worthwhile. To shut me up, my wife agreed to eschew supermarkets and clear our shelves by living off the kitchen until her exalted foot heals, just as the brave westward-ho pioneers lived off the land. As soon as I finish this portion of my work outside the home, I will return to my kitchen to stalk an envelope of macaroni and cheese. ■

Grandchildren . . . and some other relatives

Presidential grandparents
must have cold fingers

August 24, 1979

Super Grandmother had her button pushed by ex-President and Mrs. Gerald Ford. She probably will never pardon them.

(Later on in this column, I will establish a relationship between grandchildren and push buttons. That's why I cleverly said the Fords had pushed Super Grandmother's button. Otherwise, I simply would have said the Fords had surprised her unpleasantly. I used the button to provide continuity and to pique your curiosity. It's not easy being a clever columnist, let alone an accomplished piquer.)

Super Grandmother read in the newspaper that the Fords got their first look at their first grandchild on the weekend of Aug. 12. The kid was born April 22.

"I can't believe it," Super Grandmother said. "That baby was almost four months old before their grandparents saw her. Gerald Ford is rich and doesn't have a job. He would fly to Asia for a Sunday afternoon of golf with Arnold Palmer. Betty Ford would fly anywhere to confess sins to the Ladies Home Journal, or to get a face change. But they couldn't fly to Pittsburgh to see their first grandchild until she was almost old enough to start school. What kind of a family was that to have in the White House?"

When a grandchild is born, my wife believes a grandmother should immediately speed to the scene, not to intrude upon the new parents' privacy, but to do housework, such as scrub grease spots out of the hospital parking lot. If two grandmothers are present, as is often the case, the grease spots should be shared equally.

If there are older grandchildren in the home, according to my wife, it's the grandmother's job to hug them frequently so they won't be jealous of their new sibling. They get jealous anyway, but at least they know their grandmother loves them. They have the grease marks to prove it.

A grandmother shouldn't hog a new baby, thus preventing the parents from enjoying their own child, my wife says. However, if the parents are overly protective and never let go of the kid, a good grandmother should point out that too much parental attention can be smothering, and it's good for a baby to meet new people. If the par-

183

ents still won't let go, it is reasonable for the grandmother to put all grease spots back where she found them.

"How could Betty Ford possibly wait so long to see her grand-daughter? She must be a colder woman than I thought," Super Grandmother said.

It was noted that all of our grandchildren were born to our oldest daughter, while the Ford's grandchild was born to their daughter-in-law. I suggested that perhaps grandmothers react with less urgency when their relationship to the new baby is through their son.

"That's nonsense," Super Grandmother said. "If your son ever becomes a father, I'll be worried about more than grease spots. I'll want to be there even before the birth, to make sure he doesn't take his wife to the hospital on his bike."

"One thing for sure," I said, "if Gerald Ford is smart, he'll enjoy his grandchild while she's still not old enough to push buttons."

This sage observation was prompted by the experiences of the previous week when our three grandchildren, ages five, seven and 10, visited their grandparents in a big-city high rise where you can't go anywhere without pushing elevator buttons. This modern convenience makes it possible for children to warm up with an inside squabble before going out to the car to squabble over who gets to sit in the front seat next to the window.

After a stampede down the hallway, the inside squabble goes like this: "I get to push the button." "You pushed it last time; it's my turn." "I did not." "You did, too." "I did not." "You did, too." "OK, I get to push the down button on the inside." "You did it last time." "I did not." "You did, too ... "

The final decision involves who will push the button that keeps the elevator door open while funny Grandpa lies down in the hallway and pounds the floor with his head. Now that he's a grandfather, Gerald Ford may finally start wearing a helmet. ■

It's good to be sitting
on Popsicles again

May 8, 1976

My three-year-old granddaughter, Melissa, is tremendously fond of the minister of her parents' church. When he comes visiting, he eats peanut butter sandwiches with her. And sometimes he takes her out to lunch at McDonald's.

He should be nice to her, in view of what she calls him. She calls him God.

Whenever I bore you with grandchildren stories, you'll know I am tapering off after being visited by the three darlings. They are aged infant through first grade, two girls and a boy, and their last visit prompted me to lodge a complaint at City Hall in our small town.

The civil defense people explode three bombs to warn the populace that a tornado is coming. But they don't even put up a distress flag when my three grandkids cross the city limits. Three nuclear explosions not only would be appropriate, they would be a comparatively quiet introduction to the impending calamity.

Anyway, I find it isn't wise to quit vibrating cold turkey after the children head back home. Instead, I turn my son's stereo up full volume and place my strung-out body in the center of the four speakers. I have him play Frank Zappa records, reducing the volume gradually over a period of hours. I pass the time pondering the many things I had forgotten until Michele and Melissa and John arrived to bring back the memories.

It has been 15 years or so, depending on your criteria, since babies lived at our house. It's hard to say exactly when our youngest child ceased to be a baby, but I remember getting suspicious when he began changing his own diapers and heating his own bottle.

I had forgotten how it feels to hear a baby cry at 3 a.m. It took me a few seconds to remember what to do. What you do is push your foot softly to the south. If this doesn't work, you kick more firmly. Finally, your wife wakes up. You then tell her the baby is crying.

I had forgotten about that spot on a baby's neck, up under the chin, not far from the ear. That's where you nuzzle a baby. It feels great.

I had forgotten the crunchy sound of cookie crumbs underfoot.

185

I had forgotten how your heart stops, and then pounds, when you hear a baby scream and the sound of a small body going bump, bump, bump.

And I had forgotten the mixed relief of discovering he fell only two steps. A potted plant went the rest of the way.

I had forgotten to look before I sit. Have you ever sat on an abandoned Popsicle?

I had forgotten a grown man somehow can enjoy eating his dinner while watching a kid with a runny nose stick her face in chocolate pudding.

I had forgotten the most beautiful babies have fat stomachs and no fannies, and once they get walking fast, it is a fact of gravity that they are going to fall down, bam.

And I had forgotten adults are supposed to look the other way when these falls occur. This is supposed to make the kid think he is not hurt. I keep forgetting and picking the kid up and kissing his sore spot and mouthing silly "there-there-there-baby" words I'd hate to have overheard in the Alibi Bar.

I had forgotten how grand it feels to return home from work and be greeted by a little kid who wants to climb up your legs and stick his fingers in your nose. I had forgotten that babies don't watch TV and you don't have to knock on their heads to say hello.

I had forgotten the goofy pride of taking little kids into a restaurant and having strangers smile at them. I react modestly to such attention, bowing from the waist only after repeated applause. Inside my fat head I am hoping everyone will think I am the father, not the grandfather, for gosh sakes.

I had forgotten the marvelous innocence of a small baby; the trust and the dependence and the eagerness to love and be loved. I had forgotten that some smart adult like me must teach little kids how to hate, and who to hate.

I had forgotten that a little girl can eat peanut butter sandwiches with God. ∎

The years turn parents hearts to pure mush

March 27, 1978

Swoooosh! It flew over my left shoulder and then turned abruptly to the right, nicking my nose before dipping crazily into my lap. I was driving at the time, and the sudden attack nearly forced me to jerk my eastbound car into the westbound freeway.

From the backseat there came two whoops, followed by gurgly giggling.

"It certainly is nice to have the grandchildren visiting us," I said to my wife, who had crawled into the glove compartment.

We had been attacked by an escaped balloon from the International House of Pancakes.

I suspected there was going to be trouble when I first saw the inflated balloons tied to the cash register. I've never gotten along well with balloons.

Melissa is five years old and her sister Michele is eight. Naturally, they asked Grandpa to buy them balloons. That's what little grandchildren are supposed to ask their grandpas. It's a law, passed by Congress in 1953 in honor of Norman Rockwell.

"Grandpa can't afford it. He spent all his money on the movies and popcorn and Dr. Pepper and pancakes and hot fudge sundaes and nerve pills," I lied. I'm a firm believer in lying to children. The truth can only make them jump up and down and cry.

"The balloons are free," said the woman behind the cash register.

"What do balloons have to do with pancakes?" I asked her. "I have never seen a balloon salesman giving away pancakes. Why do you have to give away balloons?"

She ignored me and handed limp balloons to Melissa and Michele. Children are never given inflated balloons. Children's balloons must be blown up by their parents or grandparents. This is another law, passed by Congress in 1949 in honor of Oscar Apoplexy.

I explained to the children I was physically unable to blow up their balloons, due to a hernia suffered at a circus in 1955 while inflating a two-foot-long balloon for their mother who even then, at the age of five, was busy earning her subsequent nickname which starts with

187

"T" and rhymes with the nicknames of her siblings, Nerd and Ferd.

Melissa and Michele assured me they could blow up their own balloons. Melissa didn't appear to be nearly big enough for the job, but I didn't want to question her ability for the second time that evening. I'd already bet she couldn't eat six pancakes, a scrambled egg, a hot fudge sundae and two of Grandpa's sausages in five minutes. But she did it. When Melissa grows up, she wants to be a steam shovel.

So Melissa undertook the inflation of her balloon, in the backseat, on the freeway, and got the job almost done. You know the rest. SWOOOOOSH! Show me a motorist who retains his composure while an escaped balloon blows amok around his head, and I'll show you a motorist who is parked.

But we all survived, and Grandpa didn't do anything to embarrass Norman Rockwell. In fact, there were no reprisals at all, not even a harsh word. Melissa and Michele thought the near-accident was pretty funny, and somehow I couldn't tell them to stop laughing.

Twenty years ago, if their mother had pulled a similar stunt, I would have driven to the nearest orphanage and thrown her out of the car. Obviously, I've become the cliche grandparent. When my own kids did it, it was a crime. When my grandkids do it, it's cute.

Time is the accepted reason for this flip-flop behavior. Grandparents usually spend little time with the children, so it's comfortable to ignore their crimes for a few hours and send them home spoiled. Parents spend much time with the children, and if the darlings are spoiled, the smell soon becomes unbearable.

That's what Ann Landers and the other experts say, and there's truth in their explanation. But it's not enough.

The night of the balloon escape, I watched my granddaughters say their prayers before going to bed, and then I listened to them giggle when they should have been sleeping. Instead of telling them to shut up, I just sat and enjoyed the sound.

And I decided grandparents spoil grandchildren because grandparents are old enough to know something parents don't know. Grandparents know how fast children grow up, how swiftly the sweet times are gone, and how nice it would be to live them again.

Which is pretty mushy stuff for me to be writing, but I have to. It's a law, passed by Congress many years ago, in honor of love and balloons. ∎

A Father's Day thought for
the child who slipped away

June 13, 1980

There came a time in their marriage when, somewhat to their surprise, they decided it would be nice to have another child. They were both over 40 years old, they already had three children, and all the newspapers said the world's biggest problem was overpopulation. But still, the idea of one more little kid to snuggle was appealing.

Besides, she was already pregnant.

The husband had the most trouble rationalizing his fatherly attitude. He was strongly in favor of zero population growth. He knew there already were too many people and some of them weren't getting enough to eat. On the abortion issue, he was pro-choice, but reluctantly. He insisted birth control was the real answer and he had no patience with organizations that oppose teaching people how to avoid having children.

Of course, he hardly could claim birth control was a perfect solution. Not in the face of the wife's morning sickness, contracted at night. He simply accepted that they were among the few who lose the nearly sure bet, and he didn't care.

Despite his pro-choice leaning, there was never any discussion of an abortion because he knew the choice was hers, and she would give birth to a two-headed elephant before she would approve the killing of her unborn child. Her first three children had been delivered easily and the wife saw no reason to worry about No. 4, even though she was beyond the normal childbearing years.

So the unplanned parenthood was anticipated with growing happiness and excitement, especially when they learned their married daughter was also pregnant. The wife was scheduled to become a grandmother for the first time during the same summer she became a mother for the fourth time. Holy Moses.

When the husband wrote this double news to his mother, he pointed out that she could top him only by revealing a triple, but she had better not, seeing she was a widow. There was much of this type of silly merriment, along with the knitting of tiny garments and the reclaiming and refurbishing of baby furniture long forgotten.

The husband was insufferable macho about this proof of his

189

middle-aged manhood. During the fifth month of the pregnancy, his poker club gave him a baby shower at which he received many gifts, all ribald. The big boob was so proud of his virility he practically swung from tree limbs.

The day after the shower, the wife had a miscarriage. At the hospital, a nurse said they'd lost a son.

That sad day was 10 years ago. Lately, the husband has had good reason to remember it. He remembers their grief was brief. They realized miscarriages occur all the time, and there was no reason one shouldn't happen to them. They realized they had been much luckier on three previous attempts, and were grateful for that. Actually, it was easy to reverse the rationalizing and decide diapers wouldn't really have been all that much fun for people old enough to be grandparents, which they soon were — and a granddaughter was the best therapy possible for what ailed them.

But what the husband is remembering most about the miscarriage is the reaction of his youngest daughter, then 14. She had been looking forward to a new baby in the house. The husband remembers how she sobbed when he came home from the hospital and told her the child had been lost. He remembers taking her in his arms and trying to comfort her.

That daughter is now grown and married, and last month, with some booties already knitted, she had a miscarriage. Her father wasn't there to hug her, but he sent a note reminding her of the other miscarriage and of how it was soon forgotten.

As much as he hates cliches, he wanted to tell the daughter that life goes on, and while it's fine to mourn sadly for people lost, it's much more important to love happily the people who are here, the way he loves her.

On this Father's Day, for the husband there will be little thought of the unborn child who slipped away. If he swings from limbs, it will be because of the three kids who stuck around to make him climb walls, if not trees. ■

Love is a wonderful way
to worry about children

October 9, 1981

Emily Patricia Smith was born owing $4,694.20. Statisticians say that's her fair share of the nation's new $1,079 trillion debt limit. And she was born a few hours before the peacemaker, Anwar Sadat, was slain by warmakers. Welcome to the world, Emily.

Emily is my fourth grandchild, the first by my youngest daughter, Ferd. I worried terribly about Emily and Ferd during the last couple of months of the gestation. My wife wondered why I worried more about my pregnant daughter than I ever worried about my pregnant wife. It was a question to ponder.

Emily's projected birth date was Sept. 17, but the doctor said indications were she would arrive early, perhaps by several weeks. The suitcase for the rush to the hospital was packed by Sept. 1, and the waiting began.

Sept. 17 came and went with no baby. So did Sept. 30. Holy Moses. The impending grandfather became more worried and cranky everyday. I remembered Ferd had the same doctor a year ago, when her first attempt at motherhood ended in a miscarriage. I also remembered that, several years ago when we were old enough to know better, my wife and I tried to rust our golden years with a fourth child. Another miscarriage, same doctor.

"Maybe Ferd should get a new doctor," I suggested, minding my daughter's business from 60 miles away.

"Don't be silly," my wife said. "It's not unusual for babies to be a couple of weeks late. Our own daughter was three weeks late, an you didn't worry about that."

Ferd was three weeks late? I'd forgotten that.

When she was born, in 1956, we lived in a tiny home full of mice, a mile outside town. I remember my wife and I played a lot of Scrabble while timing contractions during the final days of that pregnancy. More than once I got the two scores mixed up and thought our baby might turn out to be a five-letter word beginning with N, such as Never.

I also remember that, for awhile, we slept in town, at a relative's home, to be nearer the maternity ward. But the baby still didn't come, and we had to move back home because if the mousetraps weren't regularly emptied and re-baited, the mice would move our home to a warmer climate.

Finally, all the forces of modern medicine were used to cause the birth of Ferd before she was big enough to go to school. Her mother induced labor by gulping castor oil. I've always remembered that because Blue Cross didn't cover the cost of the castor oil.

But I don't remember ever worrying about Ferd's delayed birth. I always knew everything was going to be all right, and it was. So why, 25 years later, was I worrying myself nuts because Ferd was going through the same thing her mother did?

After considerable pondering, I decided the difference is age. A 29-year-old father doesn't know enough to worry about anything, births or mice, but by the time he is 55, he's lived enough to know how ignorant he was when he was 29. And he knows about trillion-dollar debts and assassinations and the short supply of what the world needs most — love.

I never said it out loud, but I wasn't sure everything was going to be all right with Emily and Ferd. I felt the same way before my older daughter produced three healthy grandchildren. I knew unfortunate births sometimes happen, so why not to someone I loved? It's awful to grow old and pessimistic.

The phone finally rang Oct. 5. It was Ferd, calling from the hospital, with an eight-pound baby named Emily in her arms. No castor oil was needed, and "mother and child are doing fine." Oh boy. That's the greatest cliche in the world because it describes the greatest miracle.

I figure it's possible that my children will be giving me grandchildren for the next 12 years, by which time I will be only 68 but easily eligible to have great-grandchildren. I'm not sure I can survive such a fecund future. Love is marvelous, but it can make you worry something awful. ■

This brilliant baby has one forgetful Grandpa

August 27, 1982

"I'm making a list of all the smart things Emily can do," Grandma said.

Emily is almost 11 months old. Recently she spent her first weekend alone with her maternal grandparents, with neither parent present to prevent rampant spoiling. Grandma prepared for this most auspicious visit by vacuuming and scrubbing every rug and carpet in sight. This struck Grandpa as dumb.

"I understand why you always houseclean completely before adults come for dinner," he said. "There is always the terrifying possibility that a sister-in-law will see dust while eating roast beef under the washing machine. But I really don't think you have to worry about a tiny baby thinking you are a lousy housekeeper."

"Emily has learned how to crawl and I don't want her crawling on dirty carpet," Grandma explained.

"I can't wait until she learns how to swim so I can watch you wash the water in the swimming pool," Grandpa said. It wasn't one of his better ripostes because his heart wasn't really in it. He also didn't want sweet, precious little Emily soiled by any icky yucky old dirt. When it comes to being a cliche grandparent, Grandpa is almost as big a boob as Grandma.

It was for posterity that Grandma listed all signs of incredible intelligence demonstrated by Emily during her visit. "I'll give the list to your mummy and she can put it in your baby book," Grandma explained to Emily as the kid nodded her head understandingly while at the same time reaching for the section of the New York Times with the crossword puzzle in it.

And Grandpa, eavesdropping, felt a little twinge of sadness. Such twinges are common when the grandchildren are around. He can't remember whether he and his wife compiled baby books for their children. It has been 24 years since their last baby, and there is so much he has forgotten. Watching a grandchild perform, Grandma often says, "Remember when Eddie did that . . . " But Grandpa can't remember, no matter how hard he tries, and the failure makes him sad.

He remembers how much he enjoyed his babies, but few details. At what age did they first crawl and walk and talk? He has no idea. How did they behave the first day they went to school? He can't remember. Did they used to stick their tiny fingers into his ears, the way Emily does today? Not that he can remember. So many good times are gone forever, beyond recall, and he feels cheated by his poor memory.

Grandpa worries that maybe he didn't pay close enough attention all those years ago. Determined not to make the same mistake again, he watched Emily closely during her first solo visit. He rediscovered the pure joy of nuzzling a freshly bathed baby and the peaceful comfort of slipping into a dark room late at night to watch a sleeping baby breathe. He even contributed an item to Grandma's list of smart things done by Emily — "clapped her hands when Tiger game was switched off TV."

And he spent so much time watching her play on the clean carpet he didn't finish reading Friday's newspaper until Sunday night.

There was one slight lapse. Just out of the bathtub, Emily was nude on a blanket on the floor. Grandpa was instructed to keep his eye on her while Grandma stopped something from burning in the kitchen. He said it would be a pleasure. Emily always flails her arms and legs wildly and laughs loudly when she is undressed, and Grandpa thinks this might be the most delightful sight he ever has seen. But he was mentally distracted for a second, trying vainly to remember if any of his babies had ever flailed in the nude.

Until it was too late, he didn't notice that Emily had crawled onto the clean carpet and made it doubly impossible for Grandma to list that one of the smart things Emily can do is wait until she gets to the next gas station.

Encore: One item Grandma could have listed, but didn't get the chance, was that one of the smart things Emily can do is eat the list of smart things she can do. ■

Emily is just one more
reason to be a funaholic

January 15, 1983

Perhaps the best way to explain myself to Bob is to tell him about the afternoon I didn't get mad even though a doctor kept me waiting 90 minutes beyond appointment time and I couldn't find my way out of a multi-level parking garage.

Bob is a column reader who makes his living as a salesman and writes just for the fun of it. He sent me a sample of his fiction, strictly to get my opinion, requesting anonymity and stressing that he had no desire for the world, or even the neighbors, to read his words. In my answer to him, via mail, I included the observation that I have a tough time understanding amateur writers because writing is work to me and the only reason I do it is to pay my bills.

Bob didn't believe me. "Surely you must enjoy what you do," he wrote back. "I can't even believe that money enters into it. Frankly, I think you'd do it for half of what they pay you. Please write a column explaining yourself."

OK. I do enjoy writing for a living, but compared to what? Compared to working on an assembly line or similar jobs that ached my back and mind before I began fooling editors. But I don't enjoy writing enough to do it for nothing.

And I also don't enjoy writing enough to do it 20 hours every day. I'm always reading about super-successful people who got that way by working that kind of a schedule. I even know a few of those inspired workaholics. I admire their drive and lust after the luxurious fruits of their labor. But even if I had the talent, I wouldn't work hard enough to own 12 cars and 10 homes. I guess I'm a funaholic, and writing isn't fun to me.

My problem is time. Certain fringes invariably cling to a highly visible job like mine. Just as surely as I receive nasty letters, I also receive suggestions that I appear on TV or write books and movies. And along with these suggestions come the pointed observation that I certainly have enough time to make those attempts at becoming rich and famous.

But I don't have enough time. It's true that column-writing often leaves me with idle hands. However, it's also true that some people are born to test the devil in his playground. These people should be born wealthy, with no need to earn an income. When they're not that lucky, they're forced to manage the best they can with the lazy hours available. That's me.

My funaholic condition has worsened through the years. When I was younger, I kidded myself that someday I would begin using nights and weekends to write the great American dirty book. But since age 40, all pretense has been dropped in favor of the 30-hour work week and wanton fun.

What's fun? To each his own. To me, the trip to the doctor was fun. Actually, my wife had the appointment. I went along because we were granddaughter-sitting and I was needed to keep an eye on one-year-old Emily while Grandma had her health checked. It was supposed to take one hour but it took three because a patient's time isn't as valuable as a doctor's time.

Usually in these cases, I murder the doctor. But this time I put Emily in her stroller and pushed her to a nearby shopping mall, taking a shortcut through a parking garage. It took dumb Emily 45 minutes to find the right exit. The rest of the time I sat on a bench and watched Emily laugh and take wipes out of a box and put them back in, over and over. Wipes are new to me, sort of a damp Kleenex used to wash a kid's face when no sink is handy. My mother spit on the corner of a handkerchief.

Certainly it was no way for a grown breadwinner to spend a Friday afternoon. I didn't earn a nickel. I should have been working on a movie script. But instead I had the most fun I know how to have. And if I could afford to do it every day, I would.

I wouldn't write a word, Bob, not a word. If you want to come home from work and write for the fun of it, be my guest. I'd rather watch Emily wield wipes. ∎

Children can add such
order to a topsy-turvy world

November 30, 1983

Emotionally speaking, Thanksgiving week was up and down. One downer was actually an upper.

Two-year-old Emily visited. When she wants the immediate attention of an adult, Emily jerks on his or her pants or skirt. At one point, her grandmother was standing up in the chic sweat pants she usually wears for rolling around on the floor in front of the TV set, trying to look like Jane Fonda. The pants have an elastic waistband.

You guessed the rest. Emily jerked, and Grandma's pants came down below her knees. Onlookers applauded, and some threw money.

There were many laughs like that, thanks mainly to Emily. Watching a two-year-old, especially when she doesn't know she's being watched, is more fun than anything, even piano bars. But Thanksgiving was the first holiday I couldn't share the laughs with an older generation.

Oh, my brother-in-law Jack was there, and his age qualifies him to call me "son." But he is the husband of one of my younger sisters, so must be considered a member of my generation by marriage. The family patriarch can't be married to one of the kids.

Aunt Madeline and Aunt Florence, who always were available for holiday parties, died earlier this year. That left only my wife's mother, Ethel, eligible to make one more four-generation photo possible. That was the big downer.

A few days before Thanksgiving, the word came that Ethel had fallen and was very ill. So there was a hurried trip to the little town where Ethel has lived all of her 87 years, the last few in a nursing home. She barely realized we were at her bedside. "Are you sure that's you?' she asked her daughter.

On the way out, passing through the visitors lounge, I heard my name called. It was Isabelle, another resident of the nursing home, who had been my mother-in-law's roommate for a short time a few months earlier before being moved to another floor. Typically, she wanted to know how Ethel was.

For several summers, around 25 years ago, Isabelle was head cook at the local country club. She may have been the best cook ever born. I was a lousy golfer but I played often anyway in those days, just for the exercise, to stay slim. Thanks to Isabelle, I gained 20 pounds every golf season.

After she left the country club, I didn't think of Isabelle for many years, until one day last year when I was looking at the walls in my mother-in-law's room in the nursing home. Her new roommate, whom I hadn't yet met, had pasted up some family photos. One of them showed Stacy Keach, the well-known actor, with his arm around a young woman. How come?

I later learned Isabelle was the new roommate and her granddaughter was married to Keach. Isabelle never mentioned it. She never bragged about being related to a famous star of stage, screen and TV. That wasn't her style. She wouldn't even admit she was the best cook in the world, no matter how many times I accused her of it.

Isabelle would rather talk about my mother-in-law or my wife. She was 87 and in a wheelchair, but she worried about other people's well-being. That's how it was on the Sunday before Thanksgiving. She wanted to hear about Ethel. She wanted me to know how sorry she was that Ethel had fallen. She wanted me to be sure to tell Ethel and my wife that she loved them.

The next day, Isabelle Grumbache died.

So it was an up-and-down Thanksgiving week. It was marvelous to see Emily and her parents. And it was fun to tell my brother-in-law he always would be welcome at my home on Thanksgiving Day, just as long as he promised to stay away the rest of the year. But my mother-in-law fell, and may not get up again. Before I could tell her what Isabelle said, Isabelle was dead.

There is a grand, sensible scheme to these uppers and downers, of course. Middle-aged people see it: For every Ethel who falls, there is an Emily who jerks down Grandma's pants. We can be thankful for that. ■

A toehold on Emily's laugh
is worth more than fame

September 17, 1983

My stealthy wife sneaked up from behind and took an embarrassing photograph of Emily and me playing cards. Perhaps Adele Hast, doctor of philosophy, would like to publish it in her book.

Adele Hast is editor-in-chief of "Who's Who in America." She writes to me every couple of years to say how pleased she is to inform me that I have been selected for inclusion in the next edition. I know she is a doctor of philosophy because she signs her name with PhD after it. That little conceit is not why I never answer her letters.

I am not bugged by people who like to call attention to their education. If I were a doctor of philosophy, I'd have PhD embroidered on my nose. Medical doctors can use beepers in their pockets to let everyone in the room know their important presence is needed in surgery immediately. But it is awkward for doctors of philosophy to be summoned by beepers. What can they do — explain they must leave in the middle of dinner because the philosophy of Spinoza is very sick?

So it is not because I think she is ostentatious that I regularly ignore Adele Hast's invitations to be included in "Who's Who." All types of doctors should advertise extensively, for the good of humanity. If you fell and broke your philosophy, you would be darn grateful to look up and see the embroidery on my nose.

Also, my snub of the "Who's Who" overtures doesn't mean I'm not as vain as the next guy. I'm too cheap to buy a book just to read my name, but I wouldn't mind if my neighbors bought it and were impressed by my inclusion. I know a columnist who offers readers a free bumper sticker with his name on it, so it certainly wouldn't be too egotistical for me to suggest that you run out and get the "Who's Who" with me in it. At least you would find it easier to read in bed than a bumper.

The reason I'll never be in "Who's Who" is that Adele Hast, PhD, asks too many questions. She wants me to fill out a "biographical data form" with all sorts of information concerning such "special achievements" as my "civic and political activities, professional memberships, creative works and career-related activities." I never

199

saw so many blanks, and I just don't have time to unblank them.

I don't feel great about saying no to a doctor of philosophy, and I get no reverse-snobbery kick out of refusing to become a who's who. I am dismayed to realize I automatically have eliminated myself from any consideration when President Reagan thumbs through "Who's Who" in search of a press secretary without a rabbit fetish. But I have more important things to do than make an endless list of my special achievements.

For instance, on the same day Adele Hast's latest letter arrived, I had to take my granddaughter Emily for a walk on a long pier. I had to show her boats and ducks and how the water lapped directly below her feet. Most important, I had to show her how to spit through the cracks in the dock.

The most accurate through-the-crack spitting is done from a squatting position. Did you know a 23-month-old child can squat forever and suffer no ill effects, but a 57-year-old man who squats for three minutes can't walk properly until late the next day? It is important to know stuff like that.

Contrary to what you probably think, my most special achievement lately hasn't been spitting through cracks. It has been playing cards with Emily. That's why my sneaky wife took the aforementioned photo. She really was impressed. Emily and I hold the cards between our toes.

Sure, that's a strange way for a grown man to play cards, and should probably be listed as my most special achievement in "Who's Not." But it makes Emily laugh. You should hear her laugh.

Everybody should hear an Emily laugh. That's my philosophy, from my nose to your bumper. No charge. ■

Bridging the gap between
Emily's bears, my Tigers

October 12, 1984

Emily put her grandfather to the test during the first game of the World Series. All I wanted to do was watch the action on TV while keeping my mind and body alert and ready to erupt at the first sight of a Tiger base hit. All Emily wanted to do was sit on my lap and listen to me read a book called "Milk and Cookies."

The test would determine if, no matter how difficult the circumstances, I were man enough to stick to my theory that the only sensible way to make a little girl be a good girl is to give her everything she wants. This was, after all, the Detroit Tigers' first World Series appearance in 16 years.

On the other hand, this was a soft child, just four days past her third birthday, who wrapped her chubby arms around my neck, kissed my ear, and whispered, "Please read to me, Pappa." And if I refused, this was a noisy child, just a few decibels short of a steam whistle, who would yell loud enough to awaken her grandmother to the fact that I was keeping the little darling up too late simply to be mean to her.

Usually I like to keep Emily up too late. We have our most serious talks after everyone else has gone to bed. It is my chance to explain the world to her. Just the other night I told her why she is going to have it so easy when she gets in high school.

I'd just read that some schools now are giving class credits toward graduation to students with drug habits if they undergo anti-drug therapy. Progress and fairness being what they are, by the time Emily is a teenager, it will be possible to get class credits for skipping classes if the student attends an anti-skipping lecture.

On another night, I explained to Emily why I'd enjoyed a terrible movie that afternoon. It was while ABC-TV was in Detroit to telecast the baseball playoffs, and in a RenCen theater I sat behind Jim Palmer, the famous jock broadcaster and wearer of tight underwear.

I always feel guilty about having nothing more important to do than attend a movie matinee all by myself, and seeing a big celebrity like Jim Palmer do the same thing made me feel a lot better about my baggy boxer shorts.

Emily is bored by my late-night monologues, of course, and she probably has a right to ask me to interrupt myself long enough to read her a good book. But during the World Series?

Yes. The book "Milk and Cookies" is about a little bear who looks through a keyhole and sees his grandfather feeding a fire-spitting dragon. So the little bear goes to sleep and dreams that a dragon comes to his home and polishes off all the milk and cookies in the place, leaving nothing for the little bear, who wakes up crying.

I read that story to Emily with one eye while the other eye watched Jack Morris strike out three straight San Diego Padres with two men on base. I also read it while watching two Tigers get picked off first base and Larry Herndon hit a homer.

In all, I read that little book nine times, or once an inning, and by the time I went to bed, my eyes were farther apart than my ears.

But the ending was happy. The Tigers won, Emily hugged me every time she said, "Read it again," and Pappa passed his toughest test.

Also, the little bear's grandfather wasn't really feeding a fire-spitting dragon. He was putting wood in a furnace. ■

Adella's story shouldn't
have to be written

July 22, 1983

I gave Emily a toy telephone that talks back to her. It contains recorded messages that sound off at the punch of a button. None of the messages is: "Don't bleed all over this bathroom floor."

Three of the messages are:

"Let's be friends."

"When is your birthday?"

"What's your dog's name?"

The taped messages are delivered in a sweet child's voice. According to court testimony, it was an adult voice, live and in anger, that instructed a three-year-old girl to not bleed on the bathroom floor. A 25-year-old man said it to his girlfriend's daughter.

He was mad at her because she apparently changed her mind about going to the bathroom. So he "barged down the hall, grabbed the girl from the bed by her T-shirt and kicked her down the hall to the bathroom," the child's mother testified.

And the little girl had gall enough to bleed on the bathroom floor.

So the man "smashed" her against the wall and punched her in the stomach. And she cried: "Mommy, Mommy, please help me. Bill's hurting me."

That's enough. I picked the bleeding three-year-old's story out of the newspaper almost at random. There are child abuse articles in the paper almost every day. I can't stand to read them, but I always read them.

I can't stand to write about child abuse, either, and almost never do. I like to make people laugh.

I talked with a colleague about my reluctance to deal with such an unfunny subject. "Write about it," he said. "It doesn't hurt to remind readers that you're a warm, compassionate human being."

It does hurt. It hurts my self-esteem. I don't want readers to think I'm looking for medals for being a "warm, compassionate human being." I realize most human beings are warm and compassionate — and horrified at the thought of anyone abusing a helpless child.

There is nothing unusual or laudable about the way I feel. I don't want to take bows for hating child-beaters, any more than I want to wear the Stars and Stripes on my nose to prove I love my country. There are some things so obvious they shouldn't have to be said, and I feel silly saying them.

But my three granddaughters visited my home last week. Emily is not quite two years old, Melissa is 10, and Michele is 13.

One morning I got up to find all three of them crammed into my big leather chair, peeking over the edge of a blanket and giggling. The sight was pure joy, and I can think of no better way to begin a day.

They kissed me and said they loved me, and I said I loved them. We played with Emily's phone. I thought of how blessed I was. And I thought of all the other little kids — each one as loving and lovable as my grandchildren — who would be slugged that day by brutal adults I can't even pretend to understand.

I thought of the innocent children who are abused and taught to feel guilty for doing nothing more than being innocent children. The children to whom no adult says, "Let's be friends." The children who could get more love and affection from a toy telephone than from their parents.

Punch a button. Punch a child.

While hugging my grandchildren I thought about the three-year-old who bled on the bathroom floor and was smashed against a wall. This is not a smart thing for a man to think about. It can make him cry, and feel silly.

Thinking about a punched child also can make a man want to scream. But screaming doesn't do any good. So instead I wrote an un-funny column that says obvious things that shouldn't have to be said. And it won't do any good, either.

I'm sorry. I am so sorry.

The little girl who bled in the bathroom is named Adella. When is your birthday, Adella? What is your dog's name? Let's be friends.■

God must have a sense of humor; the wig proves it

January 1, 1977

Is there any hope for a grown man who goes to church on Christmas Eve and laughs at the creche?

(My mother just fainted. She knows I am talking about me.)

It didn't happen in 1976. This Christmas story is two years old. I am retelling it now because this is New Year's Day and you might need a laugh, especially if Michigan blows the roses.

On the other hand, you might not think it's a funny story. For some people, church is a strictly serious place. Wipe that silly grin off your face and say your prayers. Getting to heaven is no laughing matter.

Whatever. To each his own. There are even some people who will not watch football on TV today. To make you glad, or to make you mad, this is the way it was . . .

I didn't intend to laugh at the creche. But the Christ Child wouldn't stop crying. So the Chief Singing Angel came down from on high and whispered urgently into the Virgin Mary's ear. Mary and the squealing child immediately fled the scene (Nativity).

And a minute later, Mary was back with a surrogate-baby that looked like a Barbie doll wrapped in swaddling clothes.

One of the shepherds had YMCA stenciled on his turban and a wise man wore a beard you wouldn't believe. My son whispered that the beard was actually a wig borrowed from an angel.

This pantomime pageant was staged by the youth of my favorite church. The costumed kids acted out the birth of Christ while the choir sang and a narrator read the Gospel to Luke.

It was nice, and no reason for more than a holy smile. My mother and numerous nuns taught me to behave in church or a bolt of lightning would zap me into purgatory or hell, depending upon my state of grace at the time of my transgression.

But I was sitting between my two teenage children, a daughter home from college, and a son home from the nearest acid-rock concert. (Their mother was part of the heavenly chorus, in the soprano section.) It was the son who exposed me to the lightning.

He began to laugh with his mouth shut. The noise was minimal,

205

escaping in small snorts through his nose and ears. But his efforts to contain the laugh forced him to shake. It was crowded and he was shaking against me.

It did no good for me to turn my head away and pretend he wasn't laughing because I could feel him quivering and I know he was dying because he couldn't stop laughing.

This made me laugh and I tried to swallow the laughs and this made my eyes water and my jaw ache. I finally buried my face in a handkerchief, now quivering myself, and I prayed that God would forgive me and that my favorite angel in the heavenly chorus would not see me, please dear God.

Of course, I quivered against my daughter and she started to laugh and couldn't stop. The same thing happened to the two people on her left and also to a couple seated in front of us. It was a disaster.

And no one except my son knew exactly what we were laughing about. He later explained it was the three wise men who did him in. In real life they are his buddies and he recognized their bathrobes from less holy occasions. The beard that was really an upside down wig was the kiss-off. It was hilarity time in the pews.

The bearded Wise Man later confessed he had hoped his wigged chin might provide the congregation with a few chuckles. Bless him. Why not give a laugh for Christmas? And why not give it in church?

Constant readers (Mother and Aunt Madeline) will recall that I long have crusaded for less stiffness before the altar. Why not applaud a good anthem from the choir, or a good point from the pastor? Why not say an unorchestrated Amen aloud when you agree?

And why not laugh when something funny happens? God wouldn't want a man to choke to death on a laugh swallowed out of piety.

As I grow older, and my offspring spring farther away, I realize the warm value of happy memories. I am certain the laughing-in-church episode will be remembered and recounted on countless Christmas Futures.

It was a fun thing that might have occurred in the Alibi Bar. But, as a soprano voice from the heavenly chorus surely would agree, it was nice that it happened in church. ■

I'd probably have worn
lace stockings if she'd asked

May 6, 1978

The wedding is tonight, and the father of the bride-to-be feels constrained to explain how in God's name he ever became involved in such a frilly affair.

He eloped, and he has always insisted that was the only sensible way to get married. No one would ever catch him playing a major role in one of those costumed extravaganzas where you must arrive early to get a parking space. That's what he always said.

But tonight the father will wear a shirt with ruffles. He will parade down a church aisle while an organ plays and people stare. He will stand in a reception line and exchange cute remarks with dozens of strangers. How can such things happen to a shy man who skipped his own university commencement exercises because ceremony of any sort makes all of his skin crawl into his shoes?

In trying to answer that question, the father thinks back a few years to a time when the same daughter caused him to undergo a similarly traumatic experience. She was a candidate for homecoming queen of her high school.

There were five other candidates. The six girls had to parade their charms across a football field during halftime. They had to be escorted by their fathers. These things had to be done because the school principal said so. Only the most cruel father would disobey the principal and force his daughter to be the only candidate without an escort.

The father of the bride-to-be always has loathed any sort of beauty contest. He never saw a Miss America who didn't look as if she ran on batteries. He claims there's something silly about women prancing and preening before judges. He keeps looking for their leashes.

And besides, the value of a beauty crown has been decreased considerably by the frequency of the crownings. Today there are queens selected to reign over all events except funerals. And now that it's been mentioned, the U.S. Morticians Association will probably come up with a Miss Grief, in a black bikini.

207

In view of all this nonsense, how could the father possibly be an official escort for a homecoming queen candidate?

It was easy. The father not only escorted his candidate, he did it proudly, with tears in his stupid eyes. He didn't feel like a hypocrite. He felt good, and he wasn't surprised.

There is an older daughter. Tonight she will be matron of honor. In high school she was a drum major. She pranced in front of the band, and twirled a baton.

All of his life, the father of the matron of honor has made fun of baton twirling. He thinks baton twirlers are dumber than candidates for beauty crowns. But every time he saw his oldest daughter lead the band onto the football field, the big goof grinned, and leaked those stupid tears, and prayed she wouldn't drop her baton.

That's how it will be at the wedding. The father will grin, and cry, and walk proudly down the aisle, escorting his queen candidate one more time. He'll forget his lifelong scorn for pomp. He'll ask strangers to admire his ruffles. A real goof.

There is only one explanation for this remarkable change in character: Daughters are magicians. They can turn fathers into goofs. Love is the magic potion.

The father of the bride-to-be remembers the day a rather foolish woman came into his weekly newspaper office. He overheard her tell the girl at the counter that she wished she had nerve enough to ask for the editor's autograph. And the girl fell down laughing.

"He's only my father," the bride-to-be said.

And then the father automatically thought: "I'd rather be her father than anything else."

Even if, to do the job right, he has to wear ruffles once in a while.■

That little boy inside me
only has eyes for pool

July 1, 1977

There was a day when she always wanted to wear frilly dresses. She wore white gloves and patted her mouth with a lace hankie after sipping root beer at the A&W. She sat primly in the backseat of my old Plymouth and never raised her voice when telling her little brother to bug off.

Her name was Chrissie and she was six years old.

Today she is 21 and everyone calls her Ferd. She wears a plastic football helmet and rides around on the back of a Kawasaki motorcycle.

My dainty little girl on a motorcycle. How could such a thing happen? What did I do wrong?

Don't misunderstand. I am not sorry my daughter has grown up. I have no trouble adjusting to the passing years. I'm glad I'm no longer driving that old Plymouth, and it is OK with me that Ferd soon will marry the guy on the front of the Kawasaki. Let him pay her phone bills. That'll put sweat on his black leather jacket.

But a motorcycle! That's my beef. No sane person should ride a motorcycle. It is not pleasant to admit your child is an idiot, but there you are.

The highways are jammed with idiots, usually traveling in packs. They roar through downtown Detroit at 2 o'clock in the morning and the awful noise reaches our apartment on the 25th floor and knocks me out of bed.

It is depressing that my own skin and blood would skim so close to the freeway. I also am dismayed by the age of some non-relatives who ride motorcycles. I know there is supposed to be a little boy inside every old man, screaming to get out. But I like to think that men my age have sense enough to ignore the more irrational screams.

Not so. I see grandfathers in crash helmets, completely enveloping both Harley and Davidson in middle-aged spread.

When I see an old crock weaving down the road, I am reminded of a refugee fleeing a bombed city in whatever vehicle is available in the emergency. I keep expecting to see his wife trailing along behind, wheeling the family possessions in an old baby carriage.

209

I know a guy who sells Hondas, and one night, several years ago, he took advantage of my gratitude. He said he'd be over to my house that weekend to give me a ride on a 747 or whatever two-wheeled monster he was pushing at the moment. I nodded in agreement because he was kindly exercising my elbow. The next morning, when I realized what I'd promised, I jumped out of bed and left town for three weeks.

A 60-year-old friend recently told me he had his Honda going 90 m.p.h. on a country road. His teeth were still bent inward, with gravel imbedded in the cracks.

"You own a 1975 Cadillac with air conditioning and a roof. Why would you want to ride a motorcycle?" I asked him. "If God had wanted man to ride motorcycles, he would have given them leather fannies."

"It is exciting," my friend explained. "I like the wind in my face and I like the feeling of risk."

"You can get the same feeling by sticking your nose too close to an electric fan," I said. "Motorcycling is for young men with nothing to live for. You're old enough to smell the joys of retirement but you could blow the whole thing on that bike. It will be the first time I've been a pallbearer for a man dressed in a jacket with 52 zippers.

"The trouble with you is you have no sense of adventure," my friend snorted.

He is right. My idea of adventure is to sit with my wife and pretend to read the newspaper while I actually am watching Farrah Fawcett on TV. Happily, I can enjoy this type of risk despite the certain knowledge that Farrah would pick a motorcyclist over me every time. There is something to be said for being over the hill, and I just said it.

There's a little boy inside me, too. But I only let him out to shoot pool. And if he ever suggests the Honda shop will cash my Social Security check, I will flake him to death with Kellogg's All-Bran.

As for Ferd, she is still my daughter. She and her family will always be invited to my home for Christmas dinner. Just so long as they park their bikes out of my hearing and walk the last few blocks, laden with gifts.

Onward and Upward, but always on four wheels. ■

Love runs rampant when
a family gets together

November 18, 1981

After services at the First Presbyterian Church in Lapeer last Sunday, a woman told my friend Mallory Cox that he should come to church more often, not just when his granddaughter is baptized. But his granddaughter wasn't baptized; mine was.

Mallory and I are the same age and size and have the same type of Irish mug. We lived in the same small town for 25 years, and people continually got us mixed up. He worked for the state Department of Revenue and people stopped me on the street to ask questions about their tax bills. I advised them not to pay under any circumstances.

When I sold advertising for the county newspaper, people asked Mallory to sell them an ad and he told them nobody ever read the rotten rag and they should save their money.

At large parties, people accused me of spending the entire evening at the bar when actually I was there only half the time. Once, a busy bartender listened to Mallory's problem and then told me how to solve it. This is why our close friends are able to tell us apart by the puzzled expression on Mallory's face. He's still waiting to hear the solution to his problem.

So it was exceedingly nostalgic, after several year's absence, to return to the old church for the baptism of my newest grandchild, Emily, and to learn that at least one member of the congregation thought she was Mallory's granddaughter. He does have a granddaughter, but she cries more than mine.

It also was nostalgic to sit in the pew behind my youngest daughter, Ferd, and note that even though she is now a mother, she still has hippy hair. Our entire family, including three other grandchildren and sons-in-law, was there for the baptism, which is why we overflowed into two pews. Even my son showed up, arriving, as usual, from a different direction from anyone else and not fully prepared. His mother had to meet him outside the church with his dress shoes, or he would have worn ragged sneakers with his Sunday suit. Unfortunately, as his sisters quickly pointed out, sweat socks don't go well with dress shoes.

When Ferd was a teenager, she was something of a flower child,

211

wearing her blonde hair longer than her skirt, and I often described her as my hippy-haired little girl. So it was a giant pang for me, there in church, to pull that hippy hair away from Ferd's shoulder to get a better look at baby Emily, who was nestled there. Fathers whose little girls have little girls can be real goofs.

For the event, the baby was lovely in the same christening outfit her grandmother wore 53 years earlier. I whispered to my grandson that Emily's dress was even older than her Uncle Nerd's sweat socks. And someone whispered to me that, during her pregnancy, Ferd was called "the prego deaco" because she is a church deacon. As I sat there thinking of myself as the father of a church deacon, I heard the walls of the Alibi Bar crumble 45 miles away.

After church, we filled two cars and drove to the nursing home where six-week-old Emily was dropped softly into the lap of her 85-year-old great-grandmother. From Grover Cleveland to Ronald Reagan. Lips kissed, arms squeezed, words caressed, cameras clicked and the pages of Christmas catalogs flipped. The sounds of love ran rampant.

It has become a cliche to say "that's what life is all about." I've heard that said about everything from sunsets to baseball to two weeks in Aspen. To each his own. To me, life is all about hippy-haired little girls, sweat socks in church, 53-year-old christening dresses and marvelous mothers who rear children to become deacons despite their fathers.

I am waxing slightly poetic for a reason. It gives me an excuse to tell you that Emily's classiest christening gift came from the young man in the sweat socks, of all people. He gave her a book of poems by Emily Dickinson, and she probably is home reading it right now.

Even though my friend Mallory is incredibly handsome, I'll bet his granddaughter isn't reading poetry yet. ■

Maybe Nerd had too many
popcorn and pickle dinners

May 4, 1977

The first night we stayed at a motel in Louisville. Our rooms faced the swimming pool. I was awakened at 2 a.m. by a loud voice which said: "Hey Marge, come look at this. There's a guy lying on the bottom of the pool."

Then there was much exclaiming and more yells for more people to come see the nut in the pool.

There was no water in the pool. I figured my sleep was being ruined by a bunch of Kentucky drunks. In the morning I asked my family if they had also been disturbed.

My daughter Ferd said the guy in the dry pool was my son Nerd. Oh my. That's how it was driving to New Orleans in search of pralines and all that jazz.

Nerd is an 18-year-old camera freak. Mostly he takes pictures of shadows and rocks and big toes and bird droppings. His photos would probably look like stills for Swedish art movies, except he never develops the film. He has a dark room but it is also a laundry room and he can never use it because his mother is always using it to lose socks in.

Anyway, Nerd's equipment includes a tripod and timer so, when he needs a body in a picture, he can use his own body. And he thought it would be great to get a photo of a body lying on the bottom of an empty pool, snapped in available light provided by a Kentucky moon and a red neon sign saying "Admiral Benbow Inn."

You can imagine the astonishment of those motel guests, returning from the Admiral's tap room at 2 a.m. to find a long young man prostrate in the dry and spooky shadow of a a diving board. Nerd offered to take their picture if they would climb down into the pool. They declined ("Don't get too close to him, Marge").

Another noteworthy thing about Louisville is its huge movie complex. It contains seven theaters, the most I've seen in one place. But they won't give you extra salt for your popcorn. That's the same as no mustard at the World Series. My wife was sore until we reached Hattiesburg, Miss., and discovered a theater that sells large pickles.

Movie food is important when you travel with me. I insist upon checking into a motel by 5 p.m., out of respect for the cocktail hour. But it makes me uncomfortable to sit in a motel room too long, so we go to the 7 o'clock movie.

It costs around $14 for a family of four to get by the box office, leaving no money for fancy dining. When you eat dinner in a theater seat for four straight days, a Mississippi pickle can be a gourmet's delight.

The reason I often am uncomfortable in a motel is I never can coax the desired temperature out of the heating-cooling unit. The problem is the control dials are always next to the floor. A man wearing bifocals cannot read the dials unless he lies flat on the floor and eats the carpet. A man with a large stomach should dial with his toes and go to a movie.

We stopped at budget motels along the freeway so we could afford to eat in restaurants in New Orleans. There was no great disappointment until Natchez, Miss., on the way home. That's where Ferd saw me stomping on the motel floor and asked why I was dancing to no music.

Actually, I was killing a cockroach. When I flushed away the corpse, the toilet plugged. I stopped at this motel because a sign in front said it was approved by the Auto Club. I didn't realize this approval was granted because the resident cockroaches are large enough to drive autos and belong to the club.

The jazz in the French Quarter was as fine as ever. The purest stuff is still being played by old guys you never heard of in such run-down joints as Preservation Hall. But this was the kids' first time, so I took them to hear a name — Al Hirt.

For $12.50 a head you get two awful drinks and a long wait. Hirt still plays a nice horn but unfortunately he no longer is satisfied to be only a musician. He also thinks he is a philosopher and a comedian. He told five minutes' worth of Polish jokes, for Lord's sake.

And when he did shut up and play, his hucksters went from table to table selling Hirt's albums and glasses with his name on them. Hirt didn't mind that the sales pitches messed up his music, as long as his cash register kept ringing. Nuts to him, praline style.

We also spent a day at Vicksburg, Miss., touring the National Military Park. That's where thousands of soldiers died in a Civil War battle that lasted several weeks. Countless gravestones and monuments mark their graves, acre after acre. It's a sad place.

"They should all have gone to Canada instead," Nerd said.

I should have left him on the bottom of that pool in Louisville. ■

Ferd, Nerd and Karen just
doesn't have the right ring

January 16, 1978

The U.S. Supreme Court has agreed to decide if my oldest daughter's nickname can be broadcast on radio and television.

Well, that may not be precisely true. But practically.

Actually, the court will rule even on words which the Federal Communications Commission considers indecent. Newspaper reports coyly describe the seven words as "slang which depict sexual or excretory activities and organs."

Why are there seven such words, instead of six, or eight? The precise count is not the result of extensive research done by the FCC on rest room walls. It is the result of a record album made by comedian George Carlin.

The album includes a selection called "dirty words" in which Carlin says the seven words which, in his opinion, turn sensitive noses bluest fastest. When a New York man and his young son heard Carlin's record on the radio, the father complained to the FCC.

Subsequently, the FCC banned the seven words from TV and radio. But the U.S. Circuit Court of Appeals in Washington soon struck down the FCC ban, ruling that it was overly broad and vague. Now the Supreme Court will decide the issue.

I heard Carlin deliver his seven-words routine in person several years ago, in Detroit's plushest theater. I remember it was riotously funny, but no matter how hard I try, I can't remember all seven words. I can come up with only four of them for sure, and then must guess at the rest. My guesses quickly reach a total of 56, including suffixed words, so you must admit my vocabulary is better than my memory.

So I can't say for sure that my oldest daughter's nickname will be affected by the Supreme Court decision. Her nickname is in the "excretory activities" category, but it is not the most popular word in that category. Rather, it is an auxiliary word, often used by prissy people who wouldn't say the most popular word if they had a mouthful of it.

For fear of offending my wife and my editor, I won't write the nickname here. But I will give you a good hint.

215

The world has already been told, many times, that my youngest daughter's nickname is Ferd. And her little brother most commonly is called Nerd. Well, my oldest daughter's nickname begins with "T" and rhymes beautifully with the nicknames of her brother and sister.

Her given name, incidentally, is Karen. She and her family live many miles away and I see her only a few times a year. Therefore she doesn't appear in this column nearly as often as Ferd and Nerd, or even the lousy cats. Karen's friends were concerned that she might feel left out and neglected by her father.

So they gave her a nickname as distinctive as Ferd and Nerd, but certainly not as appropriate. Everyone in her little town now calls Karen by her new name. She thinks it's funny.

Her mother doesn't. When my wife first heard her firstborn child's nickname, that's when the most popular word hit the fan. Naturally, she blamed me.

I told my wife that sticks and stones might break her bones, but words would never hurt her. She told me I wouldn't say such dumb things if I weren't made of snails and puppy dog tails.

I reminded her that Ferd and Nerd had accompanied me to the show in which George Carlin had given his seven-word routine. The kids were barely teenagers then. When Carlin was through, I asked them if they'd heard any words they'd never heard around school. The answer was no.

"I don't care," my wife said. "I don't think people should have to hear those words if they don't want to, and I don't want to."

The Supreme Court may well agree with her. In which case, when Ferd and Nerd replace Donny and Marie on TV, there will be a great loss of poetical pizzazz when the FCC forces them to introduce their guest star as Karen instead of by her nickname.

"Couldn't they call her Curd?" my wife asked.

"No whey," I said. ■

Violets for Mother

Mother . . .
the last years

Volcanoes and navels
do not a mother make

May 13, 1978

For Mother's Day, a national magazine named Cher one of "The 10 Most Admired Mothers" in the world. My mother wasn't mentioned.

Cher was honored because "despite volcanic marriages to Sonny Bono and Gregg Allman, she never lets disappointments interfere with taking care of her children."

Actress Shirley Jones was the eighth most admired. "Rock star Shaun Cassidy's mother has to be super," the magazine said.

Shirley divorced Shaun's father but they remained good friends until the day he died. People named to "Best 10" lists always remain good friends with their spouses after the divorce. It's one of the requirements for nomination.

Sophia Loren was also one of the most admired mothers. The explanation was brief, but apt. "Actress Sophia Loren rounds out the list as No. 10," a news release said. Sophia would round out a list of the 10 most admired gas balloons.

The balance of the mother list was made up mostly of women who were named because of what they did before they became mothers. What they did was marry the right men. To me, this makes as much sense as naming Mrs. Dionne the bride of the year for giving birth to quintuplets. But what do I know?

Under this pre-pregnancy criteria, Jackie Kennedy Onassis obviously has twice as good a chance as most women to become a most admired mother. In naming her No. 3, the magazine said Jackie "never seems too busy with her activities to spend time with her two children."

It is easy to see why my mother didn't make the most admired list. When she was raising five children, if she wanted to spend time with one of them, all she had to do was cross a room. Jackie Onassis has to cross an ocean.

Also, unlike Cher, my mother never had a volcanic marriage. I can remember her cleaning a lot of messes off the floor, but never lava.

Mother never had to face the disappointments that Cher has to overcome to care for her children. Being in show business, Cher

219

constantly must worry about real troubles, such as her navel healing over. My mother never had to worry about anything more important than the Depression and Dad losing his job and how to pay for food.

Certainly there is nothing admirable about the way my mother didn't raise her son to become a rock star like Shaun Cassidy. She never bought me a guitar, and she never encouraged me to make terrible noises with my mouth. On the contrary, she used to tell me to shut up before the neighbors called the police.

My mother's husband was never elected president, and he never owned an island, so she couldn't use the pre-pregnancy method. All my father ever did was take good care of his family and make them laugh a lot. He was funnier than Sonny Bono, but he was a dud when it came to producing the lava a wife must swim through to become one of the world's 10 most admired mothers.

Because there was no volcanic marriage, my mother never had to divorce my father and then remain good friends. The best she could do is miss him terribly after he died.

Obviously there is no reason for a magazine to mention my mother among such internationally admired mothers as Cher and Jackie. Mother simply doesn't make the scene. She probably never even heard of Gregg Allman, for Lord's sake.

But she has been a marvelous mother for many years, and she is much admired by her children. She's nothing like Cher, but she's probably a lot like your mother.

I'm no national magazine, but I thought I would mention Mother anyway, for tomorrow, for her. ∎

Such a momma's boy
— and so proud of it

August 16, 1978

It was something like playing musical chairs, without the music. The players laughed a lot, but they weren't fooling each other. They all knew they felt like crying.

The son was there, and his wife, and his sister and her husband. They are all middle-aged, somewhat thick around the middle, and inclined to grunt when they get up out of low chairs. But on this day they felt like children again.

The son's daughter was also there, with her husband. They are the newlyweds, and they felt like ghouls. Because of their youth, they voluntarily stood first as the chairs slowly disappeared.

They had all arrived from out of town, on different highways, to meet in a small home in the city where the son and his sister had grown up, so many years ago. One couple drove a pickup, and another couple had rented a trailer for the occasion.

Vodka and tonic was served. That's why the chairs and other furniture disappeared slowly. No one was in a hurry. They moved reluctantly, and sat and sipped gratefully, even when most of the chairs were gone, and three middle-aged spreads had to fit on one couch.

They didn't want to do what they were doing. They hated doing it. They didn't want to move the chairs and other furniture out of the home and into the truck and trailer and car trunk. But it had to be done.

In the basement, the son found the wicker clothes basket. It still looks huge. Forty years ago, the son thought it was probably the biggest basket in the world.

He was surprised that he remembered. The last time he saw that basket Franklin Delano Roosevelt was president. He hadn't thought about that basket since before World War II. How could he even be sure it was the same basket?

He was sure. And the memories came back in a rush. He remembered carrying that basket when his arms were barely long enough to reach the handles on each side. The basket isn't round, like most clothes baskets, it's rectangular, and a little kid had to stretch to get a grip on it.

The son used to carry that basket from the basement to the backyard for his mother. It was always full of just-washed clothes that had to be hung out to dry. He could smell those wet clothes again, and he could remember how proud he was to lift something for his mother.

When he was a very little boy, before he became a wise-guy teenager, the son was a fool about his mother. He knew she was the most beautiful mother in the world and he wanted nothing out of life except to be near her.

He sat under the grand piano while she played "Tiptoe Through the Tulips." He was always there, begging to lick the dish, no matter what she was cooking. When she visited neighbors, he literally hung onto her skirt for fear she might get out of his sight.

There was a day when the sister was leaving on a glorious vacation to visit an aunt in Toronto. The father was certain the son was jealous, so he gave his shoulder a squeeze and promised the son that some day soon he also could visit the aunt.

"I don't want to go anywhere," the son said, almost crying. He was horrified at the idea of leaving his beautiful mother.

The son remembered these things as he looked at the old basket so many years later, on the day of the non-musical chairs. He'd forgotten what a momma's boy he used to be. He was glad to be reminded, and sad.

The chairs and clothes basket and everything else must be moved out of the home because no one lives there anymore. The woman who used to live there is now in a nursing home and, on the way out of town that day, the middle-aged son stopped to visit her.

Her health is failing and she may never live in a home of her own again. She is almost blind, and when she passes a mirror, she can't see what the son can see. She is still the most beautiful mother in the world.

The son hopes she knows how much he aches because he can no longer lift her basket for her. ■

Life would be sweeter
with a little brown gravy

November 29, 1978

The middle-aged son wonders what the people who live nearby must think as they look out their windows and see him — a stranger — empty a silver bucket into the sewer drain in the middle of their street.

He does it two or three times a month, usually around 5 o'clock in the afternoon. He is respectably dressed and doesn't appear to be a troublemaker. Close inspection would reveal the silver bucket is respectfully engraved, a goodby gift from former co-workers who evidently don't think he's some kind of a weirdo who gets his kicks from dumping his trash in other people's neighborhoods.

The middle-aged son also wonders about the neighbors who might not see the actual dumping, but pass by the sewer drain later and see his rubbish before it has melted small enough to slip through the grate. "Where in hell did the ice cubes come from?"

The people who see the man with the silver bucket probably don't feel threatened. His actions aren't sinister, or even slovenly. After all, he dumps in the daylight, he uses the sewer, and his attitude is biodegradable.

But it must be a puzzlement. "What is that stranger with the silver bucket doing in the middle of our street week after week?"

He is cleaning up after a party. He also is reaching back for yesterdays.

The middle-aged son grew up in a home that observed the cocktail hour. Not every day, but on momentous occasions, such as weekends. Nothing boozy. Two drinks, sipped, and then let's eat.

The dinners were usually roast beef or leg of lamb with mashed potatoes and brown gravy. His mother made the best brown gravy in the world. Everybody said so.

"Gertrude, I wish I knew how you made that gravy," her sister Madeline would say. Or her sister Florence would say it. Remember those old-fashioned names? Remember when every girl baby wasn't christened Karen or Michelle?

There may be nothing in a name, but a father out of a job during

223

the Depression had to be better off married to Gertrude, rather than Debbie.

But back to dinner. Father carved the meat, standing at the head of the table, armed with an enormous knife and fork. This was the ultimate position of authority. Plates were passed to the father for filling. His children always knew from whom all blessings flowed, and they respected the source.

The middle-aged son remembers ruefully. He never carved a roast in his life. His wife has always done it in the kitchen, plugged in. On Father's Day, his children pay homage to the power of a General Electric knife.

Oh well. That's today. As he dumps the silver bucket, the middle-aged son is thinking of yesterday, when the brown gravy was the best in the world . . .

His mother doesn't make brown gravy anymore. She isn't able to cook at all. She doesn't even have a kitchen to call her own. And the father who carved and filled the plates died many years ago.

There's no way to bring back the warmth and fun of those roast beef or leg of lamb dinners on a Sunday afternoon. Too many members of the cast are missing, or ailing. Besides, who would make the gravy?

But the middle-aged son and his sisters still reach back to grab what they can of yesterday. That's how the ice gets in the silver bucket.

There's also a Thermos. Inside is mostly orange juice. It's not the alcohol content that's important, it's the memories.

The cocktail hour is brought to Mother in a nursing home. For a while the conversation is bright, there is laughing, and much remembering.

And when the party's over, the middle-aged son, on the way back to the car, dumps the dregs down the sewer drain, and wonders what the neighbors think.

And then he drives out of his old hometown, wishing hard that he could pass his plate to the head of the table and taste that brown gravy just one more time. ■

Nursing home mass
is a lesson in love

February 7, 1979

The young priest walked among his elderly flock and touched their faces lightly, speaking soothing words as he called each of them by name. He told them they shouldn't be fooled by his beard: "I'm not Jesus Christ, I'm just Father Jim."

The middle-aged son was there, sitting in the back, outside the flock. He had arrived at mass much later than his mother, who was seated up front, in a wheelchair. Most of the flock were in wheelchairs, or shuffled slowly with the aid of walkers or canes.

This wasn't a church, it was a recreation room in a nursing home. Father Jim comes every Saturday afternoon to say mass at a makeshift altar. One candle was lit. There was no one to play the piano, so hymns were sung a cappella. The middle-aged son didn't know all the words.

He watched his mother as she sang. She looked toward the sound of the priest's voice, straining to see him with eyes that have failed her. He wondered how many thousands of masses his mother had heard since 1900, and how many times they had attended the same mass, with the mother up front, praying, and the son in back, a late arrival, not knowing all the words.

There were maybe 70 other patients at the mass. The middle-aged son watched them, too. There was a woman who couldn't stop her right leg from twitching violently. There was a woman who interrupted the service to say something that couldn't be understood and then slowly left the room.

Out in the hallway, there was a woman he sees every time he visits the nursing home. She can't propel her wheelchair with her hands, so she uses one foot. She thrusts the foot against the floor in front of her and drags the wheelchair forward, again and again and again. Sometimes her slipper comes off and it takes her many minutes to get her foot back into it. She doesn't want anyone to help her. She smiles at everyone.

There was an old man who wasn't a patient. He attended the mass with his wife, who appeared to be asleep in her wheelchair. The old man held his wife's head up, and he held her hand. The middle-aged

225

son later learned that the old man comes to the nursing home and sits by his wife's side all day, every day. She usually is not conscious. He usually holds her hand.

Before the mass was over, some unChristian thoughts pushed into the middle-aged son's mind. He thought of all he has read lately about suburban neighborhoods that don't want groups of old people living in their midsts. The suburbanites say the old people are breaking zoning ordinances and lowering property values. They hire smart lawyers and go to court and ask judges to order the old people to go away.

There are many younger people who claim they have nothing against old people but they "just don't like to be around them." To the middle-aged son, this is the most perplexing prejudice of them all.

You can be prejudiced against Negroes or Irishmen without worrying about waking up someday to discover you have become black or Irish. You'll always wake up the same nationality you were when you went to sleep — a native Idiot.

But someday you'll wake up old, or you won't wake up at all.

The middle-aged son was trying to decide what terrible punishment would be fitting for the idiots who run people out of neighborhoods because they're over 75. But then he remembered where he was, and he recalled that his mother had always advised him "to pay attention in church."

So he listened while Father Jim relayed the words of Jesus Christ. The priest's gentle preaching made the middle-aged son understand why some of the elderly flock might be fooled by his beard.

Toward the end of the mass, Father Jim suggested that his audience touch hands with those nearby and wish each other love and peace. The middle-aged son moved forward to kiss his mother. He wanted to tell her how sorry he was he didn't know all the words.■

The ache she left behind
is a nice one

April 18, 1979

The middle-aged son brought his mother violets for Easter. She wanted something else.

Actually, the violets were just an excuse for a visit that wasn't supposed to be made. The son wasn't scheduled to see his mother on Easter.

His large family is scattered across several cities, and there's usually no way all the members can attend the same holiday party. Most often, a few relatives get together in one town and a few others gather in other towns, and after dinner they all phone each other in memory of a departed uncle who worked for Michigan Bell.

For this Easter, the son and his mother were slated to eat ham in different towns. It shouldn't have made any difference to him. She wouldn't be alone on the important day; he had seen her the week before Easter, and he would see her again the week after.

And besides, as his wife reminded him, he always has claimed a day isn't special simply because the calendar says it's supposed to be special. When his wife says they have to be with their grandchildren on Dec. 25, he insists that Christmas is just as much fun on Dec. 27.

"The day you open the presents is Christmas, and the day you're locked out of the bank is Washington's birthday. It doesn't matter what the calendar says," the middle-aged son always growls. "A man brave enough to stretch tradition can avoid a lot of traffic by going on a Labor Day picnic in the middle of August."

His anti-calendar logic is unassailable. So how could he explain his compulsion to see his mother on Easter, even though he had a date to dine with other relatives many miles away from her? He tried flowers.

"Every son should give his mother flowers for Easter," he announced, rather stuffily. He went out and bought a dinky pot of African violets. He would have made a grander purchase, but he knew his mother already had received a huge Easter lily and other flowers from his sisters. There wasn't room for another big plant on the windowsill of her little room in the nursing home.

Why not have a flower shop deliver the violets? The middle-aged son didn't answer that question. But he did make a compromise against the calendar. He decided it really wasn't necessary to see his mother on Easter. He took the violets and drove to his old hometown the afternoon before Easter.

At the nursing home, he went directly to the recreation room where Easter mass was being said. Sunday mass is always a day early there, and it was the high point of every week for his mother. Her wheelchair was always in the same place, close to the makeshift altar. But on this Saturday, she wasn't there.

On his hurried way to his mother's room, the son talked to a nurse. He learned his mother suddenly had become very ill, while he was driving to visit her. She had been blind and weak for many months, but she had been able to visit her children and to enjoy picnic cocktail parties when they visited her. She had been his mother for more than 50 years, and he hadn't yet thought much about losing her.

He thought about it now. He mother was barely conscious. Her little sister (only 77) was at her side, as always.

"Boy, you must really be sick if you missed Easter mass," the middle-aged son said. "I hope the new pope is an understanding man."

She smiled. Perhaps she didn't really hear her son's lousy joke, but he hopes she did.

He held the little violets under her nose and asked if she could smell them. She didn't answer, ever.

It turned out that the son did see his mother on Easter Sunday. He saw her when she was transferred to a nearby hospital and tubes were inserted into her arms and nose. He watched while she struggled to breathe and the time between each breath grew longer and longer . . .

Early Easter morning, the mother died.

The middle-aged son isn't sad. He is grateful for whatever force compelled him to make an uncharacteristic visit to his mother. He is grateful for her; she was a marvelous mother. He also is grateful that she got more than violets for Easter.

What the mother really wanted was to die, and she often said so. The last year was rough on a beautiful lady who always loved to dance but could no longer see to walk. She was ready to leave.

It hurts to let go, but it's a mistake to hang on too long. The middle-aged son's ache will last much longer than the violets, but it's a nice ache that reminds him of how much his mother loved him — and how much he loved her.   ■

A party dedicated to Mother; she would have loved it

May 12, 1979

My brother-in-law from Cincinnati dropped his pants to the floor and pulled them back up in one continuous motion almost too fast to be detected by the human eye. This fleeting exposure of blue boxer shorts was offered for instructional purposes. It was not the highlight of our first family party since my mother's children became orphans.

The highlight came when this same brother-in-law, who is named Gabby, grew weary of the festivities and went upstairs to bed. As soon as he was snoring, several of Gabby's relatives filed silently into his darkened room and stood stiffly around his bed, like ghostly sentinels. Each of the relatives held a lighted candle.

This party was in the home of my sister, Terrible Jean, who lives in a suburb furnished electric power by the Detroit Edison Co. This explains the abundant availability of candles. Edison customers are frequently plunged into darkness by the failure of Edison technology to cope with drizzle weather, which is encouraging for the future. When all Edison power is furnished by nuclear reactors, customers will keep radiation-proof coveralls in their candle drawers.

Anyway, the candles around Gabby's bed were not lit out of necessity, but out of reverence, as in church. And while the small flames sent shadows flickering across the walls and ceiling, Terrible Jean led the assembled chorus in the slow singing of a mournful dirge.

The song was "Poor Judd Is Dead" from "Oklahoma" with "Gabby" substituted for "Judd." Only Terrible Jean knew all the words. She knows all the words to every song written and she keeps singing them, over and over, for fear she might forget them if she shuts up for five minutes.

"Rod Steiger played Judd in the movie version of 'Oklahoma,' " I whispered to my wife.

"It is poor taste to bore people to death while they are singing around a funeral pyre," she answered. She always has been jealous of my superior knowledge.

When Gabby opened his eyes to see what the noise was, he immediately stuck his head under a pillow. "I don't believe this is

229

happening," he said. "I can't believe that civilized adults would treat a fellow sleeping human being in such a shabby manner."

An outsider might agree with Gabby's evaluation. The people who held the candles are not silly teenagers. They are all middle-aged except for one brother-in-law, Jack, who is past middle, although a fine human being in his own right.

He married my second sister, Mary Lou, whose hair turned gray before she was 18. It wasn't until some time after the wedding, when Mary Lou dyed blond and Jack exhaled, that the generation gap became embarrassing. By then, it was too late, and there was nothing the in-laws could do except adjust to the situation graciously. When Jack comes to dinner, we always serve prunes.

However, despite his extreme maturity, Jack's presence never lends dignity to our family gatherings. In fact, he laughed loudest when Gabby dropped his pants to demonstrate how men of a certain ethnic background pull up their socks.

Once a man learns the fluid motion, he can grab the tops of his socks quicker this way than by hiking up his pant legs. It takes a lot of practice, but no one ever said it was easy being Irish.

You might think this party sounds too joyful, coming so soon after our mother's funeral. It couldn't be. No one liked a good party better than she did. During her last few months, she was no longer able to enjoy parties. But, until the day she died, she loved to hear her children tell about the good times they had while she was confined to her bed.

"Tell me what you've been doing," she always urged.

This will be my first Mother's Day without a mother. I can't tell her what her goofy kids did at their first party as orphans. Amid the laughs, they talked a lot about her. I wish I could tell her that, and I wish I could tell her about Gabby's socks, and about Terrible Jean leading the singing around Gabby's bed.

Lord, how Mother would laugh. Lord, how good it would be to hear her. ■

Her memories make an old soda jerk feel so good

May 7, 1983

There was a long-ago evening when someone decided it was again time to measure the family, to see how tall the children had grown in relation to their parents and to each other. But my mother refused to participate. That was strange.

The usual procedure was for family members to take turns standing back-to-back with each other, stiff and shoeless. There was keen competition between my younger sisters and me to see who was doing the best job of growing. We knew if we ever got as tall as Mother and Dad there was a chance that someday we might even be as big and strong as our much older sister, Terrible Jean.

It was early in 1942. I was 14 and proud to have recently landed my first real job — jerking sodas in a drugstore near our home. Mother lately had been phoning the drugstore to ask me to bring her ice cream sundaes — hot fudge on strawberry, or butterscotch on chocolate. Weird combinations. It never occurred to me there was a connection between her unusual tastes and her refusal to stand stiffly, back-to-back, with her very own children.

In declining to be measured, Mother simply explained she was too tired to stand up. We didn't believe her. We knew if, at that very moment, the doorbell rang, Mother would find the energy to dust and vacuum the entire house in the 30 seconds it took for a visitor to get inside and see if she were a good housekeeper.

But it didn't do any good to coax her. Family measuring was incomplete that night, and I didn't find out if I was as tall as Mother, which would have been halfway to Terrible Jean. We kids were puzzled by Mother's stubborn refusal; Dad probably wasn't.

The mystery was solved two months later when Mother finally decided it was time to tell her children the surprising news: She was pregnant. When a woman stands stiffly, back-to-back with someone else, it's easy to see if her stomach is swollen with child. Mother didn't want her big-mouthed kids to see too soon.

In those days it was common to keep gestations hush-hush until it was absolutely impossible for the woman to get into a non-maternity dress. And Mother thought she had an extra-good reason for secrecy.

She was 42 and it had been four years since the birth of her fourth —
and definitely last — child. As much as possible, she wanted to limit
the length of time the whole town had to talk about Gertrude
Fitzgerald being pregnant again, at her age.

Only a few weeks after Mother began wearing smocks, I came
home from the drugstore to find my aunt crying. I knew that was the
due date, and I was sure something had gone wrong.

Forty-one years later, when I remember the awful moment I saw
those tears, the terrible stab returns to my stomach .

But they were tears of joy. Mother and child were doing fine. I was
so relieved I didn't even care that I now had four sisters and still no
brother. One good thing about having a big sister like Terrible Jean is
it makes you appreciate little sisters.

On their first night out after the birth, Mother and Dad went to a
movie and then stopped at the drugstore. She was wearing a hat with
a little red bird on it and she looked like the happy mother of her first
child, not her fifth. And the soda jerk overheard a stranger whisper:
"Look at that beautiful woman!"

This Sunday I'll have Mother's Day dinner with several mothers I
love, but not with the mother I loved first. It is only my fifth Mother's
Day without her, and I'm still not used to it.

But I don't feel bad. I recall some of those lovely memories that
never dim, such as the time Mother refused to stand up and be
measured, or the night she walked into the drugstore and made me so
proud. And I feel good. ■

Peace and war . . .
and guns

You shoot your birds;
I'll eat cheeseburgers

May 27, 1976

The people of Colombia have been rescued from being beaked to death by rampaging doves.

And for writing that smartie sentence, I will have to explain once again how I can eat hamburgers.

It happens all the time.

I can't understand how hunters can enjoy killing. I laugh when they claim they are "harvesting a crop," not killing. I ask them why I've never seen a farmer drive through town with a bushel of rutabagas tied to his fender, headed for the newspaper office to have his picture taken with his vanquished vegetables?

And the hunters can't understand how I can enjoy eating steak if I am against killing animals. They laugh when I claim slaughterhouses won't bother me until they are featured on TV's American Sportsman with Rock Hudson knocking the steer's brains out with a golden hammer. They ask me how I can be so dumb as to not realize dead is dead, meat is meat, and there's not enough ketchup to change the taste?

It is a great and frequent argument which I've never won, or lost. And it's nothing personal. Some of my best friends go hunting all the time. When they return home, they always assure they never fired a shot for fear of hitting a waitress. But I think they are just trying to spare my Bambi stomach. I have been known to throw up on newspaper photos of snake hunts.

My favorite opponent is Preston Mann who operates the Hunters Creek hunting preserve about 50 miles north of Detroit. It is a slick operation with every convenience for outdoorsmen who don't have time to go outdoors. Mann's pheasants are trained to fly into the pockets of lunching auto executives and commit suicide.

Mann does not take my barbs peaceably. In fact, he is a master of the weird debate and I don't have a prayer in one-on-one combat. Just recently his local newspaper quoted him as revealing that I am actually a closet blood-sporter who lusts after innocent animals. Mann said he discovered my killer instinct during several years of watching me eat at his club. He said he could tell by the glint in my

235

eyes and the slobber on my lips everytime I bite into a cheeseburger, rare.

I mention this as some sort of solace to all of you hunters out there who, after reading this column, will want to send me nasty words. Don't bother. I've heard them all from the master, Mr. Mann. If he can't make me see the light at the end of the deer run, nobody can.

I can understand why Preston might think I eat meat with inordinate enjoyment. But he mistakes haste for lasciviousness. When dining at Preston's, I always eat the meat quickly before someone shoots it.

Actually, Mann's customers win points from me for honesty. They don't give you any harvesting baloney about killing to thin the herd or protect the grain. They go to hunting preserves for birds the same way their wives go the A&P for pork chops.

The birds are there to be killed, no other reason, and the hunter pays for every bird released in front of his gun. If he misses the first shot, the best-trained birds keep circling until hit. They get their training in carnival shooting galleries.

There is a difference between shooting pheasants at Preston's place and shooting doves in Cali, Colombia. No one could afford that much bloodshed at Preston's. The doves fly over by the thousands and, if you forget your shotgun, you can probably kill them with rocks. U.S. sportsmen can fly down for the dove hunts on Braniff Airways, which offers special excursion rates which are cheaper per bird than lunching at Preston's.

"It's like dying and going to paradise," a Bloomfield Hills attorney said as he killed doves quicker than he could count them. He was quoted in a sports page story which also said: "All afternoon they had come, a never-ending stream of gray birds. Our shoulders, which we had taken to padding with heavy handkerchiefs the day before, still ached. Earlier they had been actually bleeding from the kick of the gunstock." There is no bag limit. It is possible for one hunter to kill 600 doves in one day.

Forget about the danger to a species. Maybe Colombia has to be protected from takeover by doves. But what is the pleasure in killing them? Why would anyone spend hundreds of dollars and fly thousands of miles to shoot birds in a birdbath?

If that's sport, so is eating a hamburger.   ■

Menace of long hair
keeps Joint Chiefs busy

July 6, 1976

Several years ago, in New York, I left a dinner early to avoid hearing a speech by the nation's top military officer. Thus I probably blew my chance to learn inside information on why black soldiers tap-danced before dying in Vietnam.

I was reminded of this last week when the U.S. Senate OKd Gen. George S. Brown for a second term as chairman of the Joint Chiefs of Staff.

In 1974, in a speech to Duke University law students, Gen. Brown first went public as a bigot. You may remember. He explained that the trouble in the Mideast was that rich Jews owned all the banks and newspapers in the United States.

Gen. Brown probably felt safe parading his prejudices before a bunch of future lawyers. After all, lawyers were responsible for most of the Watergate tricks, including the famous break-in at the office of Daniel Ellsberg's psychiatrist. Everyone knows Ellsberg is not Protestant and the only reason he exposed the Pentagon Papers was so he could play the big shot at neighborhood bar mitzvahs.

But one of those Duke law students must have been a guy named Green with a nose job. Gen. Brown's speech was leaked through ivy walls and it became worldwide news, exposing him for what he really is — a typical high-ranking officer in the U.S. military.

President Ford immediately reprimanded Gen. Brown, threatening him with the loss of a valet if he didn't confine his future philosophizing to rest room walls.

And the Senate Armed Services Committee almost questioned Gen. Brown about his Duke remarks.

The proposal to grill the general finally was voted down 11-4. The senators were afraid the world might learn from the chairman of the Joint Chiefs of Staff that the United States bombed Cambodia because it was full of slant-eyed gooks.

Gen. Brown accepted amnesty gracefully. He apologized, admitting his remarks were "unfortunate and inaccurate." He promised he no longer would make speeches on subjects he knew nothing about and from then on would devote his full time to military duties.

237

At that time, I wrote that one of his military duties would be to bomb the Duke law school. In fact, I wrote several unkind things about the general and the military, including an anecdote about the time I walked out on a speech given by another chairman of the Joint Chiefs of Staff, Adm. Thomas Moorer. The result of my criticism was a widening of my experience with Joint Chiefs.

A letter arrived from Col. Norman Bedell, a former staff member of the Joint Staff, now retired in Ohio. He conceded that Gen. Brown's speech had been "ill-advised," but he chastised me for failing "to make clear that Gen. Brown's statement on Jewish influence was off the record."

I immediately wrote an apology and a clarification, pointing out that only those Duke law students were supposed to learn that this nation's top military officer was a biased jackass. If Brown wanted the entire world to know, he would have included kike jokes in his Morning Reports.

But back to the present, when the Senate committee asked Gen. Brown if he still believed what he'd said about Jews in 1974. "In all candor, I do," Gen. Brown answered.

Sen. Abraham Ribicoff, D-Conn., accused Brown of "anti-Semitism and religious bigotry." But his opinion did not prevail. The Senate voted, 57-34, to keep Brown on the job.

A lot of naive people have expressed shock that a bigot is chairman of the Joint Chiefs. This is because most people do not understand the function of the Joint Chiefs: the protection and the preservation of the short haircut. Every West Point graduate knows a short haircut is the bumper sticker of a true American. Hairy people are automatically furtive. It is much easier to find a communist in a bush if he is bald.

The test is that no lock of a man's hair should be longer than the first joint of his middle finger. It is up to Gen. Brown and the other chiefs to administer the joint test and to enforce necessary penalties.

So naturally they are called the Joint Chiefs.

Men charged with this tremendous responsibility hardly can be expected to have time for the niceties of civilization. They leave it to the pinko bleeding hearts to keep the Negroes in the front of the bus and the Jews out of the gas ovens.

The Joint Chiefs have more important things to do. They are ever-vigilant, protecting their nation from the long-hair menace.

As Gen. Brown might explain: "I can never lock up the joint and go home." ∎

Legionnaires disease
threatens our moral health

August 31, 1976

Perhaps Pennsylvania Gov. Milton Shapp could spend an evening in an American Legion post. Just to prove it is safe.

There is more than one type of Legionnaires disease, as Jimmy Carter could tell you.

A lot of people got sick, and some died, after attending a state American Legion convention in Philadelphia's Bellevue-Stratford Hotel. There never has been any proof that it was the hotel's fault, but there is always the suspicion. So tourists are staying at the Holiday Inn instead, and business is lousy at the Bellevue.

Gov. Shapp tried to do something about it. He spent the night at the Bellevue and came out alive and healthy in the morning. Which proves you don't have to worry about eating at the Bellevue if you are the governor of Pennsylvania.

I was a member of the American Legion for many years in several cities. For the first few years after World War II, when my underwear was still olive drab, I even attended some legion conventions.

Which prompted my first reaction to the mysterious Legionnaires disease. I thought some of those convention delegates might have been bored to death.

I have enjoyed some marvelous evenings in legion posts. That's where I learned how to play euchre, subsequently becoming the world's champion.

I also learned how to hold my liquor in a legion post (with both hands, and take it to the john with you).

It was mostly fun. But another thing I learned from the legion was to disappear when the meetings started. Especially if there was a visiting official from the state or national level.

It has been my experience that the higher a legion officer's rank, the more certain he is to make a 90-minute speech explaining that the only way to guarantee peace in New Jersey is to kill people in Cambodia.

You can be sure the audience was full of this type of storm trooper when Jimmy Carter spoke at the legion's national convention in

239

Seattle last week. Those guys never miss a convention, even if they have to pawn their anti-aircraft guns to get bus fare.

And when Carter said he would pardon Vietnam draft resisters, the legion yahoos booed for three minutes.

I quit paying my legion dues during the Vietnam war because of my teenage son.

The legion's national commmander was forever making brave speeches about how it was a shame that our nation's youth had to die, but their survivors should be proud that their sons had given their lives to stop the ever-widening scourge of communism.

At this same time, I was cautioning my son about the danger of leaving the house without bridge fare to Canada in his pocket. And it seemed only proper to give him the $7 a month I no longer was sending to the legion.

Fortunately, I got out before I caught the real Legionnaire disease. This is the illness which Jimmy Carter was exposed to when he dared to hint at the truth — that the young men who refused to fight an immoral war might have been right, and John Wayne might have been wrong.

The real disease can be best described by that old cliche: "Misery loves company."

Ask any veteran about the military. It is not fun and glory. It is boring and lonely at best. And at worst it is blood and misery and stink and weariness. It's degrading and stupid and cold and hot and it's the sudden loss of your best friend.

Most legionnaires know that. So why do many of them want every mother's son to become a soldier? Whey do they want revenge against any youth who refused a uniform? The answer is Legionnaires disease:

"By God, I went through the Battle of the Bulge for my country. Today's kids should do the same or first thing you know we'll no longer have the freedom to meet every Wednesday night and drink beer."

Two years ago the Detroit USO was forced to close because of failing patronage. What with no war, and no draft, there just weren't enough soldiers and sailors to keep the Ping-Pong balls bouncing.

If this marvelous trend should continue, someday there will be no legionnaires. Which is probably the only way to cure the disease. ■

Let's end wars on earth
before we take on the moon

February 7, 1977

Bob died the other day. He was my closest link to the tragedy of the Vietnam war.

I knew Bob for 26 years. We belonged to the same poker club for most of those years. We belonged to the Holiday Duffers Club which was eight men who met every warm holiday to play terrible golf together.

I don't think Bob agreed with half of the stuff I wrote through all those years. Certainly he didn't go along with my constant cooing during the Vietnam war. And for good reason.

But Bob never jumped on me for writing dumb things. Not seriously. He would call me a lousy golfer and a stupid poker player. He wouldn't call me a pinko traitor for uging amnesty for Vietnam draft dodgers. And he had good reason to call me worse than that.

A good friend can disagree with you without being disagreeable. Bob was a good friend. He was only 58 when a heart attack suddenly killed him. I find now, typing these inadequate words, that I cannot think of him without getting wet eyes.

I am thinking about a poker night in May of 1970. It was at Bob's house. It was the night I was struck by the big difference between two trips.

The Apollo 13 astronauts were on their way back from moon country. That's one of the trips. Between beers and shuffles, there was considerable talk about the three men risking their necks in space.

And later, when the space talk faded, Bob was asked the whereabouts of his wife. He explained that she was out of town but she would walk through that door at 10:20 p.m.

Which brings us to the second trip.

None of the other players asked Bob how he could be so certain of the time his wife would return. We knew. She had made the trip so many times before, and so had he, that it was easy to set the clock by their departures and arrivals.

At 10:20 p.m., she came through the back door.

For the umpteenth time, she had been visiting their son Ed at a

241

nearby veterans hospital. A year earlier, he had suffered a head wound in Vietnam. Now he was almost totally paralyzed, almost speechless.

That was seven years ago. Ed is now 29, and still spending most of his time in a hospital bed. That's the way it is going to be the rest of his life. And his mother and two brothers will spend the rest of their lives visiting him and bringing him home weekends and taking him to concerts.

That's how Bob spent the last eight years of his life, which ended way too soon. But Bob would not have complained about his burden if he had carried it until he was 95.

I haven't fully identified Bob's family because that's the way they want it. Their friends already know. They see no reason to parade their trouble before strangers. They don't want pity for their heartache. They don't want publicity for what they gave for their country.

I hope they'll understand why I find myself wondering again, the same things I wondered on the poker night of Apollo 13.

Three astronauts soared away and returned to the adulation and tears of an entire nation.

Thousands of boys went to Vietnam and returned battered, or in boxes. And only their families wept and really cared. And still care, and ache.

Sure, I was awed by the incredible technology and courage that put us on the moon. But I was saddened by a nation that sweat blood with the astronauts but didn't care that 300 men were killed in Vietnam the same week, and didn't care that hundreds more had been doomed to hospitals for life.

Who gave the most for his country? Who received the most in return? The astronauts now own airlines and make TV commercials. Ed is still paralyzed, and thousands of his fellow soldiers are still dead too young.

In 1970 I wrote: "Shoot me if you will, but I don't give a damn about trips to the moon. Not as long as my friends are making trips to that hospital."

I feel the same way today. Bob has made his last visit, but his son is still in the hospital. And this is still an armed world where we must point guns at them because they are pointing guns at us.

In memory of all the Bobs, and all the Eds, someday the guns must be put down. Someday there must be an end to the flag-draped caskets and the trips to the hospital.

Then it will be time to take a trip to the moon. ■

It's much harder being
top dog than enlisted man

June 4, 1977

A long time ago I was a sergeant about to be discharged from the Army after winning World War II. A colonel wondered if I would rather go to West Point and become an officer and a gentleman. He said he could arrange it and he obviously expected me to be overwhelmed at the honor.

I turned him down for the same reason, a few years earlier, I had rejected membership in the Boy Scouts.

Scouts must pledge to keep themselves "physically strong, mentally awake and morally straight." For me, yet today, it is a weary thing to even think of keeping such a ramrod pledge. I was always a skinny kid who fell asleep reading dirty books.

West Point cadets must pledge "not to lie, cheat, steal or tolerate those who do." I explained to the colonel that I planned to attend college with the help of the GI Bill of rights, and I planned to graduate even if I had to cheat on tests. And if I got caught cheating, I wanted to be reprimanded by the teacher, not investigated by Congress.

Subsequent events proved I was grooving on the correct philosophy. Otherwise I wouldn't be writing about it 30 years later. You think I'm going to write a column admitting I was wrong?

My philosophy can best be described through proverbs. Such as: The higher you fly, the bigger grease spot you make when your parachute doesn't open.

Or: The purer you aspire the more heads you turn when you suffer an attack of gas.

Or: Mud looks worse on a white suit.

I could open a lot more Confucius cookies but that's enough wisdom for now. You get the idea: When a truck driver murders his wife, it is back-page stuff. But when a U.S. senator clangs on a love triangle, Walter Cronkite is there before the body stops twanging.

When I rejected the Boy Scouts and West Point, I knew what I was doing. I was seeking the security of obscurity rather than risking the shame of fame.

There would never be any "Ex-Eagle Scout Robs Bank" headlines about me. There would never be any front-page stories describing

243

how I was caught cross-eyed during the West Point biology examination, with answers tattooed on my nose.

Remember three years ago, when some top Boy Scout leaders were caught cheating? The whole nation gasped.

The leaders had borrowed a trick from politicians who dig votes out of cemeteries. Paper scouts were created to meet membership quotas, impress national headquarters and qualify for a bigger allotment of sticks to rub together.

This was not nice, of course. Mythical scouts leave a lot of knots untied and a lot of little old ladies stranded on curbs. But is padding membership rolls really a front-page sin, deserving of nationwide scorn and ridicule? Only if you're the Boy Scouts.

The latest cheating scandal at West Point is just one more example of the risks involved in high aspirations. It is a marvelous thing to become a cadet. Only the finest are chosen by their congressmen. The young men become instant celebrities in their hometowns, with successful futures assured.

Unless they get caught with the answers to a math test stuck inside their olive drab socks. Then it is instant disgrace and dismissal.

Can this nation afford to be led into nuclear warfare by men who couldn't crib at arithmetic without getting caught? Certainly not.

But is the offense worthy of national trauma, with front-page confessions accompanied by box scores revealing the number of students who cheat always, some of the time or just when nobody is looking?

Only if the students are West Pointers.

I've done a lot worse things than holler "here" six times when the scout leader took attendance. I could never have passed Spanish II if I hadn't sat behind Rosita Gonzales.

But who cares? Nobody ever expected much of me anyway. That's the way I planned it.

I lived my formative years so as to make my adult years look good by comparison. My family and childhood companions have to be proudly surprised at anything I accomplish outside the occupational therapy room at the state penitentiary.

When a West Point cadet is convicted of cheating, part of his punishment is to serve two years as an enlisted man. A lot of us slobs would consider this a reward.

Enlisted men have more room to go Onward and Upward — and Sideways. ■

Guns are bad for children
who like to have their ears nuzzled

February 13, 1978

Melissa doesn't care. But Anwar Sadat, president of Egypt, says he will "raise hell" if the United States doesn't sell him as many weapons as it sells to Israel.

Melissa is only five years old. She doesn't know enough to be disturbed by the bloody fact that IRA terrorists are outshooting the police in London because the terrorists have superior machine guns — made in America.

Melissa is my granddaughter. Her youth excuses her from throwing up at the knowledge that her country makes money selling death to other countries. Adults don't have that excuse, but most of us are equally unsick in the face of the nauseating truth. It's easy to have a strong stomach when you can't see the blood spurt.

I was reminded of Melissa, and also of the most obscene advertisement ever written, when I read about Sadat's anger.

I was reading the obscene ad a couple of years ago when Melissa leaped into my lap, crushing my newspaper. And I thought how glad I was that she was so young and didn't want me to explain the world to her.

The obscene ad wasn't for a dirty movie or a massage parlor. It was for Bell helicopters. It was selling a good way to kill someone else before they kill you.

Isn't that lovely? I squeezed Melissa and nuzzled that great spot just below and behind her ear. She kicked and ripped my paper some more, and I didn't care.

The ad headline said; "Enemy Tank Attack! You Can Stop It Fast With the World's Most Effective Anti-Tank system. Bell's Armed Helicopter — the Cobra."

The weapon hucksters merchandise death with the same glibness used to erase bad breath and make your teeth sparkle.

When I first glanced a the ad, I thought it was selling war toys. Just a small obscenity. But this was the real thing. Bell builds these helicopters for just one purpose — to kill people and destroy property.

The ad bragged that the helicopters will furnish "heavy fire against hard targets."

Hard targets? How hard is a young man's head? How hard is that great nuzzling spot just below and behind a child's ear?

But don't you worry. The helicopter ad was for foreign publications only, such as the magazine Modern Asia. The hard targets are all over there. Everything is cool in the good old USA. We aren't getting bombed and we aren't bombing anybody.

Sure, our industries make the military hardware and our State Department arrange sales to warring nations. Sometimes our men teach their men how to shoot straight. But what the hell?

A guy has to make a buck, doesn't he? The ammunition industry feeds a lot of sweet American faces. If we don't sell 'em guns, Russia will. And you must remember what Kissinger always said — if Cambodia falls, there goes your neighborhood.

It is easy for me to be against all guns, wherever for whatever. I'm against fists and loud arguments. And if I won't buy my grandson a toy pistol, I sure don't want my tax money helping Jews to drop bombs on Arabs, or vice versa.

It's that simple. Also simplistic, I admit. So shoot me. You've probably got a gun handy. Not because you want to hurt anyone, but because you belong to the National Rifle Association, the world's best-regulated militia, with the most arms to bear.

There are probably some Bell helicopter executives and some Pentagon brass who favor gun controls to keep our streets safe. Think about it. Sob.

It isn't so much that I am Percy Humanitarian. I'm not nearly as interested in unloading foreign guns as I am in preserving my own skin, which pricks easily. And I feel a lot safer when there are no guns around — anywhere.

Most selfishly, I worry about the most innocent skin of all. Melissa's skin.

My Melissa, your Melissa, and their Melissa.　■

The Navy knows asbestos
can't speak for itself

May 22, 1978

The Associated Press recently reported: "The Navy banned asbestos as thermal insulation in new ships as of Jan. 9, 1973, the Navy's asbestos spokesman, Lt. Jim Bullock, said."

It should be comforting for U.S. citizens to know asbestos has a spokesman in the Navy. This nation has not always been so fortunate.

My friend Ralph was in the Navy during World War II. Yesterday he snorted when I asked him who spoke for the Navy's asbestos when he was a sailor.

"Nobody," he said. "I was stationed aboard a carrier that was completely insulated with asbestos. Many times I wondered how the asbestos thought the war was coming along but I could never find out because the asbestos had no spokesman."

To a civilian, it may seem strange. Years ago, when all the Navy's ships were full of asbestos, there was no asbestos spokesman. But today, five years after asbestos has been banned from all ships, the Navy has a full lieutenant whose job is speaking for asbestos.

If the Navy no longer has any asbestos, what does Lt. Jim Bullock find to speak about? Are the taxpayers paying him to simply holler, "There's no one here" whenever anyone knocks on the door of the room where the Navy used to keep its asbestos?

Exactly. But Bullock's job is not as frivolous as it might sound. Union executives recently have accused the Navy of using asbestos on four ships commissioned in 1976, three years after the ban was declared. If these charges weren't answered by Bullock, the asbestos spokesman, the asbestos would have to speak for itself. No one wants that.

Asbestos was banned because it causes cancer. HEW Secretary Joseph Califano recently warned that as many as 5.6 million Americans may die of cancer or other diseases as a result of exposure to asbestos in shipyards and other workplaces.

Cigarets also cause cancer, but Congress continues to force taxpayers to subsidize the tobacco industry. This is a humanitarian subsidy, designed to prevent unemployment among congressmen from tobacco states.

In some quarters, there is the suspicion that the Navy is treating the asbestos industry as kindly as Congress treats the tobacco industry. Again, the motive would be to prevent unemployment. If the asbestos industry went broke, it couldn't hire any retired admirals.

Andy Abbott is president of the Metal Trades Council at the naval shipyard in Long Beach, Calif. He says Navy officials told him new ships are being built without asbestos insulation.

"But our experience here has been that we haven't seen any come out asbestos-free yet," Abbott told the Associated Press.

Abbott named four ships that, he claimed, had asbestos insulation on pipes. The Navy confirmed the ships were built long after the asbestos ban. But was asbestos used?

Only one man could answer that question, of course. He was Lt. Bullock, the asbestos spokesman. His answer was that it would be several days before he could comment.

This nation can sleep secure in the knowledge that its Navy has an asbestos spokesman who thinks before he speaks.

Any dumb lieutenant immediately could ask the captains of those four ships to check the pipes for asbestos insulation. But such a hurried procedure could result in wrong answers. Lt. Bullock might be forced into areas beyond his qualifications. Inadvertently, he might speak for some insulation other than asbestos, perhaps even an insulation that hadn't been banned for causing cancer. This is no way to run an efficient Navy.

How does the Navy find such fine asbestos spokesmen? I asked a recruiter.

"We try to enlist men with experience," he said. "Right now I'm recruiting a man who spent 10 years as the botulism spokesman for a restaurant that banned spoiled food." ■

The little dancing girl
in the Happy Hour Cafe

February 21, 1979

Recently I mentioned spending time at Camp Polk, La., during the big war. This prompted a reader to ask if I remember the Happy Hour Cafe, where she used to be an infant waitress. Ah, yes . . .

The Happy Hour was near the bus stop in Leesville, one of the most famous Army towns of World War II. Leesville became famous when it was featured in a Life magazine article concerning the dozens of little towns that suddenly boomed when large military installations were opened nearby.

Leesville, about 10 miles from Camp Polk, was typical. It was a drowsy, one-street, one-theater, one-general-store town with elderly men sitting on benches in front of the courthouse and cows grazing on the edges of downtown.

Then the Army moved in, with the quick-buck guys following close behind. Suddenly there was package liquor for sale in dozens of "new" stores built out of old orange crates in 30 minutes. Bars grew like weeds, and traveling hookers parked their mobile homes for the duration. Business was khaki — and great.

This booze-prostitute aspect was stressed in the Life article, making Leesville sound like a wicked place indeed. I suppose it was, but I was there almost a year, and the most wicked thing I remember doing is taking one of those grazing cows into the barracks and tying it to the foot of a sleeping friend.

It was Alwynelle Self Ahl of East Lansing who reminded me of Leesville. Her grandfather, Duke Parker, owned the Happy Hour Cafe. She wrote: "I was born in Leesville in 1941, and my earliest memories are of the soldiers coming into the Happy Hour for good food and jukebox music (not liquor as the name might imply). Since 'help' was short, my parents, both teachers, helped my grandfather with his cafe on their time off, especially nights and weekends. They let me 'help,' too.

"This entailed being a waitress (memorizing orders, since I couldn't write) and helping the soldiers select music from the jukebox and, on occasion, 'dancing' by special request. I must have reminded many a soldier of a child left at home because my tips for

249

waitress service were sometimes very large indeed ($5 seemed impossibly large to me then) . . .

"I remember the excitement on a Friday about 5 p.m., waiting for the soldiers to come into the cafe and make us all busy and make the music play. I remember being sad when told that the soldiers wouldn't be coming anymore, not understanding that the end of a war was a great thing for my playmates, the soldiers . . .

"I remember Leesville and the soldiers, and your column brought back all these memories, and reminded me of the many lives that were partially lived there because of the war . . . "

Thirty-four years later, it seems unlikely that I would remember the Happy Hour Cafe. Lord knows I've been glad to forget hundreds of other restaurants I've eaten in since 1945. But I do remember the Happy Hour.

I remember it because of the cute little girl who played with the soldiers there, who reminded me of my little sisters and made me wish I could see them, even if they were terrible pests. I can't remember anything about the food at the Happy Hour, but I can remember that little girl.

And now, almost two generations later, the teenage soldier has become a grandfather; the little girl long ago learned how to write, and she has written him a letter, wondering if he might have been one of the soldiers she remembers. The nostalgia is overwhelming, and my eyes are wet, but I am not sure why.

Two years ago I returned to Leesville for the first time out of uniform. The town has grown and changed beyond recognition since 1945. The Happy Hour is no more. But Camp Polk looks much the same. It's now called Ft. Polk, a permanent Army installation where teenage soldiers still are being trained to kill.

Some things never change. Maybe that's why my eyes are wet. ■

A pot of peace would have
made it a perfect rainbow

June 25, 1979

The rainbow happened during the SALT II negotiations. I made a note of it so I wouldn't forget. I could see both ends touch the ground. I had never before seen both ends of a rainbow at the same time.

I made the note on a pad that's always on the table beside my chair at home. The chair sits beside a large window on the 26th floor. It is a marvelous spot from which to watch a rainbow. But I usually watch TV.

I felt poetic as I jotted the note. I promised myself that it later would remind me to write many lyrical paragraphs about the majesty of that magnificent rainbow. I would write that Mork and Mindy can make money, but only God can make a rainbow. Real cornball stuff. For a minute, that crazy rainbow really got to me.

But the note subsequently became lost in the clutter of clippings and trash on my table. I forgot about it, and I forgot about the rainbow.

There were more important things to think about. The SALT II treaty, for instance. That required a lot of thinking.

The way I understand it, Russia and the United States are promising each other to limit the number of nuclear weapons they will aim at each other. The only limit on the limit is that it must never be so stringent as to prevent both sides from destroying each other whenever the need arises.

The people favoring the treaty admit it falls somewhat short of tranquility, but they claim it is at least a step away from Armageddon. You have to be more than a step away to survive the fallout, but walking is good for you.

Those people opposed to SALT II have different reasons. Some Americans say they're against the treaty because the sneaky Russians will break it. Some Russians say they're against it because the shifty Americans will break it. Some citizens of both nations say they're against the treaty because it doesn't have to be broken to be no good.

I spent several days trying to make up my mind about SALT II. All this time, the rainbow note remained unread under a growing pile of Rolaid wrappers. On the evening of June 20, I had about decided to support the treaty. No matter how dismal the forecast, I always end up rooting for first steps to pick up speed and someday arrive at peace. Good lord, I still support the United Nations.

The TV news was on, but I wasn't paying much attention. Something about the fighting in Nicaragua. Something about a news correspondent being killed. What?

Holy Jesus! A soldier put his gun against the head of a civilian lying on the ground and pulled the trigger. There was a small puff of smoke. The body jerked under the impact of the bullet.

This wasn't Starsky and Hutch. This was murder. Just before the soldier shot, he kicked the newsman in the stomach. Does the SALT II treaty say anything about kicking before killing?

Civilization has become so push-button sophisticated it can wipe itself out at 3 o'clock and show film of the final writings on the 6 o'clock news. Does SALT II say anything about the last person to writhe turning off the TV set?

As long as there are guns — of whatever size — they will be shot. Total disarmament is a pipe dream for trusting fools. Peace treaties offer comfort for the hopeful, but hope never swerved an intercontinental ballistic missile.

A few minutes after the Nicaragua murder, I accidentally found the note reminding me I'd seen both ends of the same rainbow. So I quit thinking about treaties and wars and other things made by humans. Instead, I thought about the shimmer and brilliance of a perfect rainbow arched across the sky. I thought about all the splendid things human beings can't make and are too dumb to appreciate. Deep stuff.

The north end of the rainbow touched the grass in the park directly below my window. The south end touched down on the riverbank five blocks away. If you don't ask, I won't tell you there was no pot of peace at either end. ■

The delicate balance between guns and video games

May 4, 1983

Don't be dismayed by how much it costs you to furnish the weapons needed to stop the bloodshed in Central America. Never mind the confusion caused by President Reagan's speeches. Taxpayers have good reason to be grateful.

First, the Cost and the Confusion:

"The total amount requested for aid to all of Central America in 1984 is about $600 million. That is less than one-tenth of what Americans will spend this year on coin-operated video games," the president said April 27.

His meaning appeared clear: Because they spend much more playing unimportant games, taxpayers shouldn't gripe about buying important guns for Central American military forces.

But what about the speech Reagan made in March at Disney World? He told 500 teenagers:

"Many young people have developed incredible hand, eye and brain co-ordination in playing these (video) games. The Air Force believes these kids will be outstanding pilots should they fly our jets. Watch a 12-year-old take evasive action and score multiple hits while playing 'Space Invaders' and you will appreciate the skills of tomorrow's pilots."

So, will the real Mr. President please stand up and tell confused taxpayers which really is most important — helping El Salvador kill guerrillas, or training our youngsters to make multiple hits?

It's a tough question. Both actions have the same goal — to prevent bloodshed and preserve peace. And if you think supplying guns to foreign soldiers or training American youngsters to drop bombs is no way to accomplish that noble goal, you simply don't understand how to achieve modern peace.

You don't understand that the best way to save a man from drowning is to hold him under water until he stops struggling to reach shore where he would breathe free in some dumb village that will probably have to be destroyed to be saved anyway.

It would be nice to believe Reagan didn't really intend to imply that "Space Invaders" is unimportant. Many of us remember what happened during the Vietnam war when President Johnson failed to collect enough taxes to pay for both guns and butter. To prevent a similar embarrassment, it is President Reagan's duty to make sure the United States can afford both military aid and video games.

After all, what does it profit a nation if it stamps out guerrilla warfare in El Salvador but fails to produce children who know how to make multiple hits?

Sure, it will cost billions of dollars for the United States to continue pumping quarters into video machines while, at the same time, providing the weapons required to prevent the Soviet Union from circulating the writings of Karl Marx among Central American peasants and converting them from thriving capitalists into struggling socialists.

But the marvelous results — such as 12-year-olds who can take evasive action and missile bases in Costa Rica — would be worth the money.

And besides — this is what you should be grateful for — taxpayers don't have it as tough as you think. U.S. News & World Report reported it will cost taxpayers $27 million this year to provide protection, pensions and various services to our three living ex-presidents. But there was a gratifying quote concerning Gerald Ford, who gets $100,000 a year plus $249,200 for office expenses from the government to go along with the millions he earns making speeches, sitting on boards and investing wisely.

Ford is entitled to free mailing privileges for his official, but not personal, correspondence and, according to his senior aide, "Whenever we're in doubt, we put a stamp on the envelope."

Wow. Because of such freewheeling generosity, Ford sometimes may pay 20 cents for postage that rightfully should be charged to taxpayers!

Knowing that, who among you would be ungrateful enough to gripe about having to finance both military aid and video games? ■

Be on the lookout for reckless prayers for peace

August 15, 1983

Citizens of Walled Lake can breathe easier since the arrest and jailing of four people for playing peace games. Unfortunately, the situation isn't that secure in Marquette.

There were also four people arrested near Marquette for playing peace games at the K.I. Sawyer Air Force Base. Their crime included kneeling and praying. But three of them quickly were released and, at this very moment, are free to wantonly kneel and pray in unsuspecting communities anywhere in Michigan or all of the United States. You should be on the lookout for them.

Everyone knows what war games are. Military-type people gather together to shoot guns and other weapons. Tanks and planes and aircraft carriers are often used. It's just a game, but participants really must pretend they're playing for keeps or it isn't any fun.

The twofold purpose of war games is to practice for real war and to impress onlookers with a mighty show of force. It is hoped the onlookers will be so frightened, they never will raise a hand against the war-game players.

Peace games are not nearly as well-known and popularly accepted as war games. In fact, people arrested for kneeling and praying never are specifically charged with playing peace games because most police and prosecutors don't recognize a peace game when they see it. Instead, peace-game players are usually charged with trespassing.

People never are arrested for playing war games, of course. That's because the war-game players are only practicing how to kill people; they never pretend to do anything worse, such as trespass.

The twofold purpose of peace games is to practice for real peace and impress onlookers with a mighty show of pacifism. It is hoped the onlookers will be so enamored , they will touch hands with the peace-game players and ask to join the game.

Among the four peace-game players arrested at Walled Lake were such notorious kneelers and prayers as a Catholic priest and a Methodist minister. A nervous public, leery of becoming enamored, was reassured when a newspaper photo revealed police didn't take the two clergymen into open court without first chaining their hands together.

The minister and priest, along with two women, had trespassed on property owned by Williams International Corp., a manufacturer of cruise-missile engines. To commemorate the 38th anniversary of the atomic destruction of Nagasaki ("One cruise equals 16 Nagasakis"), they put burning candles and red dye in Williams' reflecting pool. For this, they got 30 days in jail plus $250 fines.

So, for a month, Walled Lake is a safer place to live. The candles and dye symbolized the Nagasaki victims who leaped into the river to ease the pain of their burns and turned the water red with their blood. It's too bad all those people were killed by an atom bomb, of course. But do we live in a civilized society, or don't we? When Williams executives look into their reflecting pool, they shouldn't have to see the debris of peace games. They should have to see themselves.

War games are much more socially acceptable than peace games. Sure, war games also leave debris behind. Sometimes that debris even explodes and kills bird-watchers. And it can't be denied that war games damage the environment and cost taxpayers millions of dollars. But at least war games don't trespass.

War games provide the practice required if a nation is to have the capability of killing lots of people and frightening onlookers. War games are an integral part of a wise national defense policy.

On the other hand, peace games are nothing less than a blatant, unforgivable violation of this nation's "No Trespassing" signs.

Don't you forget it. Also, remember what happened in Marquette and, for Christ's sake, be on the lookout for wanton kneelers and prayers. ■

A bystander never bled to death from a stray table leg

June 22, 1983

How many people have been killed by a stray table leg? Why isn't there a National Table Leg Association?

Those questions were put to my Cousin Al, a lifetime member of the National Rifle Association. He joined the NRA while still a newborn in the maternity ward because he realized he could be stuck by a stray diaper pin. Young Al's reasoning was pins don't stick people, people do, and it was his constitutional right to use a gun to protect his crib from an invasion of the pin nuts.

During a recent three-day period, in three separate incidents, three Detroiters were killed by stray bullets. In one of those cases, a young man apparently intended to shoot a neighbor, but accidentally shot his mother instead. A witness told a news reporter, "Everybody has a gun. They think this is the Wild West or something."

It is my contention no home should have a gun because people who live in homes sometimes reach for their guns during domestic arguments that could be settled with less damage if explosive weapons weren't readily available. And every time I express that type of anti-firepower wisdom, Cousin Al says if people didn't have guns to kill with, they'd break up the furniture and club each other to death with table legs.

But how many innocent people have been killed while caught in a crossfire of table legs?

Or how about kitchen knives? Cousin Al says angry people who don't own guns or table legs often reach for kitchen knives.

One of those three Detroiters killed by a stray bullet was hit while walking on the sidewalk. The shooting was part of a passing car chase, just like on TV every night. How many people throw kitchen knives at each other from moving cars? How many of those kitchen knives miss their intended targets and stray into a non-combatant's flesh?

Cousin Al said my questions were dumb. He conceded that U.S. citizens use guns more often than table legs to kill each other. "But that's only because they have guns," he said. "If they didn't have

257

guns, they'd use table legs, and just as many people would be murdered."

So in Great Britain, where there are only a few guns compared to the U.S., why aren't there more legless tables? Why aren't there anti-table-leg zealots screaming for stricter table-leg controls?

Why isn't there a British National Table Leg Association to point out that if there were a law against public ownership of table legs, only outlaws would have table legs?

Cousin Al said I was being silly, so I got serious. I told him about three young members of my family who witnessed a fistfight at the Irish Festival in downtown Detroit last week. For a few seconds they were close enough to the action to get hit with a stray punch.

What if one of those fistfighters had been an NRA member who never went downtown without a gun to implement his constitutional right to protect himself and his family against aggressive panhandlers? How would Al feel if one of his cousins were hit by a stray bullet?

"I would feel bad, but you can't have a free country without taking some risks," Al said. "If you limit my right to carry a gun, you may leave me defenseless against the outlaws who never will give up their guns, no matter what, and I'll have a lot more to worry about than getting hit with a stray bullet."

I conceded that strict gun controls — confiscation of handguns, for instance — might possibly give the outlaws an advantage in the short run, but at least they would have to furnish their own guns and couldn't depend on stealing them from their victims.

And the long-run benefit would be that in 50 years or so, our grandchildren won't be able to reach for guns when they disagree. And very few sons will accidentally kill their mothers with a stray table leg.

Onward and Upward, without a bang. ■

Children should be hugged, not dressed to kill

April 18, 1984

I'm trying to think of a peace game to counteract the war game advertised by Hudson's in newspaper ads last week. How should children dress to not kill?

A mother handed me the ad. The headline read: "Kids' Camouflage — Authentic Military Wear for Kid-size Tactics." Pictured were two little boys dressed in "Airborne" combat uniforms of muted colors designed to blend with the terrain and allow the wearer to sneak up on the enemy and shoot him in his sleep.

"Attention!" the ad read. "GI Joe gear . . . the tough new look for kids, has invaded Hudson's. And it's ready for action. From combat with the jungle-gym to roughing it on the weekends, all your backyard maneuvers will be a lot more fun in camouflage clothes. So kids, get into uniform!"

"That's just lovely," the mother said. "Now I can have my own little terrorist in my home, properly dressed for covert killing. If I can't afford to buy my son a combat uniform, the CIA probably will give me the money."

Certainly. It is important that children be properly equipped to pretend to wage war, just like real live adults. Otherwise, the kids might grow up not knowing how to wipe out entire villages and destroy tall buildings with a single bomb.

Last week in Detroit, a little boy found a real gun while visiting in a neighbor's home. He accidentally killed himself with it. His mother explained to a reporter: "He had a toy gun that he was crazy about. It was kind of hard to pull the trigger, and he discovered he could do it if he turned it around. I guess he saw this gun sticking out and . . . The bullet hit him in the forehead above the right eye. He would have been three on June 4."

I'm sorry. The loss of a child does not lend itself to sarcasm. It's not easy to write the obvious — that if the boy hadn't played with a pretend gun, he might not have known how to operate a real gun. I ache for his mother and don't want to add to her hurt. Certainly she isn't to blame for a violent culture in which real guns are so ordinary that it's hardly surprising when a child finds one under a pillow.

But I also ache when I see advertisements for "GI Joe gear" that encourage youngsters to play war games. GI Joe, the combat doll, died in 1976, struck down by anti-Vietnam-war fervor and the high price of plastic, but he's making a big comeback under the Reagan administration.

Military weapons are popular again today, and the manufacturers of GI Joe solved the plastic problem by cutting his height from 11½ to 3¾ inches. Children who remember the old GI Joe probably are told he was down-sized by the dirty Commies who used an illegal shrinking gas in a futile attempt to prevent Joe from roller skating in the Kremlin. "Combat roller skates" are part of GI Joe's official gear, honest to God.

A child's pretend world of toys always reflects the grown-up world. "With Reagan in power and defense spending up, there is a political climate in favor of guns," said Professor Brian Sutton-Smith, who has studied children's play at the University of Pennsylvania. If people believe in the president's defense policies, he said in 1982, "they will be more easygoing about their kids buying guns." Also more easygoing about their kids dressing like GI Joe in authentic military wear camouflaged for stealthy killing while playing war games. (Jacket, $18. Insignia T-shirts, $6. Pants, $18. All in cotton/polyester. Sizes S-M-L for boys' 8-20, at all Hudson's stores.)

But what would be nice in cotton/polyester for kids whose parents don't want them dressed to kill? I don't know. The extreme opposite of covertly killing people is to love them openly — and that sounds so corny I cringe as I write it.

Any fool knows how to hug a child. But no one knows how a department store can make lots of money by advertising: "Authentic Anti-war Wear for Kid-size Peace Games." ■

What's all this non-violence, for peace's sake!

March 19, 1984

It is easy to commit a crime while playing peace games, especially if you play in Oakland County, where Prosecutor L. Brooks Patterson bravely protects the public from all dangerous persons gathered together in church gymnasiums to conspire against the joys of a nuclear holocaust.

It is hard to commit a crime while playing war games, especially if you play in Washington, D.C., where violence is a trillion-dollar business and Pentagon generals retire to become highly paid "defense entrepreneurs."

A recent study by the General Accounting Office, which watchdogs government operations for Congress, charged that military spending from 1984 through 1988 likely will be around $324 billion more than original Pentagon estimates. The Pentagon said it would spend nearly $1.8 trillion but the GAO suggested the actual cost could top $2 trillion.

Although they supply the money, average taxpayers find it difficult to visualize just how much a trillion dollars is. Look at it this way: A billion is a thousand millions, and a trillion is a million millions. Multiply a trillion by a billion and you come up with the average number of times the average taxpayer is robbed by the average military procurement officer on an average Tuesday afternoon.

The GAO said its prediction of the $324 billion overrun was based on the historical fact that the Pentagon always underestimates the cost of weapons by at least 32 percent. And it is well-known worldwide that the Pentagon will go to any length to maintain its cost-overrun record, even if a general has to somehow find a defense manufacturer willing to sell a $2 tank part for $5,678 instead of the usual $3,452.

You think that's a crime? Don't be silly. Pentagon war-game players who waste taxpayers' money not only escape penalty for incompetency or thievery, they often are rewarded with far more than ordinary military pay and junkets to weapon demonstrations held in Las Vegas casinos.

A good example was provided by a recent advertisement in a

Washington newspaper. Under a headline reading "Defense Entre-preneurs" it said: "Want your own business? If you leave govern-ment, will you leave friends behind? If so, we'll set you up as a division of a national corporation and give you equity, as well as a top salary with tax sheltered benefits!!" Procurement officers due to retire and reluctant to leave the warmth of the taxpayers' pocket could respond to a box number at the Washington Post. That's nice.

After civilian auditors recently revealed the Army paid around $35 million more than it was supposed to for some helicopters, the Army didn't bother to ask the manufacturer for a refund. It is nice to know there is fruitful employment waiting for any retiring Army officer experienced enough to realize $35 million isn't worth retriev-ing, just as long as it's tax money spent on war games.

Compare the treatment of the Pentagon's wild-spending war-game players to that given the 50 people, including ever-dangerous nuns and ministers, arrested for playing peace games in Oakland County. Many of them served 30-day sentences for trespassing and blocking traffic while protesting war outside a missile-engine plant. They were prepared to accept that much punishment, just as Martin Luther King put on his going-to-jail clothes before hitting the streets. But thanks to the extreme zealousness of Prosecutor Patterson and his infiltrating troops, the peace-game players also face varied conspiracy charges that could put them in prison for a year.

Of course, we must remember it's a crime to conspire to trespass in the name of peace. But it's no crime to gyp taxpayers out of $100 tril-lion in the name of war. It's just an oversight.

If Washington's war-game players waste enough, they may become defense entrepreneurs. If Oakland County's peace-game players conspire enough, they may become convicts. That's criminal justice in the United States. Go get 'em, Brooks. ∎

Yesterdays remembered

Terrible Jean revisited:
A brother's clutching tale

May 15, 1976

Thank you, Abdullah Sheik. Now I have a name for the only right thing I ever did to Terrible Jean. It was the Camel Clutch.

I read about the Sheik on the sports page. He is a professional wrestler and he is helping train Muhammad Ali for his boxing-grappling match-bout with a Japanese wrestler next month.

Wrestling is the only thing dumber than boxing, and the Indianapolis 500 is dumber than both of them. But I still read the sports pages every day, trying to find out whatever happened to Boots Poffenberger. He pitched ball and nonsense for the Detroit Tigers many years ago, about the same time Terrible Jean's favorite sport was pounding me into the ground.

Terrible Jean is the oldest and most fearsome of my four formidable sisters. I grew up in her shadow. So did most of our neighborhood which, thanks to her, didn't need trees for shade. What I mean is she was a big girl, older, heavier and meaner than her only brother, a sweet boy who was so non-violent he protested against the Vietnam war in 1935. I watched while the Blue Water Bridge to Canada was constructed within sight of our home in Port Huron and I daily cheered the workers as they brought two great nations closer together. Even at the age of 10 I realized the bridge someday would be a great thing for draft dodgers.

Thirty-five years later I still have psychological scars from growing up in constant fear of being maimed by a shade tree with her skirt tucked into her bloomers. A scar quivered the other day when I received a letter from Dolores Messing who lives in Southfield near Terrible Jean. Mrs. Messing asked why I had failed to report that Terrible Jean recently won a tennis tournament in Oscoda. She accused me of being jealous of Terrible Jean's superior abilities. She further charged that I always had been resentful of Terrible Jean's incredible talents, even when we were small children.

It was easy to figure out what had prompted Mrs. Messing to write. Terrible Jean had dictated into her ear while sitting on her head.

I wasn't surprised to learn Terrible Jean had won a tennis trophy.

I used to be her favorite opponent and she was unbeatable. Her strategy was to smash the ball into my mouth. I was too skinny to swallow it and too weak to spit it back over the net.

Terrible Jean was a marvelous winner. To celebrate each victory she'd do something exciting such as throw me in the St. Clair River. I couldn't swim but the tennis ball stuck in my mouth kept me afloat.

In Oscoda there is probably a river awash with Terrible Jean's latest victims, bobbing.

But tennis isn't Terrible Jean's greatest sport. You should see her fist fight. She used to swing her huge meat hooks down, as if pounding nails. It usually took her 30 seconds to make me disappear into the ground, whimpering.

My only chance was to trip her, before she started pounding, and then grab her in my famous neckhold. When she was flat on her stomach I would put my knee in her back and clutch her chin with both hands, pulling back with all my strength. She would beg for mercy, and I would let her free only after she promised she never would hit me again.

I was reminded of this when I read that Abdullah Sheik's most famous wrestling weapon is his Camel Clutch. He sits on his opponent's back and pulls on his chin until he gives up or splits into two parts. I am flattered by the imitation.

And I don't care if Muhammad Ali copies Terrible Jean's defense against the Camel Clutch. All he has to do is surrender and promise to never hit the Japanese wrestler again. Then he should get up and pound the Japanese to death.

Terrible Jean used to do this while hollering what a dumb sucker I was to trust her. Ali could holler "Remember Pearl Harbor" which is more patriotic. ■

This Edmund Fitzgerald has his father's unsinkable love

June 5, 1976

The sinking of the Edmund Fitzgerald last Nov. 10, after only 17 years' afloat, reminded me it was about time for my youngest child to graduate from high school.

If that sounds confusing, be patient. This is somewhat of a ghost story, and such stories must be told slowly to retain the spookiness.

The Edmund Fitzgerald was launched May 31, 1958. At the time it was the largest ore carrier on the Great Lakes. A big boat.

On that same day, a big boy was born to my wife. We named him Edmund Fitzgerald.

It was a coincidence. When we named our Edmund, my wife and I didn't know a thing about the boat. We didn't realize there had been a twin birth until we saw the news on TV that birthday evening. The newscaster said the Edmund Fitzgerald had been launched sideways.

"So was ours," my wife groaned.

Naturally, our family followed the wake of Ed the boat closely through the years. One day we drove to Toledo where the vessel was docked. Our Edmund was five years old by then and a big ham, eager to pose for all sorts of goofy pictures with his namesake. He even came through with one of his few bright sayings:

"If this boat ever sinks," he said, "I hope I'm not taking a bath at the same time."

Another memory remains vivid. The huge Fitz clan gathered one evening for dinner at a restaurant on the bank of the St. Clair River, north of Detroit. It was our Edmund's 10th birthday. There was a grand view of the water, and an ore carrier could be seen approaching from the south.

"Wouldn't it be great if that were the Edmund Fitzgerald?" someone remarked.

It was, or I wouldn't be telling you about it. There was much exclaiming and merriment as "our boat" passed by almost close enough to touch. From the noise we created, the other people in the restaurant thought the giant carrier was coming through the window.

Everyone thought the boat's appearance at that particular time

267

was an amazing coincidence — until I explained I had chartered the vessel to sail by on Eddie's birthday.

My family was properly impressed, as was the entire restaurant when I made the announcement while standing on the bar. Easily it was the most glorious lie I ever told.

Those fun times were remembered with a bitter poignancy when our family heard the Edmund Fitzgerald had sunk in Lake Superior, in a November storm, with the entire crew lost.

We noted that our Edmund had not been taking a bath at the time, and there were some lame chuckles. And then some real tears.

I know I cried that day for more than a ship lost at sea. I also cried at the reminder that life is uncertain and full of ugly shocks — for big boats and for little boys.

The boy is no longer so little. This morning there was a long gown hanging on the inside of the bathroom door, wrinkles waiting for steam. Next week he will put on the gown to receive his high school diploma. And next month he will signal his entrance into the adult world by putting a pack on his back and beginning an open-end hike scheduled to take him down some wilderness trail in Oregon and back home again, someday, God help us all.

Too many fathers quit kissing their sons once they are out of diapers. It is acceptable for mothers to weep late at night and wonder aloud about the terrible things that might happen to their little boys "out there." But fathers are supposed to make jokes.

Eddie has been practicing for the big hike by carrying his pack around the block 30 times every evening. I told him this was the same as practicing going to the dentist.

But fathers also have their late-night moments, when they fret about the future and ponder what can happen to the bravest ships at sea. I love him, too, and I should tell him so more often.

Edmund Fitzgerald the boy, born on launching day, didn't go down the bathtub drain on Nov. 10 when Edmund Fitzgerald the boat sank, much too young.

But the spookiness lingers and twitches. Nov. 10 is my father's birthday. His name was also Edmund Fitzgerald. ∎

Five wonderful words:
'Meet me at the Statler'

June 17, 1976

To me, the saddest sight in downtown Detroit is the huge Heritage Hotel, closed because it couldn't pay its bills. The other afternoon I peeked through its dirty windows, trying to see the once grand lobby where we always met . . .

It was the Statler then. "I'll meet you in the Statler lobby at 8:30," I would tell my date. I was too young to go into the magnificent bar, or too broke. But it was great to sit in a stuffed chair in the lobby and make up stories in my mind about the rich-looking people hurrying by to the elevators. Once I saw Carole Lombard.

A favorite story in our family concerns the time my parents went to Detroit with another couple. The women went shopping while the men went to the ball game. The plan was to meet at 6 p.m. in the Statler lobby. The women showed up on time, but they couldn't find their husbands although they looked everywhere, even under the stuffed chairs.

But the two husbands were there, in the middle of the lobby, sitting in plain sight. The women never thought to look inside the new 1938 Ford which was being displayed on a revolving platform. Dad was behind the wheel.

The ball game had been boring but the husbands had enjoyed seats strategically located near a beer stand. So it seemed like a fine time for Dad, a camouflage expert, to prove you could hide an elephant if you put it where no one would think to look for it — inside a 1938 Ford in the Statler lobby, for instance.

We usually met at the Statler before going to the theater, and after. Which brings up another sad subject. The Statler (Heritage) still is surrounded by theaters. But geez, look, what it says on the marquees.

On this bittersweet afternoon, I could have seen "The Karate Killers" at the Fox. Or "Teenage Masseuse" at the Globe Art, or "three special X movies" at the Stone. The mighty Michigan, where I once got Benny Goodman's autograph, isn't even open. It just sits there, looking rotten, waiting to become a parking lot.

The main feature at the grandiose Grand Circus, where once the

269

marbled architecture reflected only the biggest stars, was something called "Poor White Trash Part II." The advertising said, "Due to the abnormal subject matter of this motion picture, absolutely no children will be allowed with or without their parents . . . special uniformed police will supervise admissions."

I entered quietly, for fear of waking the special uniformed policeman slouched nearby.

"I trust that officer lives in Detroit," I whispered to the ticket taker. "I don't want any mercenaries commuting from Bloomfield Hills to protect me from rampaging children trying to crash into this theater."

(Detroit just fired 75 cops because they don't live inside the city. There are 800 empty rooms at the Heritage. I offer this solution free to City Councilman Jack Kelly who should know what to do with it.)

As expected, "White Trash" turned out to be a lousy movie. It doesn't even have the redeeming quality of appealing to my prurient interests, which are several. The heroine wears navel-revealing hip-huggers, but she is such an insipid cluck, her pants would look sexier hanging from a doorknob.

I think this type of movie, with an all-white, all-dumbo cast, is aimed at pleasing a black audience. The idea is to give the blacks a chance to laugh and scoff at outrageous caricatures of white hillbillies. This affords a little revenge for the many years white audiences were entertained by equally outrageous, shuffling caricatures of Negroes, a la Stepin Fechit.

I'm all for equal rights, even when it comes to insulting people, but it's no fun when the barbs are only boring. After 15 minutes of "White Trash," I said to myself, in the spirit of the occasion: "Feet, don't fail me now."

Back on the street, there was one more anguished glance at the shuttered Heritage, and then I headed home before darkness came. Dark is the trouble in downtown Detroit. No one will walk the streets after it. To make a living, the muggers and the hookers must lurk around stoplights, and throw themselves in front of cars.

On a recent midnight downtown, my wife and I were about to walk two blocks from the Press Club to Howard Johnson's. Our shocked friends said we would be risking our lives. They insisted upon driving us the short distance.

But damn it, I'd rather walk.

I'd rather walk to the Statler lobby to sit in a stuffed chair and look for Carole Lombard — or for my dad, at the wheel of a 1938 Ford, revolving.

Damn it.

The world isn't ready for a funeral on Gasoline Alley

July 3, 1976

Forget Dick Tracy. He hasn't aged a day in 50 years. The guy I'm worried about is Uncle Walt.

Tracy got off the comic page and onto the front page recently when a Maine newspaper accused him of being too violent and of running around with "weirdos and sickies."

Such anti-American charges made nationwide news. Dick Tracy has been a heroic cop for as long as anyone can remember. Millions of people shouted "heresy" when the Bangor Daily News dropped the comic strip, saying "Dick is old hat. He's too much law and disorder."

Myself? I don't care. I quit reading Dick Tracy many years ago. It was the weirdos that got me. If I recall correctly, there was a character called B.O. Plenty who married Gravel Gertie and they had a baby named Sparkle Plenty who came from the moon. After years of faithful reading, I didn't think Dick Tracy had any business expecting me to believe such nonsense. Actually, I didn't even believe his wrist radio.

The only comic strip a man can have faith in is the one starring Skeezix and family. And it has recently occurred to me, tragically, like a kick in the gut, that some day Uncle Walt is going to die.

Skeezix was 55 years old last February, God help us all, and time stops for no man when he lives on Gasoline Alley.

Little Orphan Annie hasn't aged a minute in 40 years. She hasn't even changed her dress. Dondi was an Italian orphan of World War II and the poor kid is still in elementary school today. Charlie Brown has been a little leaguer for 20 years. Dagwood's wife is built better today than she was 35 years ago.

That's the way it goes in most comic strips. The characters never age — except in Gasoline Alley.

Uncle Walt found the infant Skeezix on his doorstep in 1921. Skeezix has always been five years older than I, sort of a big brother. We grew up together and went to war together. We've raised our families and wrestled with milk bills together. And now we're beginning to grow old together.

But my father died several years ago. So what about Uncle Walt?

271

He's been aging right along with Skeezix and me. He's got to be closing in on 85. He can't live forever — not on Gasoline Alley, where every birthday is counted.

I'm not sure this nation can handle the death of Uncle Walt.

Look what happened a few times on TV soap operas. A star grew sick of the suds and ran away to Hollywood. The writers explained the character's absence by having him killed in a plane crash or dying suddenly of the mange. And there was great wailing and gnashing of upper plates by viewers. Housewives demanded that Professor Bob be brought back to life or they would quit buying the sponsor's soap.

That's the type of threat that makes sponsors responsive to public opinion. So now the stars are never killed. If an actress quits, she simply is replaced with another actress. The character's sudden change from a five-foot blonde to a six-foot black is explained by an overdue visit to the most marvelous beauty shop. And everyone is happy.

But Uncle Walt cannot be replaced in this manner. His problem is not that he's fleeing to Hollywood. It's that he will begin to lose his believability when Skeezix celebrates his 90th birthday and Walt shows up at the party.

And the final loss of Uncle Walt will create a national uproar many times louder than any caused by a TV death. Soap operas are fleeting things, never lasting more than a few years at the most. But Gasoline Alley and Uncle Walt have been with us every day since 1921.

Can you imagine the mourning when Walt is erased for good? It will be the world's most watched death scene. What a funeral!

Skeezix will get a billion letters of condolence. And several newspaper offices will be stormed and bombed.

Truly, there is a sad day coming. The more I think of it, the more cataclysmic it gets. I think this tragedy must be avoided, for the good of the nation.

Uncle Walt must live.

But how?

I have a brilliant idea. How about a heart transplant from Little Orphan Annie?

I never liked the kid anyway. I used to get sick on her Ovaltine, and I never could decode anything with her lousy decoder ring.

Uncle Walt will be glad to take care of Sandy. Arf, arf.   ■

Like it or not, this old-movie buff can't keep quiet

November 29, 1976

Sammy Cahn currently is bouncing in a delightful show at the Music Hall. In fact, at one point, he tells the crowd how easy it is to sing along with him. "Just follow the bouncing Jew," he says.

The way he skips and jumps around the stage, and the way he sings bad but good, Sammy reminds me of Eddie Cantor. Eddie who?

I realize there are many disgustingly young readers out there who do not remember Eddie Cantor. So I will update him by recalling that if it weren't for Cantor, Eddie Fisher would never have married Debbie Reynolds, Elizabeth Taylor, Connie Stevens and the Radio City Rockettes.

Fisher, then just a boy, began his singing career on the Eddie Cantor radio show. This is the same show that often featured Parkyakarkas and Rubinoff and his violin. Rubinoff once made his home in the old Wolverine Hotel in Detroit. I saw the gold violin on the door of his suite.

Cantor also starred on stage and screen and even got in some TV. He had a wife named Ida and four daughters. It starred Keefe Brasselle, who later became a network TV executive and married Arlene DeMarco, one of the singing DeMarco sisters. After the divorce, she went on welfare and wrote a dirty book about him. Arlene about Keefe, not Ida about Eddie (Cantor not Fisher).

I want you to know that I spouted all that fascinating show-biz information right off the top of my head. No reference books needed. I also want you to know that I realize I am boring you. I can't help it.

I always have been a screwball about show business, especially old movies. If someone says they woke up screaming, I cannot resist the compulsion to tell them that Richard Boone played the Laird Cregar role in the remake of "I Wake Up Screaming," which starred Betty Grable, Victor Mature and Carole Landis in the original version, and Carole Landis killed herself in real life after an unhappy love affair with Rex Harrison, the same Rex Harrison who now is seen on TV having an unnatural relationship with an automobile.

That's why I got an extra kick out of Sammy Cahn's show. He wrote the lyrics for dozens of movie musicals, starting in the 1930s,

273

and when he reminisced about his early days, I had to chew on my coat to keep from hollering, "Yeah, I remember that song and I can tell you who sang it and the name of the movie and who played Bob Hope's girlfriend in it."

As it was, in an exercise of magnificent restraint, I only whispered to my wife. When Sammy began to tell how he was hired to write lyrics for Judy Garland to sing in "Romance on the High Seas," I generously informed her that Judy dropped out of that role and it was eventually played by a newcomer named Doris Day.

"Please shut up," my wife said.

Because of her obvious interest, I further told her that one of Doris Day's leading men in that long-forgotten movie was Jack Carson, not Johnny, who started out as a comedian but later played some fine dramatic roles, such as in the first remake of "A Star Is Born," the second remake of which is currently being made with a music theme, starring Barbra Streisand and Kris Kristofferson.

"Please shut up," said a woman sitting behind us.

OK, just for that, I didn't tell anyone in the theater what Sammy Cahn told me about Phyllis McGuire. I didn't even tell anyone that I'd had a couple of drinks with Sammy before the show.

But I'll tell you. You remember the singing McGuire Sisters. I think their father was Arthur Godfrey. Anyway, Phyllis now sings solo, when she feels like it, and lives in Las Vegas. She was reportedly once the girlfriend of a well-known gangster, now deceased.

The last time he saw Phyllis, Sammy said, she was wearing $3 million worth of jewelry. On one body.

You can't read that kind of stuff just anywhere. Eat your heart out, Shirley Eder.

I really did break booze with Sammy. He had straight vodka on lots of ice. He talked non-stop, sometimes burst into song, and said you can tell someone is angry at you if they bite you on the neck.

Sammy said he isn't performing at the Music Hall for money, he's doing it so people can come backstage after the show and tell him how great he was.

He is great. You should go see him and his super singers. The lovely old Music Hall is guaranteed safe, with a parking lot as bright as Phyllis McGuire's aureole.

In fact, I'm going back. If the jerk beside you says Stuart Irwin threw watermelons to Judy Garland in her first movie, it's me. ■

274

Reggie remembers home runs; I recall a galosh

December 6, 1976

While broadcasting the World Series, Reggie Jackson reminded me of some other kid's galosh.

You probably find that hard to understand. If you are disgustingly young, you might not even know what a galosh is.

A galosh is a high overshoe. Reggie Jackson is a millionaire baseball player. And this column is about remembering.

How good is your memory? Jackson said he had hit 280 home runs in his major league career and he remembered every one of them. He remembered who the pitchers were and what kind of a pitch he slammed out of the park.

I find that hard to believe.

Jackson said it was easy for him to remember every detail of every home run because home runs are his bread and butter. But I figure I've written about 2,400 newspaper columns. They are my bread and butter. And it is hard to remember what I wrote yesterday. Last year is impossible.

A voice from the bleachers might yell that I can't remember because I've never written any home runs. Jackson probably can't remember his singles, either.

There are always a lot of mouthy jerks in the bleachers.

But I suppose Jackson could be telling the truth. I've read about people who swear they can remember coming home from the hospital after they were born. Some claim they remember how it was in the womb.

For me, life began at the age of five as I was walking home from Jefferson School with some other kid's galosh on one foot.

That is my earliest memory. All that occurred before that day is a blank, and there are countless gaps in the years since then. But I've never forgotten the reckless abandon with which I got mud on that strange galosh. I hopped through every puddle.

Jefferson School was torn down several years ago. It was in Port Huron. That town, as I remember it, is crumbling in the face of dratted progress.

I delivered mail in Port Huron and, so help me, they have leveled

275

my entire route. They flattened most of my newspaper route, too.

Urban Renewal, that brutal bulldozer of boyhood memories, has replaced dozens of worn but warm homes with a few cold office buildings. I wonder where all the people went and if they are getting their mail and newspapers all right.

I soon will run out of places to drive by and point at and bore my kids talking about.

Some of the poolrooms are still there, but they look like dime stores. They even smell good, for gosh sakes, and I don't like them anymore.

I hardly can find a bartender who knows me or knows anyone I knew — not even the most famous lushes. And when I tell them, ha-ha, I paid for this bar, they just shrug and pour a drink for some 14-year-old kid who is probably 25.

I attended Jefferson for only one year — kindergarten. Two things, besides the wrong galosh, I remember most.

One is what I had to wear. Short pants and long, lumpy stockings held up by a garter belt. Anyone remember?

If my wise-guy son reads that his dad used to wear a garter belt he will fall down laughing and say I am kidding. But I can close my eyes and see again my long underwear bulking out between the tops of my stocking and the bottom of my pants.

The other thing I remember most is our kindergarten band. I played the water whistle. Is there such a thing as a water whistle today? I don't think so.

My whistle was shaped like a bird and you filled it with water and then blew through the tail. A shrill, gurgly noise came out the beak. I always have thought Lawrence Welk must have played a water whistle in school.

Our band had a recital for parents, of course. My dad complained for years after. He swore I blew and blew but no noise came out. He was right. I was nervous that day and forgot to put water in the whistle.

When you are five years old, this is a terrible thing. But it makes a lovely memory.

When you write a column like this, you can write about yesterday, today or tomorrow. When I write about today, I usually am angry about something. For tomorrow, I am hopeful, but leery.

Yesterdays are the best. The memories make me smile, and sometimes hoot, and sometimes my eyes get damp.

And almost always I go back to that first day, hopping through the puddles, and I wish I could remember if that other kid ever got his galosh back. ■

In a dry world, I still could be looking for brass holes

January 22, 1977

What's the dumbest job you ever had?

My dumbest was looking for holes in the brass at the Mueller Brass Co. in Port Huron. That was in 1948 and I hadn't thought about it in years. But then I made my first visit to Old Christ Episcopal Church and a stranger grabbed me by the arm.

Whenever a stranger confronts me in public, I immediately tell myself he or she is a reader who wants to compliment me on the brilliant column I wrote yesterday. In the winter I always carry a pencil inside my right mitten, for signing autographs.

It is true that it's not easy to recognize me from the dinky little picture that stingy editors usually run with the column. In fact, no one ever has recognized me from those pictures except my mother, once, but that was on Christmas and she knew her son was coming for dinner anyway.

I find it makes it easier for my fans if I wear a name tag, preferably one that lights up in the dark. That's why I like to attend the Michigan Press Association convention in East Lansing every January. Every delegate is given a name tag encased in plastic. These tags hold up well and will remain serviceable through the following summer if you give them proper care and don't wear them around the house — where most everyone knows your name anyway.

I was wearing a name tag at Old Christ Church, so I was prepared to be humble and gracious when that woman jerked my sleeve. I expected her to ask if I was the Jim Fitzgerald who writes the marvelous columns.

"Are you the Jim Fitzgerald who knows Jake Jacobson?" she asked. "I know him, too."

Jake Jacobson? Geez.

I admitted I once worked alongside Jake. There then followed considerable conversation about what a great and talented fellow Jake is. The woman, whose name is Sally Heberlein, used to live next door to Jake in Saginaw. She thought it was marvelous to run into someone who used to work with him. She didn't seem to know I am a

277

famous columnist, even though that information was clearly embossed on the streamer hanging from my name tag.

My wife listened with interest and later she asked what newspaper Jake and I had worked on together. I told her it wasn't a newspaper, it was the inspection line at the Mueller Brass Co. And now you know why I am thinking of the dumbest job I ever had.

I worked nights, searching for unwanted holes in various pieces of brass tubing. I did this by applying the water test, an incredible process, the memory of which still makes my socks squish.

I was stationed in front of a tank of water which had a weird air-blowing contraption suspended over it. The idea was to fit the hunk of brass into the contraption so that all authorized holes were covered tightly with rubber cups. Then I dipped the contraption down into the water and pulled a handle which sent a fearful burst of air into the brass.

If there were any unauthorized holes in the brass, I found out quickly. It was monsoon time. I got sopping wet.

Working at the water tank next to me was a beefy redhead named Jacobson. He looked like a professional wrestler who had lost every match. But, incredibly, he was forever reciting Shakespeare. He said he was going to be an actor.

Actually, it is a shame Jake didn't make a career of the water test. He was an artist at the job. He would saunter over to the drill press department and drill strategic holes into his brass pieces. Then he'd return to his water tank to wage wet war against management.

When the foreman peered over his shoulder, Jake would slyly slip a drilled piece of brass into his machine. He would dip and pull, and the foreman would get soaked in the face.

"By golly," Jake would say, "it's a good thing I found that hole."

"Nice, glub-blub, work," the foreman would say, wiping his face and hurrying on to the next tank to wake me up.

"Out, damn spot," Jake would say, evoking visions of John Barrymore in wet bib overalls.

The only time I've seen Jake since those days was on TV. He moved on to become a sports announcer, and for many years could be seen on Channel 5 in Saginaw. I'm told he is now at Channel 12 in Flint, working behind the scenes, a position more befitting his physiognomy.

You all know what happened to me. I would have stayed at the dumbest job I ever had, but I was embarrassed by people who kept asking why my name tag was all wet. ■

I'm the lucky one,
for being my father's son

June 18, 1977

During the Great Depression, my mother was a famous stretcher. She won fame by stretching food money further than any other mother in the neighborhood.

My father gave her the money, a few dollars every week. Mother had to feed from four to seven mouths with that money, depending upon the year. We were a growing family during the Depression, but the food allowance was not increased every time Mother had another baby. Mother simply squeezed harder on the dollar.

At least, that's what she claimed.

Our family ate well, and Mother's friends often asked how she possibly could provide so much food on so little money. She would take a modest bow and admit it wasn't easy. It took careful planning and exhaustive shopping, she said.

This was not true, according to my father. He said Mother stretched her food dollars so far by using the "skip-in method" of shopping.

"She phones me at work every day and tells me to skip into the grocery store on my way home and pick up a loaf of bread, a peck of potatoes and a roast of beef," he said. "Every time I skip into the store, I pay for the food out of my weekly allowance. I never get paid back.

"That is how my wife stretches her food money so far. Actually, she spends her food money on trips to Europe. I skip in and buy all the food," he said. "If more American wives shopped the skip-in way, there would be more American wives in Europe, which would make this a better country in which to live."

My father has been dead 14 years. But Sunday is Father's Day, and I am giving myself a present. I am remembering how much fun it was to be my father's son.

There was the Depression Christmas when Mother insisted she and Dad give each other practical gifts. She said that, more than anything else, our home needed two matching end tables. So she gave Dad one end table, and he gave her the other one.

The next Christmas, with great fanfare, Dad gave Mother his end table.

There was the teenage summer I worked nights in a Chrysler factory. I punched in at 11 p.m. and got back home about 8 o'clock the next morning. Except there was a bar across the street from the factory and sometimes I stopped there before work. One night I stayed too long and never got to work at all.

I arrived home at 3 a.m. The doors were locked so I pried open a porch window and began to crawl through into the living room. I saw someone peering down at me from the shadows at the head of the stairs.

"Who's there?" I asked.

"You dumb s.o.b.," my father answered. "It is 3 o'clock in the morning and you are crawling through my window. I am the one who is supposed to say 'who's there'?"

Dad couldn't drive anywhere without getting lost. In one strange town he drove aimlessly for blocks while Mother urged him to stop and ask someone for directions.

"I can't," he explained. "I don't know anyone in this town."

Dad enjoyed a few years of retirement before he died. To keep busy, he became a volunteer driver. He drove handicapped people from their homes to their doctors' offices and then home again.

Once Dad became lost in a strange neighborhood and couldn't find his passenger's home. Because of his passenger's handicap, Dad was reluctant to ask him for guidance. But he finally did and the passenger told Dad how to get to the right house.

"I am the first driver in the history of driving to get directions from a blind man," Dad later reported with pride.

Life was not all laughs for my father. His business failed during the Depression, and there must have been days when he couldn't afford to skip in and buy groceries. At the age of 42 he couldn't find employment in his hometown where he was president of Kiwanis and his father had been mayor. He had to take a job in a town 120 miles away and for many months he saw his family only on weekends.

There had to be many unhappy days, but they have faded. Memory can be marvelous. The tears are forgotten and only the sound of laughter can be heard. Dad taught his kids how great it is to laugh.

Forty years later, the stories probably aren't all that funny to strangers. Sorry. You had to be there. On this Father's Day, I am wishing so hard that I could be there one more time. ■

Old church bell's peal
softens this soulful heart

January 9, 1978

"It will be good for your soul," my wife said. She was encouraging me to return to my hometown to hear the church bell of my childhood peal once again.

Could she prove there really is such a thing as a soul? Could anyone prove it?

I first pondered this question seriously about 10 years ago. That's when I heard there was a $200,000 prize being offered to anyone who could give "some scientific proof of a soul of the human body which leaves at death."

The quote is from the last will and testament of a bachelor named James Kidd who disappeared while on a prospecting trip in Arizona many years ago, never to be found. He left his $200,000 estate to anyone who could produce convincing evidence of the existence of an eternal soul.

As far as I know, the $200,000 has not yet been awarded to anyone. But several dozen people registered claims with the judge administering Kidd's estate.

Some of the claimants are just greedy, some are kooky, and some have the noblest of motives. If I entered the race, I would have the most noble motive of all:

I would use the $200,000 to finance a search for Kidd. I would like to ask him how come he's such a troublemaker.

Think about it. If you don't believe there is an eternal soul, how would I convince you otherwise? For $200,000, or merely to make points in heaven, how would you prove there is a soul?

Everyone knows brevity is the soul of wit. A lovely person is the soul of kindness. When you're in a dark room, you can't see a soul. And when we get to the bottom of this matter, we will have arrived at the soul of it.

I know there is a soul, but I confess I can't prove it to save my you-know-what. Confession is good for the soul.

For example, as my wife had predicted, it did my soul good to hear the old bell ring again at St. Stephen's Church in Port Huron.

The bell first rang 104 years ago. It pealed in downtown Port

Huron until 1965 when the old church was torn down and the bell was stored. A new St. Stephen's was built on the edge of town, but the old bell was not included.

An energetic woman named Marian Crawford decided this was a mistake which cried out, soulfully, for correction. She headed a committee which raised $26,000 to build a tower for the old bell behind the new church.

On a recent Sunday afternoon, the bell pealed again. I was there to hear it. Actually, I was there because Mrs. Crawford had invited me to the dedication party where I knew I would enjoy seeing old friends, including my mother and Aunt Madeline. I didn't expect to get much out of hearing that bell ring again.

One church bell sounds pretty much like a thousand other church bells, right?

Upon my soul, wrong.

When that old bell clanged again, another pound of cynicism melted. It was a sound I hadn't heard in more than 30 years, but I recognized it.

I recognized it, and I remembered the nuns and the priests and the incense and the old brick church with the same old people shuffling to Holy Communion at 8 o'clock mass every morning. When that bell pealed at one minute to eight, if I wasn't kneeling with the rest of my class, I was in trouble.

For me, the resurrected bell played soul music. And later, for dinner, Mrs. Crawford served soul food — roast beef and apple pie.

But this soul-satisfying experience didn't bring me any closer to James Kidd's $200,000. I couldn't prove a thing.

Nobody can. Except at St. Stephen's I was taught that God is all soul and all souls, so he probably has the evidence. But does God need $200,000?

Sorry, Mr. Kidd, wherever you are. You'll just have to keep the faith. Bless your soul. ∎

This tree didn't even need lights; it was lit up with love

December 25, 1978

This year our Christmas tree was ordered in August, from Sears. The limbs were wrapped separately and had to be inserted into holes in the trunk. The tree doesn't smell like a forest in winter, it smells like a department store in heat. It costs $15 and should last for 15 Christmases if it doesn't get lost in summer storage.

This is the first Christmas I've spent completely ensconced in a high-rise apartment where live Christmas trees are forbidden because of the fire hazard. For the first time, I've put up a Christmas tree without getting branches up my nose or sawing off too much trunk or sobbing or swearing to never again put up a lousy Christmas tree.

In many families, it is a tradition for father to take his children into the forest to chop down the fresh tree of their choice. In our family, it was a tradition for father to tell his children if they wanted a Christmas tree, they could go get it themselves. All they had to do was walk to the church across the street and buy one from the Methodist Men's Club. I would give them the money. If they were too small to cross the street alone, their mother could take them.

The most sentimental part of our family tradition came when the children insisted they couldn't possibly pick out a tree without their father by their side. No one else could ever take my place. My children needed me to measure the tree against.

My father always had to have the tallest tree that would fit inside our home. Early in my marriage, it was discovered that if I stood on my tippy-toes and stretched both arms high into the air, I could touch the top of a tree which, with a star on stop, would be exactly the right height for our family room.

My physical presence became annually essential to the purchase of the right-sized Christmas tree. Whenever people asked why my wife never left me, I explained she needed my body once a year.

Toward the middle of every December, after my traditional protests had been ignored, I would take my children across the street and I would stand on my tippy-toes with my arms in the air while members of the Methodist Men's Club would chew on their mittens to keep from laughing out loud at the nut dancing ballet in his galoshes.

That was the Christmas tree tradition at our home until this year, when the tree came in a box from Sears and I had to lean over to put the star on top. At first, I declared it the smallest Christmas tree ever seen inside our home. But then I remembered the most beautiful Christmas tree I ever saw. It was even smaller.

Ten years ago, my family was experiencing a happier-than-usual Christmas season. My wife was with child. As editor of the local newspaper, I had modestly announced the coming birth on the editorial page. Strangers congratulated me on the street. My poker club gave me a baby shower, loading me down with ribald gifts I didn't dare bring home.

The three children were giggly at the prospect of a new little brother or sister to boss around. And the expectant parents, much to their amazement, were delighted by the idea of an unplanned addition to what they thought had been a completed family.

Under the usual big Christmas tree, there were a few gifts for the baby who wouldn't be born for a few months. But then Pat got sick. Two days before Christmas, at the hospital, the unborn baby was lost.

The kids' tears for the lost sibling soon were wiped away. The paramount problem became: Would Mother be able to come home from the hospital for Christmas? Yes, but she'd have to go right to bed and stay there.

I brought her home late Christmas Eve. What were those winking lights in our bedroom? They were hung on a green little pile of something. The kids had been concerned that Mother couldn't see the big Christmas tree from the bedroom. So they had cut enough off the big tree to make Mother a little tree, maybe the most lopsided Christmas tree ever seen.

It was beautiful. Mom and Dad laughed and cried like saps. Who needs a tippy-toed body to measure a tree against? Who needs a live Christmas tree? Who needs another kid? All we really need is each other.

Merry Christmas. ∎

Show me a pleat in the pant
and I'll show you a saner world

August 25, 1979

Sometimes something is missing for so long that you forgot it was ever there. But then it returns and you remember it fondly, and you're glad it's back. You wonder where it has been, and why it went away, and why it was returned.

That's how I feel about pleated pants.

My family chipped in and bought me a pair of off-white trousers for my birthday. I put them on and looked in the mirror, and it was a few seconds before I realized why my new pants looked different from the pants I've been wearing for so many years I can't count them. Then I put my hands in my pockets and was startled to find enough room to make fists. I pushed my fists outward and noticed the fabric billow below my belt. Pleats!

I thought of George Raft. He always had great pleats in his pants. I also thought of a slim young man whose favorite pants had belt loops several inches lower than usual. He would tighten his skinny belt and the effect was similar to tying a string around the top of a paper sack and licorice sticks. The pants bloused out below the belt and fanned out above it. He loved those pants because they were the first ones he purchased after three years in pleatless Army uniform. He was me.

The birthday pants that caused this fit of nostalgia have four definite folds across the top. Two of the folds evolve into conventional creases that descend to my shoes. The other two folds serve no purpose other than to create pleats. They are purely decorative, even frivolous, if you wish. Where have they been all these years?

I have a 21-year-old son who never has known the frivolity of pleats in his pants. He has known nothing except pants that stretch tightly and blahly across the abdomen without the slightest ripple in the fabric. He grew up believing that pant creases always have ascended no farther than the crotch.

He never has known the pleasure of putting his hands in his pockets and jingling coins. He never has carried a dime that didn't leave an impression of Franklin D. Roosevelt's face in his thigh. He never has sat down without risking embarrassment.

It is dumb enough for skinny boys to wear tight pants. But old men

285

with big stomachs also wear them, which is really stupid. Fat women can hide under full skirts, but fat men must wear pants the way apples wear peel.

At least that's been the fashion for so many years that I'd forgotten all about pleated pants. I can't remember for sure what caused their disappearance. I think it had something to do with the dramatic rise in the price of imported pleats during the 1950s. The government warned citizens not to become dependent upon foreign pleats, and there were no domestic pleats available. They all had been folded into Liberace's shirts — or something like that.

I don't know if pleated pants are making a comeback. My family might have purchased my birthday pants at an archeological dig in the ruins of an ancient Hart, Schaffner & Marx factory. I hope not.

If cleanliness can be next to godliness, comfort is certainly next to sanity. It is insane for anyone to wear too-tight pants on purpose. The return of pleated pants to the United States would serve as a sign to the rest of the world that this nation is regaining its sanity.

I walked to work in my new pants yesterday. I jingled the coins and keys in my pockets, and I luxuriated in the soft parting of my pleats. I thought about George Raft and the sane pants I bought with my mustering out pay. It was marvelous.

As I neared my office, I joined steps with a woman I know. She was tottering on spiked heels. I asked her if she knew comfort was next to sanity. She asked me if I knew my pants were baggy. I shook a fist at her without taking it out of my pocket. ■

Reviving slam books
might deflate some egos

September 5, 1979

Whatever happened to "Aw, shucks?"

It used to be that when a man received a compliment, he turned it aside modestly. He dug his toe in the dirt and said "Aw, shucks, it really wasn't anything." He might even have blushed.

Recently, Detroit Tiger manager Sparky Anderson was asked what person he most admired. He admitted he admired himself the most. Several of his players, asked the same question, said they knew no one more admirable than themselves.

This is typical of the "I-am-the-greatest" trend, and it isn't confined by a jockstrap. Recently I asked an attorney to name the best trial lawyer in his state. He named himself and took a bow. Where I work, several different people claim to be the best writer on the staff, and one of them probably is, but aw, shucks . . .

I know a TV sportscaster who is paid a huge salary to read scores and insult athletes who admire themselves most. This is a noble calling, except the sportscaster is as egocentric as the athletes. He doesn't think it's stupid that he makes seven times more than the best schoolteacher in the world.

"More people watch me than watch any teacher," he explained. "They watch me because they admire me. They admire me because I am the best sportscaster in the business."

"I admire self-effacing people," I said.

"I'm the best effacer in the world," he said, digging his toe into the tile floor.

My distaste for braggarts probably results from my childhood. I grew up during the era of the slam book, not to be confused with the slam dunk, which no one had ever heard of in 1940, but you should have seen my two-handed set shot. Slam books were used to tell people what was wrong with them.

Anyone could publish a slam book. All you needed was a spiral notebook. At the top of each page, you wrote the name of a different schoolmate. The book then was circulated throughout the school and students wrote what they thought of each person below his or her

287

name. I don't think there are such things as slam books today. Office bulletin boards are the nearest thing.

Slam books were an exercise in masochism. The kids were never as interested in writing what they thought about their classmates as they were in reading what their classmates thought about them. To facilitate this yearning for pain, the classiest slam books listed names in alphabetical order. Ziggy Zabowski started reading from the back.

The worst slam was to charge someone with being conceited. In those days, modesty really was a virtue. The populace would have been shocked if Lou Gehrig had said he was so good a candy bar should be named after him, or if Tom Harmon had celebrated a touchdown by dancing the Charleston in the end zone. It was shameful to be told you were stuck on yourself.

It wasn't only the risk of a humiliating review in a slam book that made me grow up humble. There was also the threat of my parents jumping on my ego. They taught me not only was it unseemly to brag about my own accomplishments but it also was wrong to boast about my close relatives. That's why, even today, I tell everyone that my very big sister, Terrible Jean (speaking of slam dunks), is nothing to brag about.

In the playground of my mind, I might think my two-handed set shot is pretty hot stuff. But I would never say so out loud, and if I heard someone else say it, aw shucks . . .

When I suggested to my friend the sportscaster that he might be even more admirable if he didn't force other people to blush for him, he scoffed.

"If a man doesn't have confidence in himself, nobody else will," he said. "There is nothing wrong with saying you're good if you really are good, and I am. It would be phony for me to deny it."

Boy, would I like to get that guy alone in a slam book. ■

Sliced Snickers are an offense to boyhood memories

October 26, 1979

Currently, for anniversary and dismal reasons, persons in my age group are being asked for our memories of the Great Depression. OK.

The thing I remember most is sitting on the front porch on Friday evenings, waiting for my father to come home from work. Sometimes, while waiting, I would eat a candy bar the way a candy bar is supposed to be eaten.

Candy bars have been much on my mind lately, because of a terrible thing that happened last week. In response to something I wrote, two kind readers sent me Snickers bars. My wife sliced the two bars into thin, square pieces and put them on the coffee table in a plate, with toothpicks lying beside them.

I didn't realize what was on the plate until I demanded to know where my wife had hidden my Snickers bars and she said they were sitting right under my nose. She was suggesting that tiny bits of Snickers should be speared and popped daintily into the mouth, like stuffed olives.

Snickers hors d'oeuvres, God help us all. That's worse than scraping the corn off the cob with a knife.

Eating candy bars is supposed to be fun. I learned that much during the Great Depression when I couldn't afford more than one five-cent bar a week. Forty years later I can afford a 25-cent candy bar every day, but I can't eat them because they make me fat. However, when a I receive a Snickers bar as a gift, common good manners require that I eat it. And common humanity demands that I be allowed to eat it as I did when I was a boy — directly from the wrapper, not from some dumb dish.

The important thing about eating a candy bar when I was 10 years old was to not finish my bar before my big sister Terrible Jean finished hers. If I did, she made me feel bad by shouting: "Ha, ha, ha, your candy is all gone but I still have a lot of mine left."

Habits acquired during the despair of the Great Depression are hard to break. Even today, I never consume the last bit of candy without first looking behind trees for Terrible Jean. It wouldn't be

289

surprising to find her still sucking on a Holloway sucker purchased in 1935.

The secret to the slow eating of a candy bar is judicious licking, or sucking. No biting or chewing should be done. Everything should melt in your mouth, not in your stomach. Even almonds can be sucked to death if you try hard enough.

The unwrapping of the candy is crucial to slow success. The wrapper should be pulled down the bar in half-inch increments, so as to not expose too much bar to the mouth at one time. The temptation to chomp must be avoided at all times. When the candy begins to taste like paper, it is time to resume unwrapping.

During the Great Depression, much of my candy licking was done while waiting for my dad on Friday nights because, for a long time, he came home only on weekends. His local business had failed and the only job he could find was in a town 120 miles away.

Dad drove a rickety Essex and my sisters and I would straddle the porch railing, stretching out toward the curb, competing to be the first to see the old green car coming down the street. He would always arrive to great whoops of welcome, followed by much hugging and kissing. When I try, all these years later, I still can feel the scratch of his beard against my face.

Dad was 42 years old then, the interlocutor in the annual Kiwanis minstrel show, the best after-dinner speaker in his little hometown. But he couldn't find a job there. It was many years later before I realized what a bitter experience that must have been for him.

It was also many years before I learned how broke we had been when I was a kid. I may have grown up slightly poor during the Great Depression, but all my boyhood memories are rich. It is because of those memories that I couldn't possibly eat sliced Snickers. ■

The Lord dealt him
a good hand indeed

January 23, 1980

It was a proud day for the founder of the Poker-Duffer Club. While a church full of his friends watched, his oldest son was ordained a Catholic priest.

The founder is Rod Parsch, former janitor at the Lapeer County Bank & Trust Co., in Lapeer, Mich. I met him when I moved to Lapeer in 1951 to work at the local weekly newspaper. I was freshly equipped with a Bachelor of Arts degree from Michigan State University, and thus fully qualified for my first assignment which was to go to the editor's home and help his wife move a freezer onto her back porch.

It has now been almost 30 years since Rod proclaimed that seven young men should meet regularly for golf in the summer and poker in the other seasons. The club still is meeting today, and Rod is still saying, over and over: "I don't mind losing on a good hand."

That's what he says for poker. For golf, he lets his left-handed swing do his talking. It says: "You're not going to believe this."

What you're not going to believe is that sometimes the ball goes where Rod aims it. Rod believes the entire game of golf can be controlled by the power of the swing, so it really doesn't matter which club he uses. He favors a three-wood. He drives with a swiftly-swung three-wood, and chips with a softly-swung three-wood. In between, his swing is medium, or tepid. Surprisingly, he is not the worst golfer in the Poker-Duffer Club.

Club membership has changed considerably through the year. This is what I thought about as I watched Rod's son become a priest. I thought about some of the former members who couldn't be there.

Don was a charter member. He left a factory job to start an appliance store, and then a furniture store. Slowly, he prospered. He built one of the grandest homes in town, and bought a second home in Florida. While still in his 50s, he was ready to retire. And then he got sick in his car and choked to death.

Harold liked to play golf more than anything else. He had a bad heart and sometimes the pain would hit him during a game, but no amount of urging could convince him to quit playing. He would take a pill and rest a minute, and then he would take my money. I was with Harold when he suffered his last heart attack, at the age of 42. I remember, at his funeral, hearing a strange sound and being startled to realize it was me, sobbing. I hadn't sobbed since I was a child.

And then there was Bob, another charter member. I thought about him a lot during the ordination of Rod's son. I thought about Bob's oldest son and the time he sat in for his dad in a poker game. A few days later, that tall, handsome young man went to Vietnam. He came home a paraplegic.

That son is now living out his life in a hospital. Bob used to bring him home every weekend, but he can't do it anymore. Three years ago, while still in his 50s, Bob died from a heart attack. A few days after his funeral, his second son was crippled in an auto accident.

Life goes on (you may quote me on that) and who can say why some of us draw aces and some of us tap out? I had to quit the Poker-Duffer Club four years ago when I left town. Today, there are more replacements than charter members, but the founder is still there, losing on good hands.

I remember when Rod and his wife, Shirley, had twins. It brought the total number of their children to eight. "Geez," I said, "that's almost enough for your own ... "

Rod interrupted: "We're going to play without a shortstop."

The oldest Parsch offspring is David. He used to mow my lawn. Now he is a priest. Rod is president of the bank where he used to be janitor. Last Friday I watched Rod receive Holy Communion from his son, the priest. It was a marvelous thing to see such a proud parent.

It was sad to be reminded of the losses suffered by so many of my old poker buddies and their families. But it was wonderful to watch our founder win on a good hand. Lord, but I am happy for him.■

50 years are gone,
but the memories aren't

April 5, 1980

As I proceed into the second half-century of my life, I become more and more the type of old fool who escapes from today by remembering the things I miss about yesterday. Things such as . . .

● Running boards. In the movies of my childhood, running boards were time-savers for crook-chasers. A pursuing cop didn't have to open and shut car doors. He simply hopped on the running board of a moving auto and ordered the driver to "follow that car." I always wanted to hop on the running board of a moving car, but by the time I was big enough, there were no more running boards and I hit my chin on the top of the car.

● Small, green, curved Coca-Cola bottles clunking together in the bottom of a large metal box containing ice-cold water and a block of ice. After a baseball game on a hot August day, a small boy could run to the corner gas station and get both shirt-sleeves splendidly soggy while fishing around in the bottom of the cooler for a five-cent Coke. Today my wife brings Coke home in a huge plastic jug that won't fit in the refrigerator. If I want a cold Coke, I must pour the stuff into a glass with ice cubes. Today's Coke doesn't taste half as good as it did when I had to get my sleeves wet to drink it.

● Hess & Son Grocery Store. It was two blocks from our home, and Mother sent me there with a list which I would hand to Tommy Hess. He would pack the groceries into bags and put them into my arms. If there were too many bags for me to carry, Tommy's son would drive me home in the delivery truck. I think about Hess & Son while spending two hours wandering aimlessly around a supermarket with my wife's list clutched in my fist, and then standing in line for another hour waiting to pay $50 for two bags of cans. The checkout woman wonders why I'm sobbing.

● Motel swimming pools before I could afford an air-conditioned car. My wife and three small children and I drove to Florida during the hottest months, when rates were lowest. It took three days each way. The awful heat boiled the car and made everyone cranky. I took at least one wrong freeway exit every day. When we finally checked into a motel in the late afternoon and jumped into the swimming pool, the cold water was the most fun of the vacation. Today, for me, the pleasure has been drained out of motel pools. My car is air-conditioned, and my kids are grown and gone. The only thing the same is that I still take the wrong freeway exits.

• The splendid brevity of my first presidential campaign. It was Franklin Roosevelt vs. Herbert Hoover in 1932. Once a day during the week before the election I stood in our front yard and hollered "One-two-three-four, who are we for? Roosevelt, Roosevelt. Five-six-seven-eight, who do we hate? Hoover, Hoover." That was all I did, and Roosevelt won, as I knew he would. There were no polls to pre-determine me, and no primary "winners" in third place to confuse me.

• Finally, I miss the mother who gave me the grocery list, so long ago. She died last Easter, and I remember her as I read the poem "While I Slept" by Robert Francis:

> While I slept, while I slept and the night grew colder
> She would come to my bedroom stepping softly
> And draw a blanket about my shoulder
> While I slept.
>
> While I slept, while I slept in the dark still heat
> She would come to my bedside stepping cooly
> And smooth the twisted troubled sheet
> While I slept.
>
> Now she sleeps, sleeps under quiet rain
> While nights grow warm or nights grow colder
> And I wake and sleep and wake again
> While she sleeps.